Applied ELK Stack

Data Insights and Business Metrics With Collective Capability of ElasticSearch, Logstash and Kibana

Gurpreet S. Sachdeva

Applied ELK Stack: Actionable Data Insights and Business Metrics with the collective capability of ElasticSearch, Logstash and Kibana

Gurpreet S. Sachdeva

New Delhi, Delhi

India

ISBN-13 (pbk): 978-1545022146

ISBN-10 (pbk): 1545022143

Technical Reviewers: Shyam Seshadri and Amit Singh

Source code and supplementary material referenced by the author in this book is available to readers on **https://github.com/gssachdeva/Applied-ELK-Stack**.

To my mother and father

Contents at a Glance

About the Author xi

About the Technical Reviewers xii

Acknowledgments xiii

Introduction xiv

■ CHAPTER 1: Introduction to ELK Stack 1

■ CHAPTER 2: Shipping, Filtering and Parsing Events with
Logstash 17

■ CHAPTER 3: Extending Logstash 39

■ CHAPTER 4: Creating, Indexing and Deleting Data 49

■ CHAPTER 5: Searching Data 70

■ CHAPTER 6: Mapping and Analysis 90

■ CHAPTER 7: Data Exploration with Aggregates 105

■ CHAPTER 8: Exploring Kibana 137

■ CHAPTER 9: Kibana - Data Visualization 144

■ CHAPTER 10: Kibana - Dashboard 183

■ CHAPTER 11: Designing for Scale 198

■ CHAPTER 12: ELK Stack in Production 228

INDEX 265

Contents

About the Author   xi

About the Technical Reviewers   xii

Acknowledgments   xiii

Introduction   xiv

CHAPTER 1: Introduction to ELK Stack   1

Log Analysis in Today's World   1

The ELK Stack   2

ELK Data Pipeline   4

ELK Stack Installation   5

Summary   16

CHAPTER 2: Shipping, Filtering and Parsing Events with Logstash   17

Sample Dataset   17

Logstash Configuration   19

Filtering Events   25

Shipping Events   27

Analyzing Events   31

Summary   38

CHAPTER 3: Extending Logstash   39

Plugin Management   39

Download and Installation   40

Plugin Structure   41

Build Custom Plugin   45

Summary   48

CHAPTER 4: Creating, Indexing and Deleting Data   49
Ubiquity of Data   49

Anatomy of a Document   50

Elasticsearch API   53

Index Management   56

Document Management   58

Bulk Operations   66

Conflict Management   69

Summary   69

CHAPTER 5: Searching Data   70
Search Your Way   70

Simple Searches   70

Search *Lite*   77

Query DSL   79

Summary   89

CHAPTER 6: Mapping and Analysis   90
Data Mapping and Analysis   90

Exact Values and Full Text   91

Data Analysis   94

Data Mapping   97

Summary   104

CHAPTER 7: Data Exploration with Aggregates   105
Aggregation Basics   105

Fun with Aggregation   106

Data Visualization with Bar Charts 113

Time Series Aggregations 120

Aggregation Scoping 126

Aggregations with Query Filters 129

Multivalue Bucket Sorting 132

Summary 136

CHAPTER 8: Exploring Kibana **137**
Introducing Kibana 137

Kibana Features 137

Kibana User Interface 138

Summary 143

CHAPTER 9: Kibana - Data Visualization **144**
Visualize Page 144

Building Visualization 152

Summary 182

CHAPTER 10: Kibana - Dashboard **183**
Introduction to Dashboard Page 183

Working with the Toolbar 184

Working with Dashboard Canvas 190

Debug Panel 193

Summary 197

CHAPTER 11: Designing for Scale **198**
Elasticsearch Cluster for Scale 198

Discovering Cluster Nodes 202

Removal of Nodes from Cluster 206

Upgrading Elasticsearch Nodes 209

Cluster Information 211

Scaling Options 213

Aliases 216

Routing   220

Summary   227

CHAPTER 12: ELK Stack in Production   **228**

Deployment Considerations   228

Data Management   230

Elasticsearch Tuning   236

Configuration Management   244

Monitoring and Troubleshooting   248

Logging   258

Rolling Restarts   259

Backup and Restore   260

Summary   264

INDEX   **265**

About the Author

Gurpreet S. Sachdeva is a Technology Leader with 20 years of experience working on some of the most challenging technologies related to Communication Software, Enterprise Computing and Cloud Computing. Gurpreet did his B. Tech (Computer Engineering) from NIT, Kurukshetra and M.S. (Software Systems) from BITS, Pilani. He is currently working as Director – Technology with Aricent, Gurgaon. He is a keen Java enthusiast and co-founder of Delhi - NCR - Java User Group. Gurpreet is passionate about building cloud scale software and manage it through ELK stack along with other DevOps tools.

Gurpreet is an invited speaker in prestigious conferences like Oracle – Java One, Great India Developer Summit, Indic Threads. Gurpreet blogs at http://www.thistechnologylife.com

About the Technical Reviewers

Shyam Sheshadri is currently a senior engineer at Amazon, and before that headed the engineering for Hopscotch, an e-commerce company targeted at mons, and founded Fundoo Solutions Private Limited, a Tech startup specializing in JavaScript (AngularJS & NodeJS) and Big Data. He co-authored the book on AngularJS for O'Reilly publications, and conducts hands-on AngularJS workshops across the globe. A geek at heart, even an MBA from the Indian School of Business couldn't keep him away from the technology space.

Amit Singh is the Director of Engineering with the Analytics and Information Management Practice in Cognizant Technology Solutions. He has a Bachelor of Technology Degree in Computer Science from MIET, Meerut and a Post Graduate Diploma in IT from IIIT-Bangalore. He is a seasoned Big Data Architect with expertise in Fast Data and Search based analytics. His current area of focus is IoT Analytics and is also currently pursuing his PhD in Data Science from IIIT-Bangalore.

Acknowledgements

Writing this book was a challenging task but provided me an opputunity to explore something new. As pages were created and added, I realized how difficult it is to fit all the details of ELK stack within the page limit. I hope I have done the topic justice.

This book would not have been possible without the support and encouragement of quite a few people. First of all, a big thanks to the makers of Elasticsearch, Logstash and Kibana. This wonderful stack has kept me hooked and provided the motivation to write this book.

Technical reviewers, Amit Singh and Shyam Seshadri, have done a terrific job of reviewing the contents and sharing their valuable feedback and comments. The reviewers' detailed feedback has helped me to improve the book throughout the writing process.

I remain obligated to my organization, Aricent and my colleagues for providing me oppurtunity to explore lots of interesting technologies and experiment with them.

Finally, I would like to thank my wife Ina, daughter Jasmine and son Ishu. This book would not have been possible without their unconditional love, support and encouragement.

CHAPTER 1

▦ ▦ ▦

Introduction

"In God we trust. All others must bring data. "
- W. Edwards Deming, statistician, professor and author.

We are living in an increasingly connected world what with IOT and Big Data raising the bar for the amount of data that can be comprehended. There is an increasing trend of IT infrastructure moving to public clouds like Amazon Web Services and Microsoft Azure making log analytics platforms more and more critical. Isolating performance issues becomes challenging due to factors like load fluctuation, dynamic number of users and change in environments. These issues cannot be monitored by traditional log management systems. Similarly, almost all kind of computing devices, systems and applications emit logs to indicate the state of these systems. Elasticsearch is uniquely positioned to perform log management for both cloud scale systems and traditional computing environments.

The ELK stack — Elasticsearch, Logstash, and Kibana, is a powerful combination of tools to address log management and data analytics. Elasticsearch provides deep search and data analytics capabilities. It is a distributed, multitenant-capable full-text search engine with an HTTP web interface and schema-free JSON documents. Logstash enables centralized logging, log enrichment, and parsing. It facilitates centralized data processing of all types, normalizing varying schema and formats. Kibana provides powerful and beautiful data visualizations. It provides visualization capabilities on top of the content indexed on an Elasticsearch cluster. In short, the ELK stack makes searching and analyzing data easier than ever before.

What Is This Book About?

I was first introduced to ELK stack three years back while working on a project to centralize logs and provide analytics on top of it. I was impressed by the capabilities of this suite of tools and realized it's potential to skim though huge quantities of logs and provide elegant visualizations for it. Through this book I want to showcase the amazing capabilites of Elasticsearch, Logstash and Kibana. Just as it has helped me in troubleshooting many challenging situations, I hope the readers would also benefit in the similar manner.

This book will first introduce the ELK (Elasticsearch, Logstash, and Kibana) stack, starting with showing how to set up the stack by installing the tools, and the basic configuration. Then it will demonstrate building a basic data pipeline using the ELK stack. Next, you'll explore the key features of Logstash and its role in the ELK stack, including creating Logstash plugins, which will enable you to use your own customized plugins. The importance of Elasticsearch and Kibana in the ELK stack is also covered, along with various types of advanced data analysis, and a variety of charts, tables and maps. This book would cover the practical cases where ELK stack is being used to provide actionable insights. Detailed coverage is given to production-related aspects and scaling the stack.

How is the Book Organized?

Chapter 1 emphasizes the importance of log analysis in today's big data-crazy world. It analyzes the challenges with log analysis. It presents ELK stack as a thorough solution for log analysis. Different components of ELK Stack (Elasticsearch, Logstash and Kibana) are introduced with a description of their functions and installation.

Chapter 2 gets you started with using Logstash for log generation, collection and filtering. It begins with introducing configuration settings of Logstash. It then goes on to illustrate how Logstash facilitates shipping of logs, filtering and transforming any type of data to a common format. This can further help in arriving at actionable insights.

Chapter 3 throws light on the internal organization of Logstash and its Plugins. Logstash has a diverse collection of input, filter, codec and output plugins. An overview of the common plugins is provided. It then shows you how to create and use your own custom plugin.

Chapter 4 introduces data management using Elasticsearch. This chapter shows how to add data, index it, update it, and delete it. It goes on to show how to work with distributed document stores.

Chapter 5 explores the elaborate mechanism for searching data available in Elasticsearch. It also illustrates Query DSL and Filters.

Chapter 6 examines how Elasticsearch maps data. It then goes on to show how to map data for relevant analysis.

Chapter 7 explores the subject of Aggregates. It provides a top-level view of the entire set of documents. This is unlike queries which just focus on a particular document. It also covers grouping of documents into buckets.

Chapter 8 introduces Kibana. It explains basic concepts and key features.

Chapter 9 shows how to work with Kibana by illustrating its interface to filter and visualize log messages gathered by Elasticsearch. It covers the main interface components, and demonstrates how to create searches, visualizations, and dashboards.

Chapter 10 covers the last piece in the Kibana armor: the dashboard. Various visualizations can be combined to give a holistic view using a dashboard. This serves as a single area for visualizing and analyzing data in real time.

Chapter 11 provides guidance on scaling the ELK cluster. This enhances the capability to handle more data, index many more data sets and search data faster. In these days of cloud computing and NoSQL databases, scaling is very important because there are situations when it is required to process millions or even billions of documents. It's not always possible to support this kind of load with one instance of Elasticsearch.

Chapter 12 address the key aspects of running ELK stack in a production environment. Monitoring the different components and troubleshooting any problem is quite important. Custom configurations are required for specific scenarios.

Who Should Read This Book?

This book is for anybody who is dealing with data. The ELK stack can help in solving existing problems and open the way to new features that are yet to be rolled in. This book is for beginners and experienced users alike. While the beginners will get introduced to the concepts, the more experienced reader will gain an understanding of how these concepts have been implemented and how they interact. Whether you are developing features or providing DevOps support, the use of the ELK stack will go a long way in building systems that provide amazing insights and business metrics out of different data sources.

I wish you all the best in your journey to explore the ELK stack.

CHAPTER 1

Introduction to ELK Stack

Traditionally, logs are lines of text intended for offline human consumption. With the advent of Cloud and Big Data, there is a phenomenal shift in what can be logged. Systems can now log any piece of structured or unstructured data, application logs, transactions, audit logs, alarms, statistics or even tweets. Add to this the scale of logs. The earlier methodology of human analysis would not work in this kind of scenario. There has to be some automated mechanism for log analysis and deciphering useful information from them.

This chapter begins the journey of next generation log analysis by emphasizing the importance of log analysis in today's connected world. It introduces the troika of Logstash, Kibana and Elasticsearch, which is one of the most popular open source solutions for logs management. The three products together are known as the ELK stack and provide an elegant solution for log management. Key features of each one of them would be described along with installation and configuration steps.

Log Analysis in Today's World

Almost all kinds of computing devices, systems and applications emit some kind of logs to indicate the state of the system. Put simply, a log is just a stream of messages in time-sequence. They may be directed to files and stored on a disk or directed to a log collector. Raw logs are just data but when they are processed and analyzed, they provide useful information. Log analyzers take as input the mass of data produced by our firewalls, routers, IDS, and applications and turn that data into actionable intelligence.

Whenever a Developer or System Admin faces an issue with the system, the first instinct is to go look at the logs. For a long time, we have relied on basic tools like grep, awk or perl to perform log analysis. However, with changing times and cloud scale applications, the earlier techniques no longer suffice. Imagine a system with tens, hundreds or thousands of hosts. There are multiple instances of different applications running on all these hosts. To make things more interesting, these hosts may not be located at the same geography and we may have to deal with millions of lines logs. In such a world, it is not possible to troubleshoot problems by using earlier used tools or just looking at one particular host. Add to this the fact that the logs may be generated in different time-zones, formats and even in different languages. What is required a holistic log generation, parsing, storage and analysis solution.

More and more IT infrastructure is moving to public clouds such as Amazon Web Services and Microsoft Azure making log analytics platforms more and more critical. Performance isolation is not trivial in cloud based infrastructures. There are many factors for this like load fluctuation on virtual machines, dynamic number of users and change in environment. These issues can be monitored only by a next generation log management platform which

G. S. Sachdeva, *Applied ELK Stack*, ISBN 978-1545022146

can scan through different sources like system logs, web server logs, application logs, and ELB and S3 logs on AWS. Proper log analysis can help DevOps engineers, system administrators, site reliability engineers and developers to make better decisions.

The ELK Stack

The ELK Stack - Elasticsearch, Logstash and Kibana - are open source projects that take data from any source, any format and search, analyze, and visualize it in real time. It offers a next generation log management platform which addresses the issues associated with heterogeneity and scale of logs. At the heart of ELK stack is Elasticsearch which is a distributed, open source search and analytics engine. It is based on **Apache Lucene** and is designed for horizontal scalability, reliability, and easy management. Logstash is a data collection, enrichment, and transportation pipeline. The ability to integrate connectors with common infrastructure gives Logstash the power to process multiple types of log, event, and unstructured data sources for distribution into a variety of outputs, including Elasticsearch. The ELK stack is completed by Kibana, which is a data visualization platform enabling interaction with data through stunning, powerful graphics. Kibana can bring data to life with dashboards leveraging a range of visuals from histograms to geomaps.

Let's deep dive into each of these components.

Elasticsearch

Elasticsearch is a search server based on Apache Lucene. It provides real-time, distributed, multitenant-capable full-text search engine capability. It provides a RESTful API using JSON documents. It can be used for full-text search, structured search, analytics or a combination of all three. Elasticsearch is developed in Java and is released as open source under the terms of the Apache 2.0 license. One of its key features is the ability to search fast by indexing the text to be searched.

You may be wondering that many search engines are available from a long time which can search on the basis of timestamp or exact values. So, what's the big deal about Elasticsearch? It differentiates by performing full text search, handling synonyms and scoring documents by relevance. Not only that, it can also generate analytics and aggregation from the same data in real-time. This is where Elasticsearch scores above other search engines. For once, Elasticsearch will make you fall in love with your data.

Elasticsearch is quite popular in many big companies. Some of the use cases are as follows:

- Netflix uses Elasticsearch to deliver millions of messages to customers on any given day across multiple channels like email, push notifications, text, voice calls, etc.

- Salesforce has built a custom plugin on top of Elasticsearch that enables the collection of Salesforce log data facilitating insights into organizational usage trends and user behavior.

- New York Time uses Elasticsearch to put all 15 million of its articles published over the last 160 years. This enables awesome search capability on the archives.

- Microsoft is using Elasticsearch for search and analytics capabilities across various products like MSN, Microsoft Social Listening and Azure Search.

- EBay has used Elasticsearch to build a flexible search platform and are further leveraging it for data analytics.

If the above use cases give you an impression that Elasticsearch is only for large corporations, then let me assure you that it is being used in many startups and small corporations also. The beauty of Elasticsearch is that you can run it on your laptop or scale it out to hundreds of servers and petabytes of data.

Now let's look at some of the key features of Elasticsearch:

- It provides real time search and analytics of your data.

- Elasticsearch is a truly distributed system and can run from a humble laptop to thousands of nodes.

- It can be deployed as highly available clusters with support for Multitenancy. On addition of a new node or failure of a node, it reorganizes and rebalances data automatically.

- Elasticsearch provides user friendly RESTful interface using JSON over HTTP. All data or information is stored as structured JSON documents.

- Elasticsearch is built on top of Apache Lucene and is available as open source software under the Apache 2 license.

Tip Multi-tenancy is a software architecture in which a single instance of an application or service supports multiple customers (tenants) while ensuring privacy and security concerns of these customers.

Logstash

Instead of using the traditional ways of generating and analyzing logs, which has its own pitfalls, it is much better to use Logstash which is the next generation logging framework. Logstash is essentially an integrated framework for log collection, centralization, parsing, storage and search. It is an open source software that can dynamically unify data from disparate sources and normalize the data into destinations of your choice.

Logstash enables any type of event to be enriched and transformed with a broad array of input, filter, and output plugins, with many native codecs further simplifying the ingestion process. Logstash provides insights by harnessing a greater volume and variety of data. Logstash can take input from various input mechanisms like files, Syslog, TCP/UDP, stdin and many others. There is an extensive bouquet of filters which can be applied to the collected logs to transform the events. Logstash does not disappoint while outputting data as it supports multiple options like TCP/UDP, files, email, HTTP, Nagios and many other network services.

Logstash has an extensible architecture and has a developer-friendly plugin ecosystem. Logstash is the most popular event collection framework for consumption of data shipped from mobile devices to intelligent homes, connected vehicles, healthcare sensors, and many other industry specific applications. It offers near real-time insights immediately at index or output time. Logstash offers many aggregations and mutations along with pattern matching, geo mapping, and dynamic lookup capabilities. Forwarding these logs from Logstash to Elasticsearch allows performing a diverse range of mappings, aggregations and searching.

Kibana

Kibana is an open source analytics and visualization platform which works on top of Elasticsearch. It can be used to search, view, and interact with any structured or unstructured data stored in Elasticsearch. It facilitates advanced data analysis seamlessly and enables visualization of data in a variety of histograms, charts, graphs, tables, and maps.

Understanding large volumes of data is quite intuitive with Kibana. This is enabled by the simple browser-based interface which enables you to quickly create and share dynamic dashboards which can display changes to Elasticsearch queries in real time.

Some of the key features of Kibana are as following:

- Seamless integration with Elasticsearch allows visualization of any kind of structured or unstructured data. Data pushed into Elasticsearch from any source can be visualized easily.

- Better understanding of data by representing in various forms like bar charts, line and scatter plots, histograms, pie charts and map.

- Integration with Elasticsearch's analytic capability powerful analytics capabilities helps in analyzing data from different angles.

- Easy to setup and work with. Kibana's flexible interface makes it easy to create, save, share, export and embed visualized data for further communication.

ELK Data Pipeline

The ELK stack works on the concept of chaining one component with another. This creates a data pipeline which is illustrated in Figure 1-1:

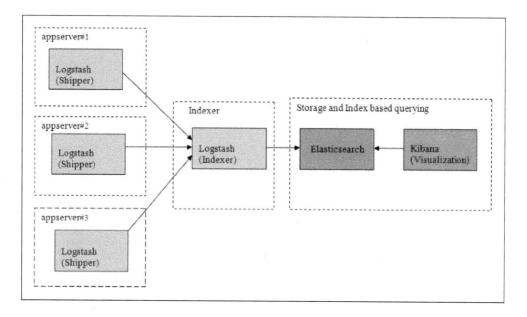

Fiure 1-1. Example of ELK data pipeline

Each application runs a **logstash shipper** at its end which pushes the logs to the central Logstash server known as **indexer**. The use of shipper at application ends avoids the need to have full installation of Logstash everywhere. As you can see the central Logstash indexer can receive logs from multiple applications. From there the logs are transmitted to Elasticsearch cluster. Kibana can be utilised to query Elasticsearch cluster to display awesome charts and build dashboards.

ELK Stack Installation

The best way to understand the capabilities of ELK stack is to get your hands dirty exploring it. The first step is to install all the three components. The pre-requisite for installing ELK stack is the latest version of Java runtime. At a minimum, **Java 7** is required although it is better to install the latest version. It is recommended to install **Java 8 update 20** or later, or **Java 7 update 55** or later. Previous versions of Java 7 are known to have compatibility issue with Elasticsearch.

The latest version of Java can be downloaded from **www.java.com**. Before proceeding ahead with the installation, verify the java version in the following manner:

```
author@DataNode:~$ java -version
java version "1.8.0_91"
java(TM) SE Runtime Environment (build 1.8.0_91-b14)
java HotSpot(TM) 64-Bit Server VM (build 25.91-b14, mixed mode)
```

Installing Elasticsearch

At the time of writing this book, the latest version of Elasticsearch is 2.3.3 and can be downloaded from https://www.elastic.co/downloads/elasticsearch.

```
curl -L –O https://download.elastic.co/elasticsearch/elasticsearch/elasticsearch-2.3.3.tar.gz
tar -zxvf elasticsearch-2.3.3.tar.gz
cd elasticsearch-2.3.3
```

■ **Tip** You can also use Debian or RPM packages provided on the download page for installing Elasticsearch. Alternatively, you can also use officially supported Pupper module or Chef cookbook.

Installing Elasticsearch is that simple and now we are ready to run it.

Running Elasticsearch

In order to start Elasticsearch, execute the following command:

```
bin/elasticsearch
```

■ **Tip** You can run it in background as a daemon by using the -d option.

It is very simple to test whether Elasticsearch is running properly or not. Just give the following command in another window:

```
curl 'http://localhost:9200/?pretty'
```

You should get the following output:

```
{
  "status" : 200,
  "name" : "Hazard",
  "cluster_name" : "elasticsearch",
  "version" : {
    "number" : "2.3.3",
    "build_hash" : "218bdf10790eef486ff2c41a3df5cfa32dadcfde",
    "build_timestamp" : "2016-05-17T15:40:04Z",
    "build_snapshot" : false,
    "lucene_version" : "5.5.0"
  },
  "tagline" : "You Know, for Search"
}
```

▒ **Tip** Name (Hazard in this case) depends on Elasticsearch version and varies across different Elasticsearch versions.

Elasticsearch Configuration and Settings

Environment Variables

The *JAVA_OPTS* passed to JVM is accessible within the Elasticsearch scripts. The most common practice is to use -**Xmx** to set maximum allowed process memory and use -**Xms** to set the minimum allocated memory for the proces.

It is a best practice to not use JAVA_OPTS but instead use *ES_HEAP_SIZE* environment variable to set the heap memory allocated to the process. It is recommended to set both the minimum and maximum process memory to the same value.

▒ **Tip** Make sure heap size is not more than 32 GB or half of RAM

System Configuration

Before starting to use Elasticsearch, increase the number of open **File Descriptors** to **32 K** (even **64K** is fine). If you want to see how many files the process can open, start it with -**Des.max-open-files** to **true**. This will print the maximum number of open files with which your installation of Elasticsearch can work with.

As part of process scheduling, almost all operating systems try to use as much memory as possible for file system caches and promptly swap out unused application memory. This in some cases may result in Elasticsearch getting swapped out. You have few options to ensure that Elasticsearch does not get swapped out.

- **Disable Swap** - If Elasticsearch is the only serving process on a system, you can simply disable swap. On Linux system you can use the following command:

sudo swapoff -a

- **Configure Swappiness** - You can reduce the kernel's tendency to swap by setting *vm.swappiness* to 0

- **mLockAll** - In this option, you can use **mlockall** on Linux/Unix systems, or **VirtualLock** on Windows, to try to lock the process address space into RAM, preventing any Elasticsearch memory from being swapped out.

Elasticsearch comes with the following configuration files:

- **elasticsearch.yml** - This is used for configuring different Elasticsearch modules.

- **logging.yml** - This is used for configuring the Elasticsearch logging.

Both these configuraton files can be found under **ES_HOME/config** folder. The configuration format is YAML.

To specify the Network Address where all components will bind and publish to, use the following settings in elasticsearch.yml:

Network.host : 10.0.0.4

The path of data and log files can be changed in the following manner:

path:
  logs: /var/log/elasticsearch
  data: /var/data/elasticsearch

It is a good practice to specify name for a cluster in production and this can be done as following:

cluster:
  name: <NAME OF YOUR CLUSTER>

⬛ **Tip** Don't reuse the same cluster names in different environments; otherwise you might end up with nodes joining the wrong cluster. For instance in order to avoid confusion, you could use logging-dev, logging-stage, and logging-prod for the development, staging, and production clusters.

In order to make troubleshooting easier, it is better to change the default node name for each node to something like the display hostname.

node:
  name: <NAME OF YOUR NODE>

Installing Elasticsearch Plugins

Elasticseach comes with a rich set of plugins that make easy the task of managing indexes, cluster and so on. Some of the more common used plugins are Marvel, Kopf, Sense, Shield and so on.

Marvel is a plugin which does management and monitoring. It has an interactive console called Sense, which makes it seamless to communicate to Elasticsearch directly from your browser. To download and install Marvel, run this command in the Elasticsearch directory:

bin/plugin install license
bin/plugin install marvel-agent

In order to disable data data collection, run the following command:

```
echo 'marvel.agent.enabled: false' >> ./config/elasticsearch.yml
```

Installing Logstash

Logstash is written in Ruby and it's available as a tarball. At the time of writing this book, the latest version of Logstash is 2.3.3 and can be downloaded from **https://www.elastic.co/downloads/logstash**.

    Tip Don't install Logstash from the Elasticsearch folder

```
curl -L https://download.elastic.co/logstash/logstash/logstash-2.3.3.tar.gz
tar -zxvf logstash-2.3.3.tar.gz
cd logstash-2.3.3
```

You are now all set to run Logstash with basic configuration.

Running Logstash

After unpacking the tarball and changing to the resulting directory, Logstash binary can be launched with command line options. The following example would demonstrate Logstash working interactively.

```
bin/logstash -e 'input { stdin { } } output { stdout {} }'
```

    Tip Start giving input data once you see the message "**Pipeline main started**"

Lets type something in the command prompt:

```
hello logstash
```

You should see the following output:
```
2016-07-04T12:07:47.446Z DataNode hello logstash
```

You can see Logstash is being run with the stdin input and stdout output and this configuration prints whatever you type in a structured format as the output. The **-e** flag enables quick testing of the configuration from the command line.

Now let's see the codec setting for output for a pretty formatted output using a configuration file. Let's call the configuration file as **sample.conf** and its contents can be seen below:

```
input {
    stdin { }
}
```

```
output {
  stdout {
    codec => rubydebug
  }
}
```

The configuration file contains two blocks - **input** and **output**. These are two of three types of plugin components in Logstash that we can use. The third type is **filter** about which more details will be covered in later chapters. Each type configures a different portion of Logstash agent:

- **inputs** - How events get into Logstash

- **filters** - How you can manipulate events in Logstash

- **outputs** - How you can output events from Logstash

Each component block can have an associated plugin. In the example above, the input block has **stdin** plugin and the output block has **stdout** plugin. The stdout plugin has a codec with value as **rubydebug** which helps in outputing each event as a JSON hash.

Now lets run Logstash with the configuration file.

```
bin/logstash agent --verbose -f sample.conf
```

Now lets give some input.

```
Hello World
```

The following is the output:

```
{
  "message" => "Hello World",
  "@version" => "1",
  "@timestamp" => "2016-07-04T12:13:22.667Z",
  "host" => "DataNode"
}
```

The generated output contains the following components:

- **"message"** - includes the complete input message or the event line

- **"@timestamp"** - includes the timestamp of the time when the event was indexed; or if date filter is used, this value can also use one of the fields in the message to get a timestamp specific to the event

- **"host"** - represents the machine where this event was generated

Logstash with Elasticsearch Output

🔲 **Tip** Make sure Elasticsearch is already running.

The most common deployment scenario in an ELK platform is to configure Logstash to output all inputs to an Elasticsearch instance:

bin/logstash -e 'input { stdin { } } output { elasticsearch { host = localhost } }'
bin/logstash -e 'input { stdin { } } output { elasticsearch {hosts => ["localhost:9200"]} }'

You can see the indexes in Elasticsearch through http://localhost:9200/_search.component

Configuring Logstash

Logstash configuration files are in JSON format having separate sections for each type of plugin that you want to add to the event processing pipeline. For example:

```
# This is a comment. You should use comments to describe
# parts of your configuration.
input {
  ...
}

filter {
  ...
}

output {
  ...
}
```

Plugins can be configured in each section. If you specify multiple filters, they are applied in the order of their appearance in the configuration file.

Often Logstash consumes significant amount of memory. This can put a tremendous stress on small machines trying to send logs. It also has some requirements like Java installation on the platform. This makes running full-blown Logstash everywhere more of a hassle. Thankfully, Logstash installation can be split into two key components:

- **Logstash Agent** - Central component which collects data from all the sources.

- **Logstash Forwarder** - The client component installed on all the machines which pushes data to Logstash agent.

In order to optimise on memory requirements, you can use the **Logstash forwarder** (previously known as **Lumberjack**). The forwarder uses Lumberjack's protocol, to ship compressed logs in a secured manner. This leads to reduction on resource consumption and bandwidth. It has a flexibility of directing output to multiple destinations. There are other options also like using rsyslong on Linux machines, or using nslog on Windows machines.

Installing Logstash Forwarder

After downloading the latest Logstash forwarder release from the download page (**https://github.com/elastic/logstash-forwarder**), prepare the configuration file. It contains input plugin details and ssl certificate details to establish a secure communication between your forwarder and indexer servers. Run the forwarder using the following command:

Logstash forwarder -config Logstash forwarder.conf

The forwarder configuration is specified in **forwarder.conf**. In Logstash, you can use the Lumberjack plugin to get data from the forwarder:

```
input {
 lumberjack {
  # The port to listen on
  port => 12345

  # The paths to your ssl cert and key
  ssl_certificate => "path/to/ssl.crt"
  ssl_key => "path/to/ssl.key"

  # Set the type of log.
  type => "log type"
 }
```

Extending Logstash Functionality

Logstash comes with several plugins which can extend its functionality. These plugins come in the form of self-contained packages called **gems** and can be found at **RubyGems**. Details of some of the major plugins can be found below:

Logstash Input Plugins

You can use input plugins to push events into Logstash. Input plugins have common configuration options.

- **Beats** - It can be used to forward logs on servers to other machines for further processing. Being lightweight it consumes minimal resources.

- **Date** - You can use this plugin to look for dates in fields. Thereafter, you can use that date as the logstash **@timestamp** for the event.

- **File** - This plugin constantly monitors files for any changes and pulls the new content as soon as it is appended. These new changes are then streamed as events.

- **Filter Plugins** - This plugin offers an optional facility wher the original events can be modified and manipulated.

- **GEOIP** - This plugin fetches geographical location information from IP addresses. The logs are then enhanced with the location information.

- **Grok** - This plugin is the "heart and soul" of Logstash filters. It is quite popular for giving proper form to unstructured data. You first define a search and then extract parts of log line into structured fields.

- **Lumberjack** - This plugin utilizes the Lumberjack protocol to receive events. The Lumberjack protocol is not only secure, but is also reliable, has low latencyoffers and needs lower resource. The use of logstash-forwarder client makes it fast and lighter as compared to logstash.

- **Multiline** - If you want to transform multiline messages from a single source into one logstash event, then go for this plugin.

- **TCP** - Best way to forward events coming over a TCP socket. Every event is treated as one line of text.

Logstash Codecs

Codecs can be used to encode or decode output or input data. Some common codecs are:

- **Default** - Use the default **"plain"** codec for plain text having no delimitation between events.

- **json** - It encodes json events in inputs and decodes json messages in outputs

- **json_lines** - Use this codec to receive and encode json events delimited by \n or to decode outputs with jsons messages delimited.

- **rubydebug** - It allows you to output Logstash events as data Ruby objects, thereby helping in debugging.

Logstash Output Plugins

Logstash outputs are the end stage of event pipeline. Before completing the event pipeline, you can use output plugins to forward the output to a particular destination. Some popular output plugins are:

- **Redis** - Redis is a very popular key-value in-memory data store and can be used as a buffer layer for the data pipeline. You can push the events to Redis by using the Redis plugin which utilizes **RPUSH**.

- **Kafka** - Kafka is a fast, scalable and fault-tolerant commit log service. It can be used to provice the functionality of a **distributed messaging system**. You can use the Kafka plugin to write events to Kafka topic by leveraging the **Kafka Producer APIs**.

- **Stdout** - This is plain vanilla simple output that prints to the stdout of the shell where logstash is running. It can be quite helpful for debugging plugin configurations

Installing Kibana

At the time of writing this book, the latest version of Kibana is 4.5.1 and is compatible with Elasticsearh 2.3.x. It can be downloaded from **https://www.elastic.co/downloads/kibana**.

```
curl -L –O https://download.elastic.co/kibana/kibana/kibana-4.5.1.tar.gz
```

```
tar -zxvf kibana-4.5.1.tar.gz
cd kibana-4.5.1
```

🔲 **Tip** Before running Kibana make sure that Elasticsearch should be installed, and its HTTP service should be running on port 9200 (default)

Run Kibana to start the node and cluster using the following command:

```
bin/kibana
```

To verify that Kibana is installed and running properly, open http://localhost:5601 in your browser (see Figure 1-2).

Figure 1-2. Kibana configuration

Kibana Configuration

Inside the Kibana installation, there is a config folder which has the configuration file (**config/kibana.yml**). Some of the important configurtion settings can be seen below:

- **port** - It controls the port to use and has the default value of **5601**.

- **host** - Property to set which host to bind with with the default value of **"localhost"**.

- **elasticsearch_url** - Use this property to point at your Elasticsearch instance, the default being http://localhost:9200

Kibana Interface

Kibana interface consists of four main components - **Discover, Visualize, Dashboard**, and **Settings**.

Discover

Kibana provides a **Discover** page for exploring matching data as per selected index pattern. On this page, you can query data, search with filter and view data from document. You can also see the count of matching results and statistics related to a field. If you configure the **timestamp** field in the indexed data, it will also display, by default, a histogram showing distribution of documents over time.

Visualize

Kibana provides Visualize page to create new visualizations. These can be on the basis of different data sources - an already saved search, a new search or a saved visulization. You can create the following visualization with Kibana 4:

- **Area chart** - Use area charts to see the overall contribution of several different series.

- **Data table** - In case you have raw data of a composed aggregation, you can use Data Table to see it.

- **Line chart** - Makes it conveneint to compare different series.

- **Markdown widget** - Expose free-form information or instructions about your dashboard.

- **Metric** - Great for displaying a single number on your dashboard.

- **Pie chart** - Makes it easy to visualize each source's contribution to a total.

- **Tile map** - Ties together the results of an aggregation with geographic points.

- **Vertical bar chart** - It's a general-purpose chart.

These visualizations can be saved, used individually, or can be used in dashboards (see Figure 1-3).

Figure 1-3. Kibana visualization

Dashboard

Dashboard is a collection of saved visualizations in different groups. You can arrange these visulization freely with a drag and drop kind of feature. They can be ordered as per the importance of the data. Dashboards can be easily saved, shared, and loaded at a later point in time.

Settings

You can use Settings page to configure Elasticsearch indices that you want to explore. You can also specify various index patterns. This page shows various indexed fields in one index pattern and data types of those fields. You can It also create scripted fields, which are computed on the fly from the data.

Summary

This chapter covered a basic understanding of ELK stack. It also elaborated why we need log analysis, and what makes ELK stack so popular. Step by step instructions were provided to install, configure and run Elasticsearch, Logstash, and Kibana.

The next chapter will show how to use Logstash for building a data pipeline for analysis.

CHAPTER 2

▦ ▦ ▦

Shipping, Filtering and Parsing Events with Logstash

In the previous chapter, you saw an overview of each component of ELK Stack - Elasticsearch, Logstash and Kibana. All these components were installed and configured. The importance of log analyses was stressed and challenges associated with log analysis were specified. Cloud and Big Data, have led to a variety of log formats tailored for specific applications.

In this chapter, you will be shown how to ship log events, filter them and send the output. This will enable you to build your first basic data pipeline using the components of ELK stack. It will demonstrate the power and simplicity of the components of ELK stack to build an end-to-end data pipeline.

Before starting with the examples of this chapter, make sure that you have already installed Elasticsearch, Logstash and Kibana as described in the previous chapter.

Sample Dataset

For our purpose, we are going to use the daily maximum temperature from 1st January, 1986 to 31st December, 2010 recorded at PASADENA, CA, Station 046719. This information is provided by The Carbon Dioxide Information Analysis Center (CDIAC). This organization has served as the primary climate-change data and information analysis center of the U.S. Department of Energy (DOE). This data set serves the purpose to understand the concept of log analysis using ELK stack.

▦ **Tip** This dataset can be downloaded from the following location:

http://cdiac.ornl.gov/ftp/us_recordtemps/sta424/tmax_serial/CA_6719tmax.txt

---

The sample data has the following fields:

© Gurpreet S. Sachdeva 2017
G. S. Sachdeva, *Applied ELK Stack*, ISBN 978-1545022146

- Station number (i.e., 046719: 2-digit state code, followed by 4-digit station code)

- Day of year (1-365)

- Year

- Month

- Day of Month

- Tmax (Maximum Temperature)

For the purpose of our analysis, I have used the data starting from 1st January, 1986. I have removed the data field Station Number, as it is a constant in our data set. I have also removed records where there is no valid value for Tmax.

Data Format

The most significant fields are timestamp and the daily maximum temperature. A snippet of the data can be seen in Table 2-1:

Table 2-1. Daily Maximum Temperatures

Station Number	Day of Year	Year	Month	Day of Month	Maximum Temperature
046719	1	1986	1	1	62
046719	2	1986	1	2	63
046719	3	1986	1	3	65
046719	4	1986	1	4	66
046719	5	1986	1	5	66
046719	6	1986	1	6	73
046719	7	1986	1	7	74
046719	8	1986	1	8	72
046719	9	1986	1	9	76
046719	10	1986	1	10	82

Since, the station number is redundant; I have removed it for the purpose of analysis. The year, month and day of month have been combined to provide the timestamp.

This data has to be put in a format and location which is accessible to ELK stack. Let's see how the csv data looks like by using the UNIX **head** command:

```
$ head tmax.csv
1,1986-01-01,62
2,1986-01-02,63
3,1986-01-03,65
```

4,1986-01-04,66
5,1986-01-05,66
6,1986-01-06,73
7,1986-01-07,74
8,1986-01-08,72
9,1986-01-09,76

Each row corresponds to the maximum temperature of a day. Now that you are familiar with the data set, let's see how to set up the ELK data pipeline by processing the data using Logstash, indexing it in Elasticsearch and visualize the data using Kibana.

Logstash Configuration

Before proceeding with log analysis, logstash has to be configured to accept input from a particular source and in a particular format. In order to read, parse and filter different types of data, logstash enables you to specify different types of inputs, outputs and filters. This is facilitated by a diverse set of plugins. In order to read data from a file, the **file** plugin can be used.

Each line in the source file is treated as a separate event and streamed by file input plugin. In running systems, typically the log files rotate. The file input plugin has the ability to detect file rotation and handle it accordingly. This it does by maintaining the last read location. New data is automatically detected if correct configuration is done. Files are read in the following manner:

tail -0f

File input configuration typically looks like as follows:

```
input {

    file {
        path => #String (path of the files) (required)
        start_position => #String (optional, default "end")
        tags => #array (optional)
        type => #string (optional)
    }

}
```

A brief description of the configuration settings can be found below:

- **path** - It is the only mandatory field in file input plugin and is used to specify the path of the file from where input events have to be received and processed.

- **start_position** - Logstash can start reading from any point in the source file and this point is specified by **"start_position"**. It can take the value of **"beginning"** or **"end"**. In order to read live streams, specify the default value of "end". Only if you want to read any historical data, you need to specify value as "beginning".

- **tags** - This field helps in filtering and processing events. Any number of filter strings can be specified as an array for this purpose.

- **type** - In order to mark specific type of events, you can categorize specific type of events by using this field. Type is added to document that is indexed in Elasticsearch. It can be later viewed in Kibana under the **_type** field. For example, you can assign type as **"critical"** or **"warning"**.

⬛ **Tip** Put tmax.csv at the path /opt/logstash/input

Since the data set we are going to analyze is in a source file, we are going to use the file input plugin and the configuration would look like as follows:

```
input {
  file {
    path =>"/opt/logstash/input/tmax.csv"
    start_position =>"beginning"
  }
}
```

The path of input CSV file is specified as the **path** attribute. Since the dataset is historic, the **start_position** is specified as **"beginning"**.

⬛ **Tip** If there are more than one input files, then corresponding sections can be specified for file input plugin.

⬛ **Tip** You can use glob expressions to specify a group of files.

The configuration varies according to the plugin type. Often there are cases that a plugin may require the value to be of a certain type such as string or array. The following value types are supported:

- **Array** - If you want to specify multiple values, then use the Array type. Specifying the same setting multiple times appends to the array. Let's look at the example below for illustration:

  ```
  path => [ "/var/log/*.log", "/var/log/postgresql/*.log" ]
  path => "/var/log/apache/*.log"
  ```

  As you can see, the above example specifies **path** to be an array with an element for each of the strings.

- **Boolean** - Value of Boolean type can be either **true** or **false**. Take care that the true and false keywords are not within quotes. For example:

```
ssl_enable => false
```

- **Bytes** - This field is a string field representing valid unit of bytes. It provides convenient way to use specific sizes in plugin options. It support both **base-1000 SI** (k M G T P E Z Y) and **base-1024 Binary** (Ki Mi Gi Ti Pi Ei Zi Yi) units. Not only are these fields case-insensitive but also accept space between value and unit. In case, no unit is specified, the integer string stands for the number of bytes.

```
my_bytes => "1345"   # 1345 bytes
my_bytes => "20MiB"  # 20971520 bytes
my_bytes => "200kib" # 204800 bytes
my_bytes => "290 mb" # 290000000 bytes
```

- **Codec** - This field represents name of the Logstash codec being used for input or output. **Input** codecs facilitate decoding data before actual processing. **Output** codecs facilitate encoding data before outputting it. By using input or output codec, you eliminate the need for using a separate filter. See below for example:

```
codec => "plain"
```

- **Hash** - It is a collection of **key value pairs** in the form "field1" => "value1". Comma separator is used to separate multiple key value entries. See below for example:

```
match => {
  "key1" => "value1"
  "key2" => "value2"

  ...
}
```

- **Number** - It represents valid **numeric** values (floating point or integer). For example:

```
num_descriptor => 25
```

- **Password** - It represents a string which will be neither **logged** nor **printed**. For example:

```
admin_password => "password"
```

- **Path** - It is used to specify a valid system path. For example:

```
log_path => /var/opt/log
```

- **String** - String values are single character sequence enclosed in **quotes** (double or single). You need to use **backslash** to escape literal quotes if they are of the kind as the string delimiter. You need to escape both double quotes within a double-quoted string and single quotes within a single-quoted string. For example:

```
name => "Good Bye"
name => 'It\'s a hot afternoon'
name => "I like \"red\" shirts"
```

Comments

You can put comments in configuration file in the same way as done in perl, ruby and python. You can start the comment with a # **character**, and it can be in any position in a line. See below for example:

```
# Comment from start of the line
input { # Comment at the end of line
  # ...
}
```

Configuring for Events

Logstash event pipeline consists of 3 stages - **inputs, filters** and **outputs**. Events are generated by inputs and modified by filters. Events are shipped by outputs. The event properties are referred to as "**fields**" by Logstash. For e.g., a HTTP request would have HTTP verb like GET or PUT. There can be event specific configuration done in Logstash. Since, events are generated by inputs; the event specific configuration applies only after the input phase. The event specific configuration works only within filter and output blocks.

■ **Tip** Event specific configuration does not work in the inputs block.

Field References

It can be more intuitive to refer a field by name and this is exactly what the Logstash field reference syntax achieves. You can access a field by **[fieldname]**. For **top-level fields**, just **omit** the [] and simply use fieldname. For **nested fields**, specify the full path to that field: **[top-level-field][nested field]**. For example, the following event has two nested fields and one top level field.

```
{
  "network": {
    "ip": [ "192.168.1.21" ],
    "timeout": 20,
  },
  "path": "/var/log/syslog"
}
```

To reference the **timeout** field, you specify **[network][timeout]**. To reference a top-level field such as **path**, just specify the field name.

sprintf format

You can use field reference format in sprintf format also. This way you can refer to field values from within other strings. For example, the statsd output can increment field values like timeout.

```
output {
  statsd {
    increment => "syslog.%{[response][status]}"
```

```
}
```

Conditionals

In certain scenarios, you may want to filter or output an event under certain conditions. This is where you can use a conditional. Logstash conditionals are pretty similar to their programming language counterpart. It supports if, else and else statements which can be nested also. The syntax looks like the following:

```
if EXPRESSION {
  ...
} else if EXPRESSION {
  ...
} else {
  ...
}
```

Comparison uses boolean logic to arrive at the correct path. Following comparison operators can be used:

- **equality** - ==, !=, <, >, <=, >=

- **regexp** - =~, !~ (checks a pattern on the right hand side against a string value on the left hand side)

- **inclusion** - in, not in

You can use the following binary operators:

- **and, or, xor, nand**

You can use the following unary operator:

- **!**

There are lots of permutations and combinations possible with expressions. They can include other expressions or group few expressions using parenthesis (...). In the below expression, a conditional check is used to take an action, which in this case is to **drop** events which contain DEBUG or INFO level log information.

```
filter {
  #Rest of the processing

  if [type] == "linux-syslog" and [messagetype] in ["DEBUG", "INFO"] {
    drop {}
  }
}
```

Multiple expressions can be combined in a single condition.

```
output {
  # Send production errors to stdout
  if [loglevel] == "ERROR" and [type] == "apache-error" {
    stdout { codec => rubydebug }
  }
}
```

23

Metadata

From Logstash 1.5 onwards, you can specify metadata with events. It is a neat way to extend and build event fields with field reference and sprintf formatting. The metadata information is specified by using **@metadata** field.

A common use for metadata tag could be to handle logs of different applications running on the same machine. Each application emits its own logs in a separate log file. The local Logstash reads all the messages, processes and forwards ahead to central Logstash server or Elasticsearch server. It can be challenging to ensure that the correct filters & output run on the logs. Adding "tags" field to input and checking for it in filters and output is a common practice. This requires some discipline in removing the tag in the output. But more often than not, the tag stays in output and leads to unexpected results. This can now be avoided by intelligently adding metadata to events. In fact, metadata tag can be used to form an independent Logstash pipeline for each application running on the same system without the need of running multiple instances of Logstash.

The below mentioned example shows how to use metadata tags for RabbitMQ logs. On reading logs from a RabbitMQ topic and processing them, each type of log is dumped into its own RabbitMQ topic (based on the type field of event)

```
# separate-logs.conf
input {
  rabbitmq {
    zk_connect => 'zookeeper.foo.com:3182'
    topic_id => 'logstash_logs'
    add_field => { "[@metadata][route]" => "separate-logs" }
  }
}

filter {
  if [@metadata][route] == "separate-logs" {
# If error in parsing logs, then drop it.
if "_jsonparsefailure" in [tags] {
      drop {}
  }
 }
}

output {
  if [@metadata][route] == "separate-logs" {
    kafka {
      topic_id => "%{[type]}"
      broker_list => 'rabbitmq.foo.com:9093'
    }
  }
}
```

As you can see, the use of metadata makes it easier to create individual Logstash pipeline. This facilitates easier troubleshooting and fewer bugs.

Filtering Events

Before proceeding with log analysis, logstash has to be configured to accept input from a particular source and in a particular format. In order to read, parse and filter different types of data, logstash enables you to specify different types of inputs, outputs and filters. This is facilitated by a diverse set of plugins. In order to read data from a file, the **file** plugin can be used.

After configuring the input file, appropriate filter needs to be applied on the input so that only useful fields are picked and analyzed. For this purpose, a **filter** plugin can be used to perform intermediate processing on the input event. This filter can be applied on selective fields based on conditions. As our input file is in CSV format, it is best to use the **csv** filter. On receiving the input event, the csv filter parses it and stores its individual fields. Besides comma, it can parse data with other separators also. Generally, csv filter looks like following:

```
filter {
    csv {
        columns => #Array of column names.
        separator => #String ; default -","
    }
}
```

Optionally, the attribute **columns** can be used to specify the name of fields in input csv file. The default nomenclature would be column1, column2, and so on. The **separator** attribute species the character to be used to separate the different columns in the file.

■ **Tip** The default separator is **comma**, but you can specify any other character also.

For our example, let's use the following csv filter:

```
filter {
    csv {
        columns => ["day_of_year","date_of_record","max_temp"]
        separator => ","
    }
}
```

As you can see, the column names are the same as the ones in the input CSV file. The separator has been explicitly specified as comma to avoid any confusion. After doing csv filter configuration, the next step is to associate specific data types with columns. The first step is to identify which column is going to represent the **date** field. This is important as this field can then be explicitly indexed as date type and the event can be filtered based on date. There is a specific **date filter** in Logstash and it looks as following:

```
filter {
    date {
        match => # array (optional), default: []
        target => # string (optional), default: "@timestamp"
        timezone => # string (optional)
    }
}
```

The match attribute is associated with an array in the format [field, formats]. It is followed by a set of time formats which can be applied to the field. In case, the input events have multiple formats, the following code can be used:

```
match => [ "date_field", "MMM dd YYY HH:mm:ss",
        "ISO8601", "MMddYYYY", "MMM  d YYY HH:mm:ss" ]
```

▦ **Tip** Logstash supports multiple Date formats as per the JodaTime DateTimeFormat library:

http://joda-time.sourceforge.net/apidocs/org/joda/time/format/DateTimeFormat.html

---

Based on the input event date format, the date filter would be the following:

```
date{
    match => ["date_of_record", "yyyy-MM-dd"]
    target => "@timestamp"
}
```

The matching timestamp is mapped using the **target** filter. The default value is **@timestamp** (the time when the event was captured). For our purpose, since we are dealing with historical data, it would be misleading to have event capture time (the time when event was processed by Elasticsearch) to be in **@timestamp**. It rather should be the date of record. The **date** field would be mapped to **@timestamp**. This is not mandatory but recommended to use.

Once the data type of **date** fields are updated, the next step is to update the data type of fields, which are required for **numeric** comparison or operation. The default value would be **string** data type. It will be converted to **integer** so that operations like **aggregations** and **comparisons** can be performed on the data. For conversion of fields to a specific data type, the **mutate** filter can be used. This filter performs general mutations such as modification of data types, renaming, replacing fields and removing fields. It can also perform other advanced functions like merging two fields, performing uppercase and lowercase conversion, split and strip fields and so on.

Generally, a **mutate** filter looks like following:

```
filter {
    mutate {
        convert => # hash of field and data type (optional)
        join => # hash of fields to be joined (optional)
        lowercase => # array of fields to be converted (optional)
        merge => # hash of fields to be merged (optional)
        rename => # hash of original and rename field (optional)
        replace => # hash of fields to replaced with (optional)
        split => # hash of fields to be split (optional)
        strip => # array of fields (optional)
        uppercase => # array of fields (optional)
    }
}
```

The mutate filter in our case looks like as follows:

```
mutate {
    convert => ["max_temp","integer"]
}
```

The convert functionality is being used to convert max_temp (maximum temperature) to integer.

Shipping Events

After transforming data into csv format, configuring Logstash to accept data from a csv file and process based on the specified data type, we are all set to ship the events. In our example, Logstash would fetch the data from csv file and ship it to **Elasticsearch**, where the different fields can be indexed. This would facilitate the visualization of data using **Kibana** interface. The **output** plugin of Logstash can be used to get output in a form acceptable by Elasticsearch.

Generally elasticsearch plugin configuration looks like the following:

```
output {
    elasticsearch {
        action => # string (optional), default: "index"
        hosts => # array
        document_id => # string (optional), default: nil
        index => # string (optional), default: "logstash-%{+YYYY.MM.dd}"

        path => # string (optional), default: "/"
        timeout => # number
    }
}
```

A brief description of key components of elasticsearch plugin follows:

- **action** - What action to take on incoming documents. The default action is "**index**" which can be changed to "delete". For indexing a document, use the "index" value and for deleting a document use the "delete" value.

- **hosts** - IP Address or hostname(s) of the node(s) where Elasticsearch is running. In case multiple hosts are specified, requests will be load balanced. For e.g., single host can be specified as "127.0.0.1" and multiple hosts can be specified as ["127.0.0.1:9200", "127.0.0.2:9200"].

- **document_id** - Document Id of index, useful to delete or overwrite the existing entries

- **index** - Index name where incoming events have to be written. The default action is to index based on each day and name it as "logstash-%{+YYYY.MM.dd}". The timestamp value is based on the filter criteria (event capture time or event raising time).

- **path** – HTTP path at which Elasticsearch is accessible.

- **timeout** – Timeout value for network requests and requests send to Elasticsearch.

The **elasticsearch** output configuration for our case looks like following:

```
output{
```

```
  elasticsearch {
    host => "localhost"
  }
}
```

■ **Tip** Logstash is assumed to be installed at **/opt/logstash**

Default values have been used for most of the settings include index. After looking at configuration of individual plugins in a piecemeal fashion, let's see what the overall Logstash configuration looks like:

```
input {
  file {
    path =>"/opt/logstash/input/tmax.csv"
    start_position =>"beginning"
  }
}

filter {
  csv {
    columns => ["day_of_year","date_of_record","max_temp"]
    separator => ","
  }

  date {
    match => ["date_of_record", "YYYY-MM-DD"]
    target => "@timestamp"
  }

  mutate {
    convert => ["max_temp","integer"]
  }
}

output {
  elasticsearch {
    hosts => "localhost"
  }
}
```

■ **Tip** Before running Logstash with this configuration, ensure that Elasticsearch is running as per the instructions given in previous chapter.

```
$ bin/logstash –f config/tmax.conf
```

On running with the defined configuration, Logstash will keep on indexing all incoming events to the Elasticsearch indexes. You can see an output similar to this on the console:

```
[2016-07-29 13:25:33,330][INFO ][node                    ] [Vermin] version[2.3.3], pid[2101],
build[218bdf1/2016-05-17T15:40:04Z]
[2016-07-29 13:25:33,355][INFO ][node                    ] [Vermin] initializing ...
[2016-07-29 13:25:39,249][INFO ][plugins                 ] [Vermin] modules [reindex, lang-expression, lang-
groovy], plugins [], sites []
[2016-07-29 13:25:39,681][INFO ][env                     ] [Vermin] using [1] data paths, mounts [[/ (/dev/sda1)]],
net usable_space [352.7mb], net total_space [6.7gb], spins? [possibly], types [ext4]
[2016-07-29 13:25:39,682][INFO ][env                     ] [Vermin] heap size [1015.6mb], compressed ordinary
object pointers [true]
[2016-07-29 13:25:39,684][WARN ][env                     ] [Vermin] max file descriptors [65535] for
elasticsearch process likely too low, consider increasing to at least [65536]
[2016-07-29 13:26:07,730][INFO ][node                    ] [Vermin] initialized
[2016-07-29 13:26:07,741][INFO ][node                    ] [Vermin] starting ...
[2016-07-29 13:26:08,536][INFO ][transport               ] [Vermin] publish_address {127.0.0.1:9300},
bound_addresses {[::1]:9300}, {127.0.0.1:9300}
[2016-07-29 13:26:08,596][INFO ][discovery               ] [Vermin]
elasticsearch/rKNxtWEyQGKWAD7QcGUNEg
[2016-07-29 13:26:11,890][INFO ][cluster.service         ] [Vermin] new_master
{Vermin}{rKNxtWEyQGKWAD7QcGUNEg}{127.0.0.1}{127.0.0.1:9300}, reason: zen-disco-
join(elected_as_master, [0] joins received)
[2016-07-29 13:26:12,040][INFO ][http                    ] [Vermin] publish_address {127.0.0.1:9200},
bound_addresses {[::1]:9200}, {127.0.0.1:9200}
[2016-07-29 13:26:12,044][INFO ][node                    ] [Vermin] started
```

You can query the document indexing status at Elasticsearch by giving the following command:

```
curl -XGET 'http://localhost:9200/_cluster/health?pretty=true'
```

You should get response response similar to the following:

```
{
  "cluster_name" : "elasticsearch",
  "status" : "red",
  "timed_out" : false,
  "number_of_nodes" : 1,
  "number_of_data_nodes" : 1,
  "active_primary_shards" : 2188,
  "active_shards" : 2188,
  "relocating_shards" : 0,
  "initializing_shards" : 4,
  "unassigned_shards" : 5560,
  "delayed_unassigned_shards" : 0,
  "number_of_pending_tasks" : 1676,
  "number_of_in_flight_fetch" : 0,
  "task_max_waiting_in_queue_millis" : 466560,
  "active_shards_percent_as_number" : 28.224974200206397
}
```

Reloading Configuration File

From Logstash 2.3 onwards, it is possible for Logstash to detect and **reload** configuration changes automatically. To enable this, Logstash should be started with the **--auto-reload** (or **-r**) command line options. See below for example:

bin/logstash –f logstash.config --auto-reload

The default configuration is that Logstash checks for configuration changes every **3 seconds**. If you want to change the monitoring interval, use the **--reload-interval <seconds>** option, where seconds specifies the monitoring interval.

In case Logstash is already running without auto-reload enabled and you want it to reload config file and restart the pipeline, just send a SIGHUP (signal hangup) to the Logstash process. See below for example:

kill -1 3452

where, 3452 is the **process Id** of Logstash.

■ **Tip** In Unix environment, you can find out process id by using "**ps**" command

---

Whenever there is a change in configuration and Logstash detects it, without restarting the process, it stops the pipeline. It then tries to create a new pipeline with the updated configuration. Once the syntax of the new configuration is validated, Logstash ensures that all inputs and outputs can be initialized. If inputs and outputs are working fine, then Logstash replaces the existing pipeline with the new pipeline. If there is a challenge with inputs and outputs, the old pipeline keeps on running and error message is displayed on console.

Multiline Event Configuration

Often there are cases when events span **multiple** lines. For Logstash to correctly handle these multiline events, proper confiugration is required. Multiline event processing is not trivial and requires proper event ordering. The best practice is to incorporate the processing early in the pipeline and the preferred way is to use multiline codec. This codec merges lines from a single source of input by using simple set of rules. The key things to keep in mind while configuring multiline codec are as following:

- **pattern** - This option specifies a regular expression. Lines matching specified regular expression are assumed to be either **continuations** of a previous line or the start of a new multiline event. Grok regular expression template is the best fit for this option.

- **what** - This option can take two values - **next** or **previous**. The previous value is used to specify that lines matching the pattern option value are part of the previous line. The next value, on the other hand, specifies that lines matching the pattern option value are part of the following line.

- **negate** - This option applies the multiline codec to lines not matching the regular expression specified in the pattern option.

Let's see how multiline configuration can be used to parse Java application logs. A typical **exception log** for Java application looks like the following:

```
SEVERE: Exception:
java.lang.BufferOverflowException:
  at Foo.main(Foo.java:25)
```

Let us see another example with a longer stack trace:

```
SEVERE: Exception:
java.io.FileNotFoundException: Bar.log (No such file or directory)
  at java.io.FileInputStream.open(Native Method)
  at java.io.FileInputStream.<init>(FileInputStream.java:146)
  at java.io.FileInputStream.<init>(FileInputStream.java:101)
  at java.io.FileReader.<init>(FileReader.java:58)
  at Foo.main(Foo.java:20)
```

Grok filter in combination with multiline filter can be used to parse Java application logs. A typical multiline filter configuration would look like following:

```
codec => multi-line {
  pattern => "^[a-zA-Z]{3} [0-9]{2}"
  what => "next"
  negate => true
}
```

The default logging configuration for Java is to record log entries starting with a three-letter month followed by the day. Whenever the multi-line filter comes across this pattern, it treats it as a new event. This configuration makes sure that Logstash treats every pattern match as a new event and treat the following lines that don't match the pattern as part of the same event.

Analyzing Events

Once the events are processed and filtered by Logstash and further shipped to Elasticsearch, it is now time to analyze these events. Kibana is an excellent tool for analyzing events with some amazing visualization. After you have verified that data is indexed in Elasticsearch successfully, look at the Kibana interface to get some useful analytics around the data.

As per the instructions given in previous chapter, start Kibana from the installation directory using the following command:

```
$ bin/kibana
```

After startup, Kibana can be accessed from the browser. It can be accessed using the following URL:

```
http://localhost:5601
```

The running Kibana would appear similar to the screenshot in Figure 2-1:

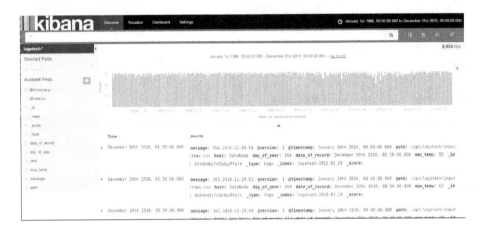

Figure 2-1. Kibana Discover Page

Since Kibana is set up to take **logstash-*** indexes by default, it would show the indexed data as a **histogram** of counts. The associated data fields are shown in **JSON** format. The first step should be to set the date filter to filter based on date range so that analyses can be based on the same. Since, the data was taken from 1st January, 1986 to 31st December, 2010, the date filter will be configured for the same. By clicking on the Time Filter icon at the extreme top-right corner, you can set **Absolute Time Filter** based on the range as shown in Figure 2-2:

Figure 2-2. Kibana Time Filter

Let's build beautiful visualizations on the collected dataset using the rich set of features that Kibana provides. An important step before building visualization is to confirm whether all fields are indexed properly with their associated data types so that appropriate operations can be performed. In order to do this, click on the Settings page at the top of the screen and select the logstash-* index pattern on the left of the screen. The page would look like Figure 2-3.:

Figure 2-3. *Kibana Settings Page*

As you can see, it displays all the fields that were indexed, their data types, index status, and popularity value.

Data Visualization

Let's start by building some basic visualization which can be later used in dashboard. First click on the visualization page link at the top of the Kibana home page and then click on the new visualization icon. This page would show various types of visualizations made possible by Kibana.

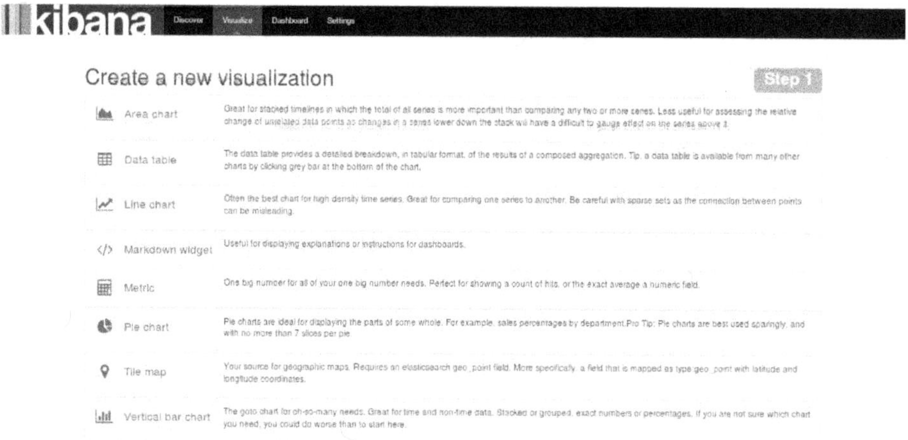

Figure 2-4. *Kibana Visualization Menu*

Building a Line Chart

Line chart would be the first visualization to be build and it would show daily movement of maximum temperature over a period of 25 years. First select Line Chart from the visualization menu. Then select Y-Axis metrics as Max and Field as tmax. In the buckets section, chose Aggregation as Date Histogram based on the @timestamp field with Interval as Daily and click on Apply.

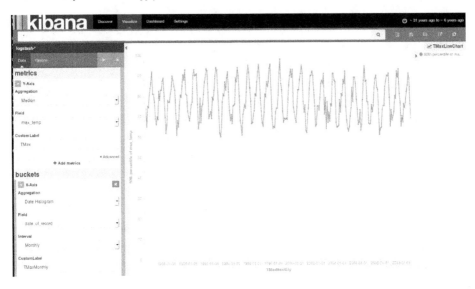

Figure 2-5. Kibana Line Chart

Give a name to the Line chart and save it. The name would help in pulling the line chart later in dashboard.

Building a Bar Chart

Let's now build a vertical bar chart depicting the movement of daily maximum temperature over a period of 25 years. First select Vertical Bar Chart from the visualization menu. Thereafter, select Y-Axis Aggregation as Sum and Field as tmax. In the buckets section, chose X-Axis Aggregation as Date Histogram with Field as @timestamp and Interval as Daily. On clicking on Apply button, you will see a vertical bar char representing the daily maximum temperature over a period of 25 years.

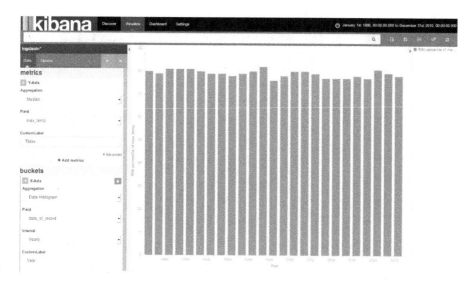

Figure 2-6. *Kibana Bar Chart*

Give a name to the Bar chart and save it. The name would help in pulling the bar chart later in dashboard.

Building a Metric

If you want to showcase one big number related to data, then Metrics is the way to go. Let's see the Highest maximum temperature recorded in a day over a period of 25 years. First select Metric in the visualization menu. Then select Metric Aggregation as Max, Field as tmax. On clicking on Apply button, you will see the result of visualization on the right as shown in Figure 2-7:

Figure 2-7. *Kibana Highest Maximum Temperature Metric*

Give a name to the metric and save it. The name would help in pulling the metric later in dashboard. Similarly, let's see what the metric for lowest temperature would like.

Figure 2-8. Kibana Lowest Maximum Temperature Metric

Building a Data Table

Data tables serve the purpose of showing detailed breakdowns in a tabular format for results of some composed aggregations. Let's create a data table of Monthly Average maximum temperature over a period of 25 years. First select Data table from the visualization menu. Then click on split rows and select Aggregation as Average and Fields as tmax. In the buckets section, chose Aggregation as Date Histogram, Fields as @timestamp, and Interval as Monthly. On clicking Apply button, you will see the Figure 2-9:

Figure 2-9. Kibana Datatable

Give a name to the data table and save it. The name would help in pulling the data table later in dashboard.

Now that we have built quite a few visualization, let's build a dashboard which includes all of these visualizations. First select the Dashboard page link at top of the page. Then click on Add Visualization link to select visualizations from the saved visualizations and arrange them. The final Dashboard would look like Figure 2-10:

Figure 2-10. Kibana Dashboard

You can now save this dashboard using the save button. It can be pulled later and shared easily. Dashboards can even be embedded as an IFrame in other systems or can be directly shared across as links. For sharing dashboard, click on the share button:

Figure 2-11. Kibana Share Options

If you have been with me till this point, then let me congratulate on successfully setting up your first ELK data pipeline.

Summary

In this chapter, you saw how to utilize different Logstash plugins like input, filter and output to gather, parse and index data to Elasticsearch. This indexed data is later analyzed by using the Kibana interface which provides visualization layer over Elasticsearch indexes. You also saw how to create visualizations. The highlight of this chapter is that you successfully created your first ELK data pipeline. In the coming chapter, an indepth analyzes of individual components would be done.

CHAPTER 3

Extending Logstash

In the previous chapter, you saw how to leverage different Logstash plugins like input, filter and output to parse and prepare data. This data can be indexed at Elasticsearch and analyzed using Kibana interface. Different type of visualization and metrics can be built using Kibana. This chapter covers advanced concepts for Logstash plugins. An overview of plugin management in Logstash would be provided, how to download and install community managed plugins and extend Logstash functionality by building custom plugins.

Plugin Management

Logstash has an extensive collection of plugins (**inputs, filters, outputs, codecs**). These plugins are developed by Elasticsearch but have significant contribution from the community also. The biggest forte of Logstash is ease of availability of plugins and flexibility of adding new ones to provide more features. It can be judged from the fact that close to **200** plugins are available for you to choose from and work with.

Plugins in Logstash are not part of core package. Ruby is used to develop Logstash plugins. Ruby programming language comes with a package manager by the name of RubyGems. This package manger specifies a common format for distributing programs and libraries build in Ruby. It manages installation and distribution of gems. RubyGems is used to make Logstash plugins available as separate self-contained packages. RubyGems provides the support required for release of plugin updates independently from Logstash releases. This approach ensures that the size of Logstash core package does not go beyond reasonable limits.

Key advantages of moving plugins away from the Logstash core are as following:

- Logstash release can be independent of plugin updates.

- Developers can release new features and bug fixes for plugins without being tied to Logstash release plan.

- Easy to describe external dependencies.

- Leaner core Logstash distribution package.

Logstash plugins, both core and community ones, can be downloaded from *https://rubygems.org/*

The GitHub repository is another place where you can access all the Logstash plugins:

https://github.com/logstash-plugins

Download and Installation

You can visit *https://rubygems.orgs* and search for **Logstash** to explore what all plugins are available. Figure 3-1 shows the list of plugins available:

Figure 3-1. Logstash Plugins

Plugin Installation

Let's say you want to install **logstash-output-mongodb** plugin. You can issue the following command from Logstash installation folder:

■ **Tip** Logstash installation folder in unix environment is /opt/logstash.

$bin/logstash-plugin install logstash-output-mongodb

The specified command will install the **logstash-output-mongodb** plugin to the Logstash installation. If you want to install a particular version, you can specify the **--version parameter**.

■ **Tip** logstash-output-mongodb plugin formats output in a format which is understood by mongodb.

Incase you have made a plugin locally and it is not yet released and hosted on RubyGems.org, you can use the following command to **install**:

```
$bin/logstash-plugin install path/to/<plugin-name>.gem
```

Updating Plugin

Whenever a new version of a plugin is released, you may want to upgrade the existing installation of that plugin. This can be done by using the following command:

```
$bin/logstash-plugin update logstash-output-mongodb
```

The above command will **update** the logstash-output-mongodb plugin to its latest version.

Uninstallation

If you no longer wish to use a particular plugin, you can uninstall it in the following manner:

```
$bin/logstash-plugin uninstall logstash-output-mongodb
```

The above command will **uninstall** the logstash-event plugin from the Logstash installation.

Plugin Structure

Elastic provides a great way to examine plugin structure by maintaining sample plugins for each type:

- **inputs** - https://github.com/logstash-plugins/logstash-input-example

- **outputs** - https://github.com/logstash-plugins/logstash-output-example

- **filters** - https://github.com/logstash-plugins/logstash-filter-example

- **codecs** - https://github.com/logstash-plugins/logstash-codec-example

Examining these sample plugins is the best way to know about the structure of a Logstash plugin and also access all the boilerplate code. You can start by cloning the plugin you need. Run the following commands to add the sample repository as a remote, and pull master from there.

```
mkdir logstash-input-foo
cd logstash-input-foo
git init
git remote add example git@github.com:logstash-plugins/logstash-input-example.git
git clone https://github.com/logstash-plugins/logstash-input-example.git
```

 ▓ **Tip** All logstash plugins should follow the naming pattern: **logstash-[type]-[name]**

Prerequisite

After getting the sample code, you can start replacing the sample information with your custom details.

```
mv logstash-input-example.gemspec logstash-input-foo.gemspec
mv lib/logstash/inputs/example.rb lib/logstash/inputs/foo.rb
mv spec/inputs/example_spec.rb spec/inputs/foo_spec.rb
```

■ **Tip** It is recommended that you use JRuby as your local Ruby interpreter.

Next step is to change the plugin details in the **logstash-input-foo.gemspec** file. Details regarding the project such as **author**, **website** and **dependencies** are kept in this file. Let's start with changing the author and project details. Ensure that the bundler knows that we would be using **JRuby** by changing **Gemfile** like this:

```
source 'https://rubygems.org'
ruby "1.9.3", :engine => "jruby", :engine_version => "1.7.19"
gemspec
```

You can now install all of the plugin's dependencies by running bundle install.

■ **Tip** Before updating dependencies, install the bundler gem on your system. It can be installed by running **gem install bundler**.

Basic Structure

Structure of all Logstash plugins follows the same pattern. A brief outline can be seen below:

```
# Required dependencies
require "logstash/inputs/base"
require "logstash/namespace"
require "stud/interval"
require "socket" # for Socket.gethostname

# Class definition
class LogStash::Inputs::Example < LogStash::Inputs::Base
  # Readable name for the plugin
  config_name "example"

  # If undefined, Logstash will complain, even if codec is unused.
  default :codec, "plain"

  # The message string to use in the event.
  config :message, :validate => :string, :default => "Hello World!"
```

```
# Set frequency of messages.
# Default value of 1 sends a message every second
config :interval, :validate => :number, :default => 1

public
# Setup phase
def register
  # Perform one time long running tasks here
end # def register

# Actual processing phase
def run(queue)
  # Generate events and push them to the queue
end # def run

# Shutdown phase
def stop
  # Close connections, cleanup temporary files, terminate threads
end
end # class LogStash::Inputs::Example
```

Tip Plugin outline varies for different types of plugins

In order to initialize instance variables and to execute actual operations, each plugin type provides certain methods which have to be implemented.

- **Input Plugin** - You need to implement the **register** and **run** methods. The register method initializes the instance variables. The run method transforms the stream of incoming messages to events for further processing.

- **Filter Plugin** - You need to implement the **register** and **filter** methods. The register method initializes the instance variables. Actual filtering of events happens in the filter method. You can use config parameters set using '@' prefix to have event properties available as event hashmap.

- **Output Plugin** - You need to implement the **register** and **run** methods. The register method initializes the instance variables. Events are processed in the receive method before forwarding them to the output destination.

- **Codec Plugin** - Codec plugin is used with other plugins to decode an input event or encode an output event. You need to implement **register** method and either **encode** or **decode** method. The register method initializes the instance variables. Encode method transforms event to another format. Decode method transforms incoming data to event.

Logstash plugin development consists of four major parts.

Configuration

First of all the required dependencies are specified. Among the first requirement is to load the **logstash/namespace.rb** file. It defines the modules namespace for the input, filter, output, and codec plugins. For filter plugin, you will need the dependency for filter - **/logstash/filters/base**. If you are developing an input plugin, then you can add **/logstash/inputs/base**. Similarly, for output plugin you can add **/logstash/outputs/base**.

Each plugin has its own class and should include the required **Base class**. In the sample configuration given above, the base class is included.

class LogStash::Inputs::Example < LogStash::Inputs::Base

At the beginning of the plugin class, there are various methods used to define the plugin. The plugin **"header"** specifies basic meta information, configuration and behavior of the plugin. Next step is to use the specified configuration options to set up the plugin. There are many configurable options available and you should try to use as many as possible. The name of plugin to be used in the Logstash configuration is done by declaring **config_name**:

config_name "example"

■ **Tip** Rather than hardcoding a value, make it as a configurable option.

You can define as many configuration options as required for your plugin. You can specify the name of the option, its data type and default value in the following manner:

- **:validate** - Helps in specifying the datatype for the option. You can chose from :string, :number, :array, :hash and :boolean.

- **:default** - Use it to specify the default value.

- **:required** - Specify whether a particular option is mandatory or not. Possible values are true or false.

Setup

The **register** method of your plugin will be called once when **initializing**. This is a trigger for the plugin to initialize or start anything needed later. One time tasks should be performed here. Possible candidates are tasks like initializing connections, clients or lists. All this would happen before start of event processing by Logstash.

Execution

The **run** method is invoked when Logstash starts event processing. A SizedQueue is passed as parameter to run method and new events have to be pushed in this SizedQueue. The information contained in Events is defined by **Logstash::Event** class. You can use **decorate** method to add fields and tags before pushing them onto the queue.

Teardown

It is always a good practice to do proper **cleanup** before Logstash stops to run. Take care to close connections, clean up files, terminate threads and any other resources which were created when the plugin was running.

Build Custom Plugin

After going through all the details of plugin development, I am sure you must be excited to build a custom plugin of your own. Now we will leverage the knowhow of previous sections to create a simple filter plugin. Let us assume that we have incoming sequence of numbers in a stream. These numbers reflect the money worth in **Euro**. We want to convert them in **USD** value. The Euro value will be passed as parameter to the plugin. For this particular exercise, I have assumed exchange rate of **1.12** between USD and Euro. I will set the exchange rate as configurable value, which can be changed to reflect real conversion ratio.

 Tip Create your custom plugin in the local github repoLet us see how this simple exchange filter plugin looks like:

```
# Convert Euro to USD value
#

require "logstash/filters/base"
require "logstash/namespace"

# Class definition
class LogStash::Filters::Exchange < LogStash::Filters::Base

  config_name "exchange"

  config :rate, :validate => :number, :default => 1.12

  public
  def register
  #do nothing
  end

  public
  def filter(event)
    if @rate
      msg = @rate * event["message"]
      event["message"] = msg
    end
  end

end
```

 Let us now examine how the filter plugin is organized.

 Tip Make sure you add the dependency for required classes to start with.

The dependencies are added in the following manner:

```
require "logstash/filters/base"
require "logstash/namespace"
```

Next step is to define the filter class:

```
class LogStash::Filters::Exchange < LogStash::Filters::Base
```

It is essential for the filter to have a name. In this case filter is coined the name, **exchange** using **config_name**.

```
config_name "exchange"
```

Now comes the point when the configuration option need for this filter should be specified. In this case it is the exchange rate of conversion from Euro to USD and is defined as follows:

```
config :rate, :validate => :number, :default => 1.12
```

As there is no need for any instance variable, the **register** method is empty in this case.

```
public
def register
#do nothing
end
```

Now comes the point when the business logic has to be defined in the filter method. This method will take an event and apply the logic for currency conversion.

```
public
def filter(event)
  if @rate
    msg = @rate * event["message"]
    event["message"] = msg
  end
end
```

The filter method first checks the value of the name filter. If it is present, the value will be assumed to be in Euro and converted into USD value. Otherwise it will be ignored. You can use the filter in the following manner:

```
filter {
  exchange{
    rate => 1.12
  }
}
```

If your input indicates 150 Euro, then after applying this filter, the output from the Logstash filter plugin will look like this:

```
{
"@timestamp" => "2016-08-15T11:09:37.117Z",
"message" => "168",
}
```

Plugin Packaging

After creating the plugin, save it as **exchange.rb** with the following folder structure:

```
logstash-filter-exchange
    └──lib
|      └──logstash
|          └──filters
|              └──exchange.rb
Gemfile
    └──spec
|      └──filters
|              └──logstash-filter-exchange.gemspec
```

Next step is to have a **gemfile** and a **gemspec** in the **logstash-filter-exchange** top folder so that a **RubyGem** can be created. Let's add some specifications to our gemspec file:

```
Gem::Specification.new do |s|
  s.name = 'logstash-filter-exchange'
  s.version      = '0.1.0'
  s.licenses = ['Apache License (2.0)']
  s.summary = "This plugin converts Euro to USD."
  s.description = "This plugin is used to convert Euro values to USD values. It assumes a default rate of 1.12"
  s.authors = ["Gurpreet Sachdeva"]
  s.email = 'gurpreets@yahoo.com'
  s.require_paths = ["lib"]

  # Files
  s.files =
Dir['lib/**/*','spec/**/*','vendor/**/*','*.gemspec','*.md','CONTRIBUTORS','Gemfile','LICENSE','NOTICE.TXT']


  # Special flag to let us know this is actually a logstash plugin
  s.metadata = { "logstash_plugin" => "true", "logstash_group" => "filter" }

  # Gem dependencies
  s.add_runtime_dependency "logstash-core", '>= 1.4.0', '< 2.0.0'
  s.add_development_dependency 'logstash-devutils'
end
```

Save the **logstash-filter-exchange.gemspec** file under the root plugin folder as depicted in the folder structure. You would need Ruby gem builders to build gems based on these files. It can be installed on Ruby console using:

```
$gem install bundler
```

You can build the gem by the following command:

```
$gem build logstash-filter-exchange.gemspec
```

You are almost done. Check the folder for gem which has been created by the name of **logstash-filter-exchange-0.1.0.gem**. You can install it to the existing Logstash installation easily.

```
$bin/plugin install file:/path/to/ logstash-filter-exchange-0.1.0.gem
```

Check the plugin in the listing:

```
$bin/plugin list
```

We can quickly test the plugin using the **logstash -e** flag option:

```
bin/logstash -e 'input { stdin{} } filter { exchange {  rate => 1.12 } } output {stdout { codec => rubydebug }}'
```

See that any number you write is multiplied by 1.12 to convert Euro value to USD value:

```
150
{
    "message" => "168"
    "@version" => "1",
    "@timestamp" => "2016-08-15T11:09:37.117Z",
    "host" => "elknode"
}
```

You can see the incoming value of 150 being converted to 168. With this you have successfully created your first Logstash filter plugin and tested it successfully. In a similar fashion, you can create and deploy plugins of input, output and codec types.

Summary

In this chapter, you were introduced to different plugins available for Logstash and where to access them. An overview was provided for accessing and installing plugins. Thereafter, different types of plugins were covered. This chapter also gave details of what goes towards making a Logstash plugin. You were taken across the whole process of plugin creation, deploying and running it.

CHAPTER 4

Creating, Indexing and Deleting Data

In the previous chapter, you were introduced to the Logstash plugin ecosystem. The entire process of developing, deploying and running plugin was covered. In this chapter, we will shift gears and talk about the fundamental piece in ELK stack - Elasticsearch. Besides covering the features of Elasticsearch, we will also look into DNA of Elasticsearch which makes it an apt platform for performing search and analytics in this era of Big Data and Cloud Computing. Before proceeding with this chapter, make sure that you have installed Elasticsearch and configured the data pipeline as per the instructions given in Chapter 2.

Ubiquity of Data

We are living in an increasingly connected world what with IOT and Big Data raising the bar for the amount of data that can be comprehended. There is an increasing trend of IT infrastructure moving to public clouds moving to Amazon Web Services and Microsoft Azure making log analytics platforms more and more critical. Isolating performance issues becomes challenging due to factors like load fluctuation, dynamic number of users and change in environment. These issues cannot be monitored by traditional log management systems. Similarly, almost all kind of computing devices, systems and applications emit logs to indicate the state of the system. Elasticsearch is uniquely positioned to perform log management for both cloud scale systems and traditional computing environments.

The most popular way of abstracting data is to encapsulate it into objects. The object oriented programming paradigm has been hugely popular and has been successful to a large extent. There is no better way to represent and handle real-world entities with complex data structures. However, when we need to store these entities things become challenging.

The most popular way is to store these entities in Relational Databases arranged in columns and rows. The Relational Databases work by organizing data into structure of tables and rows which are also known as **relations** and **tuples**. In this model, a tuple is a set of name-value pairs and a relation is a set of tuples. This provides a simple and elegant solution but not without its limitations. The most crucial limitation is that the values in a relational tuple have to be simple. They cannot be structures like nested records or lists. This leads to an **impedance mismatch** between the in-memory entity representation and relational storage.

© Gurpreet S. Sachdeva 2017

G. S. Sachdeva, *Applied ELK Stack*, ISBN 978-1545022146

During the 2000s, there was an increasing shift to **web services** with applications communicating over **HTTP**. This enabled use of richer data structures which were more often than not nested. The best way to represent these data structures is using **XML**, or in recent times, by **JSON**. This representation reduces the number of round trips involved in the interaction. Use of web services popularized JSON and it became the de facto standard for exchanging data. Another thought came around that lets store objects as objects rather than as relations. This would eliminate the impedance mismatch between application and database. The rise of **NoSQL** databases was a result of moving away from a strict schema to a schema less storage. JSON became one of the most popular representations to store data in NoSQL databases. In simple terms, an object serialized into JSON can be called as a **JSON document**.

Elasticsearch is a search and analytics platform that uses a document storage system. Elasticsearch can be considered as a **NoSQL document database**. Just like all NoSQL document databases, it provides facility to store data in an unstructured way which cannot be queried using SQL. Elasticsearch is feature rich with a strong focus on search capabilities. Complex data structures can be stored as serialized JSON documents and can be retrieved from any node in an Elasticsearch cluster.

Elasticsearch Cluster

An Elasticsearch cluster is a collection of one or mode nodes (servers) that together holds the indexed data. Elasticsearch provides **federation** of **indexing** and **search** capabilities across all nodes. You can identify Elasticsearch cluster by a cluster name. By default it is set as **"elasticsearch"**. You can configure it by changing the value of **cluster.name** property in **elasticsearch.yml** configuration file.

Node

A single running instance of Elasticsearch is known as node. The default behavior is for node to join the cluster named **"elasticsearch"**. The node settings can be configured in **elasticsearch.yml**. Different nodes can have different settings.

The different types of roles played by nodes are as following:

- **Data node** - The job of indexing documents and executing search queries on indexed documents is performed by data nodes. In order to increase performance, you can add more data nodes.

- **Master node** - Cluster management is performed by master node. It does not store indices or perform searches. While for smaller Elasticsearch cluster, even one master node may suffice, but for larger clusters, the recommendation is to have three dedicated master nodes (**one primary and two backup**)

- **Load Balancer node** - This node performs the job of load balancing or routing of requests for searches or indexing the document to appropriate nodes. It does not perform the role of either data node or master node. The routing node plays a crucial part in case of high volume searches or index operations.

Anatomy of a Document

Document is the central part in the entire Elasticsearch storage ecosystem. Put simply, a document is the serialized state of an object in the form of JSON. A JSON document has **keys** and **values**. The name of a field or property is referred to as key and the corresponding values can be of different types like string, number, Boolean, object or array of values. See below for an example of an Employee document:

```
{
    "name": "Tom Smith",
    "id":        33124,
    "manager":      "Rob Stewart",
    "department":    "sales",
    "contact details":    {
        "mobile phone": "+12072553130",
        "email": "tom.smith@foo.com"
    }
}
```

A basic unit inside a document is referred to as **field**. In the preceding example, following key-value pair can be classified as a field.

```
"name": "Tom Smith"
```

There is a tendency to use the terms object and document interchangeably. They are similar but there is a subtle difference. The term object refers to any JSON object which contains information in the form of hashmap, dictionary or associative array. It may contain a nested object. However, the term document refers to the top-level or root object which is serialized into JSON. Elasticsearch stores this object with a unique ID.

Metadata Information

Besides containing data, each document also has associated metadata information. The three key metadata components are:

- **index** - Area of storage of document

- **type** - Category of object represented by the document

- **id** - Unique identifier of the document

Let's look into some more details the components of the metadata information.

Index

Index is a place to **store** and **index** documents that have some common characteristics. It is analogous to **database** in a relational database.

■ **Tip** An index spans multiple shards, which are the actual places where documents are stored.

Index consists of multiple types, which in turn consists of multiple documents. Each document can contain multiple fields. Index stores multiple JSON documents. An Elasticsearch cluster can have multiple indices. You can either let Elasticsearch use the default index name or can specify your own index name criteria also. You can query and search an index by using the following URL:

http://localhost:9200/[index]/[type]/[operation]

Elasticsearch maps each field of the document with its associated data type which can be any of string, integer, float, double, and so on. A **mapping** for fields is created during index creation. These mappings can be queried or updated based on any specific requirement.

Type

Elasticsearch Indices are logically partitioned using type. Similar kinds of documents are represented by the same type. This concept is borrowed from the way Relational Databases store objects. In Relational Databases, similar objects are stored in the same table and they all share the same schema. Each type has its own mapping, which specifies the data structure for documents of that type. This is similar to columns in a database table.

An index can consist of more than one type, which can be defined as per context. For e.g., the index for LinkedIn can have connections as one of the index types and post as another.

The following diagram illustrates the relationship among cluster, node, index, type and document.

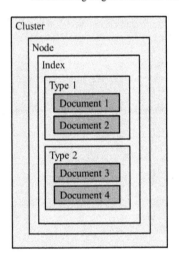

Figure 4-1. Document storage in an Cluster

Id

The Index and type, combined with the Id string, can uniquely identify a document. You can either specify your own Id while creating a new document. Otherwise, Elasticsearch will automatically generate the Id.

Shard

Shard is the actual physical area where documents are stored. Index is just a logical namespace that references one or more shards. Applications need not be bothered with the details of shards and they can perform all operations using index.

Primary and Replica Shard

In order to maintain availability of data in an Elasticsearch cluster, all documents are stored on one **primary** shard and multiple **replica** shards. When document is indexed, it is first stored in its primary shard and then on corresponding replica shard. The default number of primary shards is **5** and it can be configured as per our needs. Replica shards generally reside on a node different from primary shard. Replica shards load balance requests to take care of high load and play a key role in case of failover.

The figure below illustrates the relationship among the primary and replica shards:

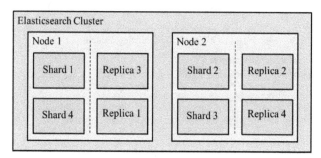

Figure 4-2. Shards and Replicas

Elasticsearch API

Elasticsearch provides powerful REST based APIs for performing various tasks like index management, document operations and support of various types of search queries. Knowledge of the Elasticsearch APIs helps in performing complex operations with elegance. All APIs have the following generic syntax:

```
$curl -X<VERB>
'<PROTOCOL>://<HOST>:<PORT>/<PATH>/<OPERATION_NAME>?<QUERY_STRING>' -d '<BODY>'
```

A brief overview of each part is given below:

- **VERB**: First thing is to specify the HTTP operation to be performed. You can perform HTTP **GET, POST, PUT, DELETE** or **HEAD** operation.

- **PROTOCOL**: It can be either **http** or **https**.

- **HOST**: Specify the hostname of Elasticsearch node. In case you are running query on local installations, you can specify either "**localhost**" or "**127.0.0.1**".

- **PORT**: Elasticsearch runs on this port with the default being **9200**.

- **PATH**: The name of the index, type or ID to be queried is specified here.

- **OPERATION_NAME**: Specify the operation to be performed on Elasticsearch. For example, _search, _count, etc.

- **QUERY_STRING**: An optional parameter which can be used to specify query options. For e.g., **"?pretty"** can be specified for pretty printing of documents.

- **BODY**: Body Text

Cluster Health and Configuration

Elasticsearch provides APIs not only for document and index operations but also checking its **internal health** and **configuration**. You can list all nodes in the cluster by giving the following command:

```
$ curl -XGET 'localhost:9200/_cat/nodes?v'
```

This command will collect information about all the nodes and display in the following fashion:

```
host      ip        heap.percent ram.percent load node.role master name
127.0.0.1 127.0.0.1      61          97 2.66 d      *        Bruiser
```

This information is based on the documents created as part of setting up the data pipeline in Chapter 2. As we have a single node cluster, the above snippet shows only one node and its related memory characteristics.

Elasticsearch has a crisp interface for checking the cluster health. Cluster health is a combination of various factors and can change due to these. The following command can be used to check the **cluster health**:

```
curl -XGET 'http://localhost:9200/_cluster/health?pretty=true'
```

This command will display the cluster health information in the following format:

```
{
  "cluster_name" : "elasticsearch",
  "status" : "yellow",
  "timed_out" : false,
  "number_of_nodes" : 1,
  "number_of_data_nodes" : 1,
  "active_primary_shards" : 3876,
  "active_shards" : 3876,
  "relocating_shards" : 0,
  "initializing_shards" : 0,
  "unassigned_shards" : 3876,
  "delayed_unassigned_shards" : 0,
  "number_of_pending_tasks" : 0,
  "number_of_in_flight_fetch" : 0,
  "task_max_waiting_in_queue_millis" : 0,
  "active_shards_percent_as_number" : 50.0
}
```

The combined status of this cluster is shown as **"yellow"**. The different colors in the Elasticsearch health status have the following significance:

- **Red** - Some or all primary shards are not ready to receive the requests.

- **Yellow** - All primary shards are allocated but some or all of the replicas are unallocated. For single node clusters, the normal status should be yellow as no other node is available for replication.

- **Green** - All shards and their replicas are well allocated and the cluster is working fine.

You can check health of not only the entire cluster but also of a particular **shard** or **index**. Give the following command to check the status of shards:

```
curl -XGET 'http://localhost:9200/_cluster/health?level=shards&pretty=true'
```

This will display the status of all the shards, a snippet of which can be seen below:

```
.........................................
"indices" : {
  "logstash-1993.01.24" : {
    "status" : "yellow",
    "number_of_shards" : 5,
    "number_of_replicas" : 1,
    "active_primary_shards" : 5,
    "active_shards" : 5,
    "relocating_shards" : 0,
    "initializing_shards" : 0,
    "unassigned_shards" : 5,
    "shards" : {
      "0" : {
        "status" : "yellow",
        "primary_active" : true,
        "active_shards" : 1,
        "relocating_shards" : 0,
        "initializing_shards" : 0,
        "unassigned_shards" : 1
      },
      "1" : {
        "status" : "yellow",
        "primary_active" : true,
        "active_shards" : 1,
        "relocating_shards" : 0,
        "initializing_shards" : 0,
        "unassigned_shards" : 1
      },
      "2" : {
        "status" : "yellow",
        "primary_active" : true,
        "active_shards" : 1,
        "relocating_shards" : 0,
        "initializing_shards" : 0,
        "unassigned_shards" : 1
```

```
        },
```

....

Similarly, you can **check health of indices**. Give the following command to check the status of indices:

curl -XGET 'http://localhost:9200/_cluster/health?level=indices&pretty=true'

This will display the status of all the indices, a snippet of which can be seen below:

....

```
 "indices" : {
  "logstash-1993.01.24" : {
    "status" : "yellow",
    "number_of_shards" : 5,
    "number_of_replicas" : 1,
    "active_primary_shards" : 5,
    "active_shards" : 5,
    "relocating_shards" : 0,
    "initializing_shards" : 0,
    "unassigned_shards" : 5
  },
  "logstash-1993.01.23" : {
    "status" : "yellow",
    "number_of_shards" : 5,
    "number_of_replicas" : 1,
    "active_primary_shards" : 5,
    "active_shards" : 5,
    "relocating_shards" : 0,
    "initializing_shards" : 0,
    "unassigned_shards" : 5
  },
  "logstash-1993.01.22" : {
    "status" : "yellow",
    "number_of_shards" : 5,
    "number_of_replicas" : 1,
    "active_primary_shards" : 5,
    "active_shards" : 5,
    "relocating_shards" : 0,
    "initializing_shards" : 0,
    "unassigned_shards" : 5
  },
```

....

Index Management

Elasticsearch has crisp APIs for Index management to index documents and make them **searchable**.

Specify Id

Elasticsearch has crisp APIs for Index management to index documents and make them **searchable**. You need to first decide where the document will reside. As has been mentioned in earlier sections, a document is uniquely identified by its **index**, **type** and **id** values. You can either specify the id value or let Elasticsearch generate one.

Custom Id

Often there are chances that the document you want to index, contains a field which can serve as an identifier. Some examples could be bank account number, employee id or student id, etc. In such cases, you may like to provide your own id, using the following API.

```
PUT /{index}/{type}/{id}
{
"field": "value",

...

}
```

Let's take example of Employee information system in a company (Let's call it **Foo**). The name of the company can be the index and **eis** (short for Employee Information System) can be the type. Let's choose the employee id as document id. The request for indexing the document would be like this:

```
curl -XPUT "http://localhost:9200/foo/eis/33124" -d '
{
    "name": "Tom Smith",
    "id": 33124,
    "manager": "Rob Stewart",
    "department": "sales",
    "contact details": {
        "mobile phone": "+12072553130",
        "email": "tom.smith@foo.com"
    }
}
'
```

The response from Elasticsearch is as follows:

```
{
    "_index":"foo",
    "_type":"eis",
    "_id":"33124",
    "_version":1,
    "_shards":{
        "total":2,
        "successful":1,
        "failed":0
    },
    "created":true
}
```

If you look at the response, you would realize that the request has been successful and Elasticsearch outputs the index, type, id and **version**. When a document is first created a version number is associated with it. Thereafter, for all changes, the version number is incremented.

Auto-Generated Id

In case your data does not have a field which is a natural fit for being a unique ID, you can let Elasticsearch take care of this by auto generating a unique id. You have to use a different request verb. Instead of **PUT** verb ("store the document at specified URL"), you have to now use **POST** verb ("store the document under specified URL"). There is no need to specify any id. You can see below that the request contains only the index and type:

```
curl -XPOST "http://localhost:9200/foo/eis" -d '
{
    "name": "Eric Anderson",
    "id": 45796,
    "manager": " Marcus Benson",
    "department": "hr",
    "contact details": {
        "mobile phone": "+12074235478",
        "email": "eric.anderson@foo.com"
    }
}
'
```

Elasticsearch stores the document with auto-generated id and gives the following response:

```
{
    "_index":"foo",
    "_type":"eis",
    "_id":"AVbA4WNg7uqRWQFJiJSn",
    "_version":1,
    "_shards":{
        "total":2,
        "successful":1,
        "failed":0
    },
    "created":true
}
```

You can see that Elasticsearch responds in a similar manner with a notable exception that the **_id** field has been **auto-generated**. Elasticsearch generates 22 characters long Id, which is URL-safe and Base-64 encoded **UUID (Universally Unique Identifiers)**.

Document Management

In this section we shall explore Elasticsearch APIs for performing various operations on documents like creation, retrieval, update, etc.

Document Retrieval

You can use _index, type and _id to fetch the document from Elasticsearch using the HTTP GET verb:

```
curl -XGET "http://localhost:9200/foo/eis/33124?pretty"
```

In response you would get the metadata elements and the source field which contains the original JSON document:

```
{
  "_index" : "foo",
  "_type" : "eis",
  "_id" : "33124",
  "_version" : 1,
  "found" : true,
  "_source" : {
    "name" : "Tom Smith",
    "id" : 33124,
    "manager" : "Rob Stewart",
    "department" : "sales",
    "contact details" : {
      "mobile phone" : "+12072553130",
      "email" : "tom.smith@foo.com"
    }
  }
}
```

■ **Tip** In order to **pretty-print** the JSON response, add **pretty** to the query string parameters.

Since, the document was retrieved successfully; Elasticsearch sets the value of field "**found**" as "**true**". This is a confirmation that the document was indeed found. In case you request a document that does not exist, you would get an error JSON response with the value of "**found**" set as "**false**". The HTTP response code would be **404 Not Found** instead of **200 OK**. You can verify this by passing the argument "**-i**" to curl, which then displays the response headers also:

```
curl -i -XGET "http://localhost:9200/foo/eis/73124?pretty"
```

You will get the following response:

```
HTTP/1.1 404 Not Found
Content-Type: application/json; charset=UTF-8
Content-Length: 80

{
  "_index" : "foo",
  "_type" : "eis",
  "_id" : "73124",
  "found" : false
}
```

Partial Document Retrieval

The default behavior of GET request is to return the whole document associated with the **_source** field. There may be cases when you may be interested in only particular fields. For example, you may be interested only in knowing the department to which an Employee belongs to. You can utilize the _source parameter to request for specific fields. You can also request for multiple fields by specifying them as a comma separated list:

```
curl -XGET "http://localhost:9200/foo/eis/33124?_source=name,department"
```

You can see the _source field now contains only fields that were requested and has filtered out rest of the fields.

```
{
  "_index" : "foo",
  "_type" : "eis",
  "_id" : "33124",
  "_version" : 1,
  "found" : true,
  "_source" : {
    "name" : "Tom Smith",
    "department" : "sales",
  }
}
```

In case you want to fetch just the _source field without any metadata, you can simply use the _source endpoint:

```
curl -XGET "http://localhost:9200/foo/eis/33124/_source "
```

The response has just the _source field without any metadata:

```
{
  "name" : "Tom Smith",
  "id" : 33124,
  "manager" : "Rob Stewart",
  "department" : "sales",
  "contact details" : {
    "mobile phone" : "+12072553130",
    "email" : "tom.smith@foo.com"
  }
}
```

Document Existence

There could be times when instead of fetching the complete document, you just want to check whether the document **exists or not**. The **HTTP HEAD** method comes quite handy in this kind of situation. HTTP HEAD requests just do a dip check on the REST end point, but don't return the body. See for yourself:

```
curl -i -XHEAD http://localhost:9200/foo/eis/33124?pretty
```

In this case Elasticsearch returns **200 OK** status code if the document exists:

```
HTTP/1.1 200 OK
```

```
Content-Type: text/plain; charset=UTF-8
Content-Length: 0
```

Now let's try to check for a document that does not exist.

```
curl -i -XHEAD http://localhost:9200/foo/eis/33129?pretty
```

Elasticsearch would return a **404 Not Found** in this case.

```
HTTP/1.1 404 Not Found
Content-Type: text/plain; charset=UTF-8
Content-Length: 0
```

Multiple Document Retrieval

Elasticsearch allows you to fetch multiple documents in a faster manner rather than fetching them one after another. You can use **multi-get** or **mget** API to give a single request instead of retrieving document by document. The mget API takes the **docs array** as parameter. Each element of this docs array should contain the type and id of the document which you want to retrieve. In case you want to fetch one or more specific fields, you can use the _source parameter.

```
curl -XGET "http://localhost:9200/_mget" -d '{
    "docs" : [
        {
            "_index" : "foo",
            "type" : "eis",
            "_id" : "33124"
        },
        {
            "_index" : "foo",
            "type": "eis",
            "_id" : "AVbA4WNg7uqRWQFJiJSn",
            "_source" : "department"
        }
    ]
}'
```

A docs array is returned in the response body. This docs array contains response per document and it is in the same order as specified with the request. You can see that each of these responses is same that is expected from an individual get request. Since, we had specified only one particular field, i.e. **"department"** for the second document; you can see that for the second document only this particular field is present in the response body.

```
{
"docs":[{"_index":"foo","_type":"eis","_id":"33124","_version":1,"found":true,"_source":
{
    "name": "Tom Smith",
    "id": 33124,
    "manager": "Rob Stewart",
    "department": "sales",
    "contact details": {
    "mobile phone": "+12072553130",
    "email": "tom.smith@foo.com" }}
```

```
},
{"_index":"foo","_type":"eis","_id":"AVbA4WNg7uqRWQFJiJSn","_version":1,"found":true,"_source":
{
    "department": "hr",
}
}]}
```

In case the documents you want to retrieve have the same _index value, you can just specify the default _index in the URL.

```
curl -XGET "http://localhost:9200/foo/_mget" -d '{
    "docs" : [
        {
            "type" : "eis",
            "_id" : "33124"
        },
        {
            "type": "eis",
            "_id" : "AVbA4WNg7uqRWQFJiJSn",
            "_source" : "department"
        }
    ]
}'
```

Similarly, if the documents have the same _index and _type value, you can specify the _index and _type values in the URL. You can pass an array of ids instead of complete docs array.

```
curl -XGET "http://localhost:9200/foo/eis/_mget" -d '{
    "ids" : [ "33124", "AVbA4WNg7uqRWQFJiJSn" ]
}'
```

Document Updates

An interesting facet of Elasticsearch is that the documents are **immutable**, i.e., we cannot change them. Does this mean we can't modify them? Not exactly. If you want to update an existing document, then you would have to either **reindex** or **replace** it. The Index API can be used to perform this operation. Let's try to update an earlier created Employee document.

```
curl -XPUT "http://localhost:9200/foo/eis/33124" -d '
{
    "name": "Tom Smith",
    "id": 33124,
    "manager": "Rob Stewart",
    "department": "sales",
    "contact details": {
        "mobile phone": "+12072553130",
        "email": "tom.smith@foo.com"
    }
}
'
```

The response from Elasticsearch is as follows:

```
{
    "_index":"foo",
    "_type":"eis",
    "_id":"33124",
    "_version":2,
    "_shards":{
        "total":2,
        "successful":1,
        "failed":0
    },
    "created":false
}
```

Note that Elasticsearch has incremented the **_version number**. Also, the **created** flag is set to **false** as a document with the same index, type and Id already exists. Internally, Elasticsearch marks the old document as deleted and adds a new document. The old documents are not cleaned up immediately but a background job does that after some time.

Updating Documents Partially

You can make partial updates to existing documents by using the **update** API. Documents in Elasticsearch, as mentioned earlier, are **immutable**. They can only be replaced and not changed. While using the update API it might appear that actually the existing document is getting modified. However, internally the update API just retrieves the document and reindexes it. A key difference is that all this happens within a shard which avoids network overhead of multiple requests. This also helps in avoiding conflicts.

The best way to give an update request for partial document update is to use the **doc** parameter. This would ensure that the objects merge together, existing scalar fields are overwritten and any new fields are added. Let's try to add a "role" field to the Employee document.

```
curl -XPOST "http://localhost:9200/foo/eis/33124" -d '
{
    "doc": {
        "role": "Analyst"
    }
}
'
```

The best way to give an update request for partial document update is to use the doc parameter. This would ensure that the objects merge together, existing scalar fields are overwritten and any new fields are added. Let's try to add a "role" field to the Employee document.

On successful execution of the request, Elasticsearch gives the following response:

```
{
    "_index":"foo",
    "_type":"eis",
    "_id":"33124",
    "_version":3,
    "_shards":{
```

```
      "total":2,
      "successful":1,
      "failed":0
   },
}
```

If you retrieve the document you will see the _source field has been successfully updated.

```
{
  "_index" : "foo",
  "_type" : "eis",
  "_id" : "33124",
  "_version" : 3,
  "found" : true,
  "_source" : {
    "name" : "Tom Smith",
    "id" : 33124,
    "manager" : "Rob Stewart",
    "department" : "sales",
    "contact details" : {
      "mobile phone" : "+12072553130",
      "email" : "tom.smith@foo.com"
    }
    "role" : "Analyst"
  }
}
```

Partial Updates with Scripts

You can also use scripts in update API to modify the contents of the _source field. The _source field is referred as ctx._source inside the script. For example, you can use script to add a new field in the document. In this case, the new field is specified as a parameter rather than hardcoding it in the script. This adds the flexibility of reusing the script in future without recompilation.

Let's see you want to add a new field, **"area"** to the employee document. You can do it as following:

```
curl -XPOST "http://localhost:9200/foo/eis/33124/_update" -d '
{
    "script" : "ctx._source.area = \"west\""
}'
```

■ **Tip** Dynamic scripting is disabled by default.

You can also remove the field in the following manner:

```
curl -XPOST 'localhost:9200/test/type1/1/_update' -d '{
    "script" : "ctx._source.remove(\"area\")"
```

64

}'

■ **Tip** The default scripting language is **Groovy**. It is similar to JavaScript in syntax and is fast and expressive language.

Conflicting Updates

Elasticsearch allows parallel update requests and it can lead to conflict situations. During an update, the document is first retrieved and then reindexed. If the window between retrieve and reindex is small, then probability of conflict is less. However, there is still a chance of conflict. It is quite possible that another process gives a request to change the document before update could reindex it. In order to avoid these kinds of situations, the update API fetches the current _version of the document in the retrieve step. This _version is passed to the index request during the reindex step. If another process changes the document, the _version number will not match and this would cause the update request to fail.

There could be some interesting scenarios when it doesn't matter if a document has been changed. Let's take the case when two processes are both incrementing a counter. It does not matter in which order it happens. If a conflict indeed happens, the next step should be to reattempt the update. This task can be done automatically also by setting the **retry_on_conflict** parameter to the number of times that update should retry before failing. The default value is **0**.

Document Creation

Often while creating documents, there are chances that you may be overwriting an existing document with the same co-ordinates (index, type, and id). You might wonder whether it is possible to be sure of uniqueness of a document. It has been mentioned in earlier sections that the combination of index, type and id uniquely identifies a document. The simplest way to ensure newness of a document is to let Elasticsearch auto generate the id. Elasticsearch ensures that the auto generated ids are unique. You can use POST to create documents:

```
curl -XPOST "http://localhost:9200/foo/eis" -d '
{ ... }
```

But what to do if your document already has an associate id which you want to use. In this case, you would have to indicate to Elasticsearch that it should accept your index request only if a document with the same co-ordinates does not exists already. There can be two ways of doing this:

- **Use of op-type** - You can specify query-string parameter with op-type.

  ```
  curl -XPUT "http://localhost:9200/foo/eis/33124?op_type=create"
  ```

  ```
  { ... }
  ```

- **Use of _create endpoint** - You can use _create endpoint in the URL:

  ```
  curl -XPUT "http://localhost:9200/foo/eis/33124/_create"
  ```

  ```
  { ... }
  ```

For a successful request, Elasticsearch will return the metadata and HTTP response code of **201 Created**. In case, if there is already a document with the same index, type and ide, Elasticsearch will return **409 Conflict response code**. An error message like the following would also be returned.

```
{
"error" : "DocumentAlreadyExistsException[[foo][4] [eis][123]:
document already exists]",
"status" : 409
}
```

Document Deletion

The way to **delete** a document is similar to how you can create or update documents. The big difference is the use of **HTTP DELETE** verb.

```
curl -XDELETE "http://localhost:9200/foo/eis/33124"
```

If the document exists, Elasticsearch will delete it and return HTTP response code of **200 OK**. It will also return response body like the following:

```
{
    "found":"true",
    "_index":"foo",
    "_type":"eis",
    "_id":"33124",
    "_version":4,


    }
```

You may have noticed that the **_version number** is incremented. In case the document does not exist, Elasticsearch returns a **404 Not Found** response code and a body like the following:

```
{
    "found":"false",
    "_index":"foo",
    "_type":"eis",
    "_id":"33124",
    "_version":4,
}
```

In this case, although the document does not exist, the **_version number** is still incremented to care of internal bookkeeping. This takes care that changes are applied in the same order across multiple nodes of a cluster.

Bulk Operations

Just like mget can be used to fetch multiple documents in one request, similarly bulk API allows performing multiple create, index, update or delete requests in a single step. This can be of great help while indexing a data stream such as log events, which can be first queued and then indexed in batches of hundreds or thousands. The bulk request has the following format:

```
{ action: { metadata }}\n
{ request body }\n
{ action: { metadata }}\n
{ request body }\n
...
```

This format looks like it is a stream of valid single liner JSON documents joined together by newline (\n) characters. It has following key aspects:

- Each line has to end with a **newline character** (\n). This rule applies even for last line. The newline character is used as marker for efficient line segregation.

- It is not allowed to have unescaped newline characters as it would create problems while parsing. This essentially means that JSON should not be pretty-printed.

The action to be taken is specified by the action/metadata line. The action can be one of the following:

- create - Document creation only if the document does not exist already.

- index - New document creation or replacement of existing document.

- update - Partial update on document.

- delete - Delete a document

The metadata should consist of _index, _type and _id of the document. As an example, a delete request can be given as following:

```
{ "delete": { "_index": "foo", "_type": "eis", "_id": "33124" }}
```

The document _source (fields and values) are present in the request body. This is used for document creation, indexing and update. A notable exception is delete operation which does not require any request body. Let's see an example with complete set of bulk requests.

```
{ "delete": { "_index": "foo", "_type": "eis", "_id": "33124" }}
{ "create": { "_index": "foo", "_type": "eis", "_id": "33124" }}
{ "name": "Tom Smith", "id": 33124, "manager": "Rob Stewart", "department": "sales" }
{ "index": { "_index": "foo", "_type": "eis" }}
{ "name": "Bob Dillon", "id": "54798", "manager": "James Owens", "department": "finance" }
{ "update": { "_index": "foo", "_type": "eis", "_id": "33124", "_retry_on_conflict": 4 }}
{ "doc": {"manager" : "Lew Grey"} }
```

All the requests except delete request have a body. Elasticsearch responds with an items array, where each array element corresponds to the result of each request, in order in which they were requested:

```
{"took":89,"errors":false,"items":[{"delete":{"_index":"foo","_type":"eis","_id":"33124","_version":4,"_shards":{
"total":2,"successful":1,"failed":0},"status":200,"found":true}}]}
{"took":121,"errors":false,"items":[{"create":{"_index":"foo","_type":"eis","_id":"33124","_version":1,"_shards"
:{"total":2,"successful":1,"failed":0},"status":201}}]}
{"took":156,"errors":false,"items":[{"create":{"_index":"foo","_type":"eis","_id":"AVbR2mhj7uqRWQFJiJSv","
_version":1,"_shards":{"total":2,"successful":1,"failed":0},"status":201}}]}
```

{"took":76,"errors":false,"items":[{"update":{"_index":"foo","_type":"eis","_id":"33124","_version":2,"_shards":{"total":2,"successful":1,"failed":0},"status":200}}]}

{

    "took":89,
    "errors":false,
    "items":[
        {"delete":{
            "_index":"foo",
            "_type":"eis",
            "_id":"33124",
            "_version":4,
            "_shards":{"total":2,"successful":1,"failed":0},
            "status":200,
            "found":true
        }},
        {"create":{
            "_index":"foo",
            "_type":"eis",
            "_id":"33124",
            "_version":1,
            "_shards":{"total":2,"successful":1,"failed":0},
            "status":201
        }},
        {"create":{
            "_index":"foo",
            "_type":"eis",
            "_id":"AVbR2mhj7uqRWQFJiJSv",
            "_version":1,
            "_shards":{"total":2,"successful":1,"failed":0},
            "status":201
        }},
        {"update":{
            "_index":"foo",
            "_type":"eis",
            "_id":"33124",
            "_version":2,
            "_shards":{"total":2,"successful":1,"failed":0},
            "status":200
        }}
    ]
}

The Bulk request handles individual request failures by executing them independently. This ensures that if one sub request fails, then other sub requests will not be impacted. However, in this case the top level error flag is set to **true**. The error details can be found under the relevant requests.

In the preceding example, you can see that it failed to create document 33124 as it already existed. However, the subsequent index request for document 33124 does succeed. This indicates that bulk requests are not atomic as each request gets processed individually. This means status of one request would not impact that of others.

Bulk Request Size

When a node receives bulk request, the entire request has to be loaded into memory. This constrains the memory available for other requests. There are optimal values for what the size of bulk request should be. If request size is more than optimal size, then you will not see any advantage in performance. On the contrary, performance may suffer and drop. To make things more interesting, optimal size is not a fixed number. It depends on various factors like hardware, size of document and its complexity, ongoing indexing and search load.

Finding the optimal size is not too difficult. You can index typical documents in batches and keep on increasing their size. The tipping point is when performance starts to drop off. It indicates that your batch size is beginning to be over the cutoff. Start with small size of batches and then increase them incrementally.

Conflict Management

The process for updating documents with index API is to read the original document, do the changes and in the end, reindex the whole document. Indexing is successful for the most recent request. The document to be indexed last gets stored in Elasticsearch. If some other parallel request was given to change the document, then it would fail.

This behavior may or may not be a problem. In your solution, there may be little chance of two parallel requests on the same document. It might also happen that losing some change is not crucial for the system behavior. But it might be crucial also in some situations. Consider, Elasticsearch being used to store bank transactions (may be just for search purpose). In this case, order is important. We can take a leaf out of the database world to deal with conflicts.

- **Pessimistic Concurrency Control** - This is a popular technique used in relational databases which works on the assumption that conflicts are likely to happen and therefore blocks access to resources so as to prevent conflicts. A common example is locking of rows before reading from the row, thereby ensuring that only the thread with the lock makes the changes to the row data.

- **Optimistic Concurrency Control** - This approach is used by Elasticsearch and is based on the assumption that conflicts are unlikely to happen. Therefore, operations are not blocked from being attempted. If the underlying data gets modified in between reads and writes, the updates will fail. The application now has to decide how to make sense of the data. There are multiple options like reapplying the update, use of fresh data or report error to the user.

Summary

In this chapter you were introduced to Elasticsearch and its different features were covered. An overview was given to create documents, index documents, partial and full updates, delete operation, bulk operations. The Elasticsearch API for performing different operations was covered. There can be conflicting situations in Elasticsearch and an overview of different conflict resolution strategies was covered

CHAPTER 5

Searching Data

In the previous chapter, you were introduced to Elasticsearch. An overview of its different features to create documents, index documents, partial and full updates, delete operation, bulk operations was given. Different operations were performed elegantly using the Elasticsearch API. The goal of this chapter is to explore the elaborate mechanism for searching data available in Elasticsearch. It covers both the search query variations - Search Lite and Full Body Search. Then it illustrates Query DSL and Filters.

Search Your Way

What good a storage engine would be if it doesn't offer comprehensive search mechanism to explore the stored data. Just like Relational Databases, Elasticsearch provides elaborate search mechanisms - from basic search APIs to query DSL and Advanced Search mechanisms. The real power of Elasticsearch is to turn huge amount of stored data into tangible information. Use of structured JSON documents rather than data blobs enables Elasticsearch to index data in order to provide a powerful search mechanism. All the fields are indexed and can act as potential keys for search. Not only that, Elasticsearch leverages all these indices to perform search at an astonishing speed. This is where Elasticsearch scores ahead of Relational databases.

You can not only perform basic search operations but also search using multi-index or multi-type. You can also have pagination of your search response. Elasticsearch has an elaborate query DSL. You can have search responses filtered.

If you want more flexibility when querying data or more specific responses, you need to move beyond the match query. You should have a good understanding of your data in order to explore it better. Knowledge of each query's contribution to the **relevance** score helps in optimizing the queries. This would ensure that the documents that best fit the search criteria appear first and less relevant documents are towards the end. Let's start by using basic search mechanism to perform structured search.

Simple Searches

A straightforward search can be one of the following:

© Gurpreet S. Sachdeva 2017

G. S. Sachdeva, *Applied ELK Stack*, ISBN 978-1545022146

- **Structured Query** - This is similar to the queries you would give using SQL to a relational database. For e.g., querying on distinct fields like bank account number or account type, which can be sorted by a field like balance amount.

- **Full Text Query** - These types of queries find documents by matching search keywords and response is sorted by relevance.

- **Combination of above two**

For the most part, you can query by just giving some matching or search criteria. However, in order to leverage the full power of Elasticsearch, it would be helpful to understand which components of Elasticsearch map and search data:

- **Mapping** - Interpretation of data in a field.

- **Analysis** - Processing of full text to make it search ready.

  Query DSL - Query language used by Elasticsearch which provides powerful and flexible searching.

In this chapter we will cover all the three above listed components starting with the search API. For the purpose of exploring Search API, load the sample document containing information about some of the works of William Shakespeare and Charles Dickens. The sample document can be loaded by using bulk request having following contents:

```
{ "create": { "_index": "ws", "_type": "author", "_id": "1" }}
{ "name": "William Shakespeare", "born": "1564-04-26", "died": "1616-04-23", "country": "United Kingdom" }
{ "create": { "_index": "cd", "_type": "author", "_id": "2" }}
{ "name": "Charles Dickens", "born": "1812-02-07", "died": "1870-06-09", "country": "United Kingdom" }
{ "create": { "_index": "ws", "_type": "play", "_id": "3" }}
{ "author": "William Shakespeare", "play": "Comedy of Errors", "published": "1589" }
{ "create": { "_index": "cd", "_type": "play", "_id": "4" }}
{ "author": "Charles Dickens", "play": "The Pickwick Papers", "published": "1836" }
{ "create": { "_index": "ws", "_type": "play", "_id": "5" }}
{ "author": "William Shakespeare", "play": "Henry VI", "published": "1590" }
{ "create": { "_index": "cd", "_type": "play", "_id": "6" }}
{ "author": "Charles Dickens", "play": "Oliver Twist", "published": "1837" }
{ "create": { "_index": "ws", "_type": "play", "_id": "7" }}
{ "author": "William Shakespeare", "play": "Richard III", "published": "1592" }
{ "create": { "_index": "cd", "_type": "play", "_id": "8" }}
{ "author": "Charles Dickens", "play": "Nicholas Nickleby", "published": "1838" }
{ "create": { "_index": "ws", "_type": "play", "_id": "9" }}
{ "author": "William Shakespeare", "play": "Taming of the Shrew", "published": "1593" }
{ "create": { "_index": "cd", "_type": "play", "_id": "10" }}
{ "author": "Charles Dickens", "play": "The Old Curiosity", "published": "1840" }
{ "create": { "_index": "ws", "_type": "play", "_id": "11" }}
{ "author": "William Shakespeare", "play": "Romeo and Juliet", "published": "1594" }
{ "create": { "_index": "cd", "_type": "play", "_id": "12" }}
{ "author": "Charles Dickens", "play": "David Copperfield", "published": "1849" }
```

■ **Tip** There should be an extra newline in the end of the bulk request contents file.

Let's call the bulk contents file as **plays.json**. Give the following command to load the bulk contents:

```
curl -XPOST 'localhost:9200/_bulk?pretty' --data-binary "@plays.json"; echo
{
  "took" : 4343,
  "errors" : false,
  "items" : [ {
    "create" : {
      "_index" : "ws",
      "_type" : "author",
      "_id" : "1",
      "_version" : 1,
      "_shards" : {
        "total" : 2,
        "successful" : 1,
        "failed" : 0
      },
      "status" : 201
    }
  }, {
    "create" : {
      "_index" : "cd",
      "_type" : "author",
      "_id" : "2",
      "_version" : 1,
      "_shards" : {
        "total" : 2,
        "successful" : 1,
        "failed" : 0
      },
      "status" : 201
    }
  }, {
    "create" : {
      "_index" : "ws",
      "_type" : "play",
      "_id" : "3",
      "_version" : 1,
      "_shards" : {
        "total" : 2,
        "successful" : 1,
        "failed" : 0
      },
      "status" : 201
    }
  }, {
    "create" : {
```

```
    "_index" : "cd",
    "_type" : "play",
    "_id" : "4",
    "_version" : 1,
    "_shards" : {
      "total" : 2,
      "successful" : 1,
      "failed" : 0
    },
    "status" : 201
  }
},
...........................
}]
}
```

Search Without Parameter

The simplest use of search API is to search without any parameters. No query is specified and it simply responds with all documents in every index of the cluster:

```
curl -XGET 'localhost:9200/_search?pretty'
```

The response would look like the following:

```
{
  "took" : 9,
  "timed_out" : false,
  "_shards" : {
    "total" : 10,
    "successful" : 10,
    "failed" : 0
  },
  "hits" : {
    "total" : 12,
    "max_score" : 1.0,
    "hits" : [ {
    }, {
      "_index" : "ws",
      "_type" : "author",
      "_id" : "1",
      "_score" : 1.0,
      "_source" : {
        "name" : "William Shakespeare",
        "born" : "1564-04-26",
        "died" : "1616-04-23",
        "country" : "United Kingdom"
      }
    }, {
```

```
  "_index" : "ws",
  "_type" : "play",
  "_id" : "3",
  "_score" : 1.0,
  "_source" : {
    "author" : "William Shakespeare",
    "play" : "Comedy of Errors",
    "published" : "1589"
  }
}, {
................
  } ]
 }
}
```

hits

In case you are wondering, hits is the most significant section of the response. It indicates the total number of documents matching your query. It also contains a hits array which contains the first **10** documents which matched the search criteria. Every result in the hits array has the **_index**, **_type** and **_id** of the matching document. It also has the **_source** field. This is significant as the entire document is available straightway from the search results. This is where Elasticsearch scores above other search engines which just return **document Id**, necessitating another query for fetching the document contents.

You may have noticed that each entry also has a **_score** field. Its value indicates the extent of matching of the document with the query. The default behavior is to return most relevant documents first, i.e. in descending order of score. In this scenario, since no specific query was specified, all documents have same relevance and thereby _score of **1** for all results. The highest _score of any document matching the query is specified in **max_score** field.

took

The took field specifies time taken to execute search query in **milliseconds**.

shards

Multiple shards are typically involved in a search query and **_shards** field indicates the number of **participating shards**. It also specifies how many shards were successful and how many of them failed. Most of the times, all the shards are successful, but there can be cases when one or more shards fail. In case of a major disaster, there is a high chance that both the primary and replica copy of the same shard are lost. In such a case, search requests for the shard would not be serviced as no copy of the shard is available. In such scenarios, Elasticsearch reports the shard as **failed** but still fetches results from the remaining available shards.

timeout

Whether the query timed out or not is indicated by the **timed_out** field. The default behavior for search requests is to **not time out**. If you want response within a certain time period, specify timeout value. For example, in the following GET query a time period of 20 milliseconds is specified:

```
curl –XGET 'localhost:9200/_search?timeout=20ms&pretty'
```

Elasticsearch will return only those results which it could gather from each shard during this time period.

■ **Tip** Timeout indicates to the coordinating node to return results obtained so far and close all connections. Use Timeout to fetch results in case if you have a SLA to meet.

Multi-Index, Multi-Type

In the preceding example, the response for the empty search consisted of documents of different types - authors and plays from two different indices - **ws** and **cd**. We had not constrained the search to a particular index or type and thereby searched across all documents in the cluster. Elasticsearch sent the request in parallel to a primary or replica of every shard in the cluster. The results were gathered to select the overall top 10, and sent in response.

Most of the times you would not want your search to be so broad based. You would like to search within certain index and type. You can do this by passing index and type as parameters in the search query as shown in the Table 1-1

Table 1-1. Search Criteria Combinations

Query	Search For
/_search	All types in all indices
/ws/_search	All types in the ws index
/ws,cd/_search	All types in both the ws and cd indices
/w*,c*/_search	All types in any indices beginning with w or beginning with c
/ws/play/_search	Type play in the ws index
/ws,cd/play,published/_search	Type play and published in both the ws and cd indices
/_all/play,published/_search	Types play and published in all indices

Searching within a single index requires Elasticsearch to forward the search request to primary or replica of all shards in that index. Thereafter, results are gathered from all the shards. However, searching within multiple indices requires looking in exactly the same way but with more shards being involved.

Pagination

The previous section about **empty** search indicated that there are **12 documents** that match the criteria. You might have noticed that there were only **10 documents** in the **hits array**. This is due to the upper limit on the number of documents which the hits array can contain. You might wonder how to fetch other documents? Not to worry.

Elasticsearch has borrowed the pagination concept from SQL. Just like in SQL, you can use **LIMIT** keyword to return all results in a single page, similarly Elasticsearch uses the **from** and **size** parameters:

- **from** - Number of initial results to be skipped. Default value is **0**.

- **size** - Number of results to be returned. Default value is **10**.

Let's see if you want to show three documents per page then pages 1 to 5 could be requested as follows:

```
curl –XGET 'localhost:9200/_search?size=3&pretty'
curl –XGET 'localhost:9200/_search?size=3&from=3&pretty'
curl –XGET 'localhost:9200/_search?size=3&from=6&pretty'
curl –XGET 'localhost:9200/_search?size=3&from=9&pretty'
curl –XGET 'localhost:9200/_search?size=3&from=12&pretty'
```

You should be cautious while paging **too deep** or fetching too many results in one shot. One of the costliest steps while generating results is to sort the results before returning them. More often than not a search request spans multiple shards leading to increase in the cost. After a shard generates its results, they have to be sorted. Once all shards generate their results, it has to be centrally sorted to make sure that the overall order is correct.

■ **Tip** In distributed systems, as we page deeper and deeper, the cost of sorting results grows exponentially.

Search *Lite*

Search API comes in two forms:

- **Search Lite** - Query string which requires all the parameters to be passed in the query string.

- **Query DSL** - Full body query with a JSON request body and use of rich search language known by the name of query DSL.

The query-string version has utility in performing ad hoc query searches from the command line. For e.g., the following query finds all documents of type **"play"** that contain the word **"The"**.

```
GET /_all/play/_search?q=play:The
```

You can combine different criteria together in the same query string. Let's say you want to search for all plays with **"The"** in the title and published in **"1840"**. The query would like the following:

```
+play:The +published:1840
```

After the percent encoding the query string parameters look like the following:

```
GET /_search?q=%2Bplay%3AThe+%2Bpublished%3A1840
```

The + **prefix** is used to specify the conditions that must be satisfied for query to match. In the same way, - **prefix** is used to specify the conditions that must not match. Any condition without a + or - is optional.

The _all Field

The simplest way to look for all documents containing the word "**Shakespeare**" is following:

```
GET /_search?q=Shakespeare
```

In previous section, we looked for words in the play or published fields. This query however returns documents matching "Shakespeare" in the following fields:

- Author with name as Shakespeare

- Play with author as Shakespeare

Interesting thing is Elasticsearch has found results in two different fields. The foundation for this is laid at the time of indexing. At that time, Elasticsearch uses the string values of all of its fields to concatenate them into one big string, which is then indexed as the special _all field. For e.g., look at the following document:

```
{
    "author": "William Shakespeare",
    "play": "Richard III",
    "published": "1592"
}
```

If you deep dive into how Elasticsearch stores this document, it would appear as if there is an extra field called _**all** with the following value:

"William Shakespeare Richard III 1592"

If no other specific field is specified in the query string, then this _**all** field is used for search request.

Query Mashup

Let's try to use different combinations for searching plays based on the following criteria:

- The play field contains either "**The**" or "**or**"

- The published year is greater than **1838**

- The _all field contains either of the word **Shakespeare** or **Charles**

The query string would like the following:

```
+play:(The or) +published:>1838 +(Shakespeare Charles)
```

After proper encoding this query string would like following:

```
?q=%2Bplay%3A(The+or)+%2Bpublished%3A%3E1838+%2B(Shakespeare+Charles)
```

It might come as a surprise, but this query string is extremely powerful. The elaborate query syntax facilitates construction of quite complex queries. The flip side is that its brevity can make it cryptic. It is also error prone as even a single misplaced - or + can return in error. The query-string search mechanism is quite useful for running slow and heavy queries on any of the fields. However, in production using the full-featured request body search API is preferred.

Query DSL

In previous section we have seen that Search Lite is useful for ad hoc queries, it is not very flexible and if result set is large then the whole process becomes quite slow. We now come to another mechanism for searching data - Query DSL. It is quite flexible and uses an expressive language to perform the most intense queries through a simple JSON interface. If you want to search data in production environment, then Query DSL is the way to go. It makes queries more precise while keeping them simple and easier to debug.

Let's see a basic use of Query DSL by passing a query in the query parameter:

```
curl -XGET 'localhost:9200/_search?pretty' –d '
{
    "query": ACTUAL QUERY
}'
```

Performing an empty search {} gives the same results as the match_all query clause and returns all documents.

```
curl -XGET 'localhost:9200/_search?pretty' –d '
{
    "query": {
        "match_all": {}
    }
}'
```

Query Clause Construction

Typically, a query clause should have the following construct

```
{
    QUERY_NAME: {
        ARGUMENT: VALUE,
        ARGUMENT: VALUE,...
    }
}
```

If you want to refer one particular field, then use the following construct

```
{
    QUERY_NAME: {
        FIELD_NAME: {
            ARGUMENT: VALUE,
```

```
      ARGUMENT: VALUE,...
    }
  }
}
```

For e.g., if you want to find out plays that have the word **"The"** in their title, you can query using the match clause in the following manner:

```
curl -XGET 'localhost:9200/_search?pretty' –d '
{
   "query": {
     "match": {
        "play": "The"
     }
   }
}'
```

Working with Multiple Clauses

Query clauses are like lego blocks which can be combined to create complex queries. There are two types of clauses:

- **Leaf Clauses** - They are used to compare field(s) to a query string, similar to the match clause.

- **Compound Clauses** - They are used to combine other query clauses. For e.g., bool clause can be used to combine other clauses that either must match, must_not match, or should match if possible:

```
{
  "bool": {
     "must": { "match": { "author": "Dickens" }},
     "must_not": { "match": { "play": "The" }},
     "should": { "match": { "published": "1838" }}
  }
}
```

You can use compound clause to combine multiple query clauses, including other compound clauses. They have the ability to nest within each other which can lead to potentially complex logic. In order to demonstrate the combination of queries, let's load the following data:

```
{ "create": { "_index": "entertainment", "_type": "motion picture" }}
{ "movie": "Hollywood", "name": "Pulp Fiction", "actor": "Bruce Willis", "date": "1994-05-12", "genre":
"action", "director": "Quentin Tarantino" }
{ "create": { "_index": "entertainment", "_type": "motion picture" }}
{ "movie": "Hollywood", "name": "Armageddon", "actor": "Bruce Willis", "date": "1998-07-01", "genre":
"science fiction", "director": "Michael Bay" }
{ "create": { "_index": "entertainment", "_type": "motion picture" }}
{ "movie": "Hollywood", "name": "The Sixth Sense", "actor": "Bruce Willis", "date": "1999-08-02", "genre":
"horror", "director": "M. Night Shyamalan" }
{ "create": { "_index": "entertainment", "_type": "motion picture" }}
```

```
{ "movie": "Hollywood", "name": "The Fast and the Furious", "actor": "Vin Diesel", "date": "2001-06-18",
"genre": "action", "director": "Rob Cohen" }
{ "create": { "_index": "entertainment", "_type": "motion picture" }}
{ "movie": "Hollywood", "name": "The Pacifier", "actor": "Vin Diesel", "date": "2005-03-04", "genre": "action",
"director": "Adam Shankman" }
{ "create": { "_index": "entertainment", "_type": "motion picture" }}
{ "movie": "Hollywood", "name": "The Last Witch Hunter", "actor": "Vin Diesel", "date": "2015-10-23",
"genre": "action", "director": "Breck Eisner" }
```

Let's call the bulk contents file as plays.json. Give the following command to load the bulk contents:

```
curl -XPOST 'localhost:9200/_bulk?pretty' --data-binary "@movie.json"; echo
```

For example, the following query snippet searches for **Hollywood** movies in which either **"Vin Diesel"** has starred or those action movies with **"action"** genre but not directed by **"James Cameron"**:

```
{
  "bool": {
    "must": { "match": { "movie": "Hollywood" }},
    "should": [
      { "match": { "actor": "Vin Diesel" }},
      { "bool": {
        "must": { "genre": "action" }},
        "must_not": { "director": "James Cameron" }}
      }}
    ],
    "minimum_should_match": 1
  }
}
```

You can see that the compound query clause combines both lead clause and other compound clause to create a single query.

Filter and Query

The common perception is to think of only query DSL, however there are two types of DSLs - query DSL and filter DSL. Both have similar clauses but somewhat different purposes.

- **Filter** asks a yes or no question of each document and is useful for fields that contain exact values:

    o   Is the published date in the range *1850 - 1900*?

    o   Is the state field reflecting *success*?

    o   Is the distance covered more than *50km*?

- **Query** is pretty similar to filter but adds value by ascertaining how well the document matches? A query figures out how relevant a document is and on that basis assigns it a relevance score. This score is later used to sort matching documents for the most relevant result. This concept of relevance is apt for full-text search, where there is **"no"** correct answer. Some scenarios where query can have added benefit:

  o   Best match for the words full text search

  o   Containing the word play, but maybe also matches playing, player or sprinter

  o   Containing the words sphinx, black and quartz. The closer the words are, the more relevant the document is.

Performance Concerns

More often than not, output from filter clauses is a simple list of matching documents, which is fast to compute and easily stored in cache. It uses only **1 bit per document** and can be reused efficiently for subsequent requests. Queries have to do a much harder job of finding documents with an exact match and also calculate relevant score for each document. This makes query more demanding as compared to filter. To make matters worse, results from a query cannot be cached.

Generally, a cached filter way outperforms a query consistently. This is due to the less number of documents examined by the filter.

■   **Tip** The rule of thumb is to use query clauses while doing full-text search and use filter clause for any other search.

Key Filters and Queries

Elasticsearch offers many filters and queries to work with, however only a handful of them are commonly used.

term Filter

The term filter sifts documents by exact value, whether it is of type number, date, Boolean or not_analyzed exact-value string field.

```
{ "term": { "cost": 500 }}
{ "term": { "date": "2016-09-04" }}
{ "term": { "status": true }}
{ "term": { "label": "full_text" }}
```

terms Filter

It is similar to the term filter but with a crucial difference that in this case you can specify multiple values to match. The document is considered matching, if the field contains any of the specified values.

{ "terms": { "tag": ["foo", "bar", "null"] }}

range Filter

The range filter is useful for searching numbers or dates within the specified range.

```
{
   "range": {
      "income": {
         "gte": 100000,
         "lt": 150000
      }
   }
}
```

Table 1-2 depicts the operators that are allowed:

Table 1-2. Ranger Filter Operators

Operator	Function
gt	Greater than
gte	Greater than or equal to
lt	Less than
lte	Less than or equal to

exists and missing Filters

The exists and missing filters help in fetching documents with specified field occurring one or more times (exists) or not being present at all (missing). Corresponding operations in SQL are **IS_NULL** (missing) and **NOT IS_NULL** (exists).

The following code snippet demonstrates example for **exists** filter.

```
{
   "exists": {
      "field": "tag"
   }
}
```

The following code snippet demonstrates example for **missing** filter.

```
{
   "filter": {
      "missing": {
         "field": "tag"
      }
   }
}
```

bool Filter

This filter combines multiple filter clauses by using Boolean logic. It accepts the following three parameters:

- **must** - The clauses *must* match, like and.

- **must_not** - The clauses *must not* match, like not.

- **should** - At least one of the clauses *must* match, like or.

These parameters can take only one filter clause. In case, more than filter clause needs to be specified, they have to be put in an array and then passed along with these parameters.

```
{
   "bool": {
      "must": { "term": { "movie": "Hollywood" }},
      "must_not": { "term": { "actor": "Bruce Willis" }},
      "should": [
         "must": { "genre": "action" }},
         "must_not": { "director": "James Cameron" }}
      ],
   }
}
```

match_all Query

The match_all query is the default query to be used when no other query has been specified. It essentially matches all documents.

```
{ "match_all": {}}
```

This query is commonly used in combination with filters. For e.g., to fetch all movies from the movie database. In this case, all documents have equal relevance so they all get a neutral score of 1.

match Query

Whenever you want to query for full text or exact value in almost any field, then you should go for the match query. While running match query against a full text field, the query string analysis would be done using the appropriate analyzer for that particular field before starting the search:

```
{ "match ": { "play": "Comedy of Errors" }}
```

While using on a field with an exact value like number, age, date, the query would search for that exact value:

```
{ "match ": { "income": 100000 }}
{ "match ": { "date": "1812-02-07" }}
{ "match ": { "label": "full_text" }}
```

Match query is different from query-string search using String Lite mechanism. The match query does not need a query syntax like +play:The +published:1840. It looks for the specified words making it safe for exposing it to users from a search field.

multi_match Query

The multi_match query enables the same *match* query to be run on multiple fields.

```
{
    "multi_match": {
        "query": "full text search",
        "fields": [ "label", "name" ]
    }
}
```

bool Query

Just like bool filter, the bool query can be used to combine multiple query clauses. There are some subtle differences though. While filters return binary yes/no answers, queries compute a relevance score instead. The bool query chains together the score obtained from each must or should clause that matches. Following parameters are acceptable:

- **must** - The clauses that *must* match for document inclusion.

- **must_not** - The clauses that *must not* match for document inclusion.

- **should** - Matching of these clauses leads to increase in relevance score, without having any other effect. These clauses are helpful to refine the relevance score of each document.

The following query fetches documents corresponding to **Hollywood** movies in which "**Bruce Willis**" has not acted. If any document (movie) belongs to action genre and released before **1st January, 2000**, it will be ranked higher than others. Documents matching both conditions would rank even higher.

```
{
    "bool": {
        "must": { "match": { "movie": "Hollywood" }},
        "must_not": { "match": { "actor": "Bruce Willis" }},
        "should": [
            "match": { "genre": "action" }},
            "range": { "date": { "lte": "2000-01-01" }}}
        ],
    }
}
```

Filter-Query Combination

Queries and Filters are used in their respective context. If you go through Elasticsearch API, you will quite frequently come across parameters with query or filter in the name. They expect only a single argument with either a single query or filter clause respectively. This establishes the outer context as either query context or filter context.

Both compound query and filter clauses can wrap other query and filter clauses, respectively. However, it is recommended to apply filter clause to query clause. To aid in this, there are specific query clauses which wrap filter clauses, and vice-versa. This allows switching from one context to another. It is crucial to select the correct combination of query and filter clauses for most efficient mechanism.

Filtering a Query

Let's assume you want to execute the following query:

```
{ "match": { "movie": "Hollywood" }}
```

Let's combine it with the following term filter, which matches only documents corresponding to movies where "Vin Diesel" is the actor.

```
{ "term": { "actor": "Vin Diesel" }}
```

As mentioned in an earlier section, the search API takes only a single query parameter, so the query and filter need to be encapsulated in another query, which we can call as the filtered query:

```
{
    "filtered": {
        "query": { "match": { "movie": "Hollywood" }},
        "filter": { "actor": "Vin Diesel" }}
    }
}
```

You can now pass this filtered query to the query parameter of the search API:

```
curl -XGET 'localhost:9200/_search?pretty'
{
    "query": {
        "filtered": {
            "query": { "match": { "movie": "Hollywood" }},
            "filter": { "actor": "Vin Diesel" }}
        }
    }
}
```

Only Filter

In the context of query, if you only want to use filter without any query (for e.g., all movies where Vin Diesel is the actor), just omit the query:

```
curl -XGET 'localhost:9200/_search?pretty'
```

```
{
   "query": {
      "filtered": {
         "filter": { "actor": "Vin Diesel" }}
      }
   }
}
```

In case no query is specified, the default behavior is similar to using the match_all query. So, the above query is equivalent to the following:

```
curl -XGET 'localhost:9200/_search?pretty'
{
   "query": {
      "filtered": {
         "query": { "match_all": {}},
         "filter": { "actor": "Vin Diesel" }}
      }
   }
}
```

Filter via Query

There can be occasions when you may want to use a query while being in a filter context. This can be done using the query filter, which just encapsulates a query. The following example shows one method to exclude movies where Vin Diesel has acted:

```
curl -XGET 'localhost:9200/_search?pretty'
{
  "query": {
    "filtered": {
      "filter": {
        "bool": {
          "must": { "term": { "movie": "Hollywood" }},
          "must_not": {
            "query": {
            "match": { "actor": "Vin Diesel" }
          }
         }
        }
      }
    }
  }
}
```

■ **Tip** You may need to use a query as a filter when you need full-text matching while in filter context.

Query Validation

Queries tend to be complex, especially in combination with different analyzers and field mappings. This makes it little difficult to follow. The validate query API checks whether a query is valid.

```
curl -XGET 'localhost:9200/ws/play/_validate/query?pretty'
{
    "query": {
      "play" : {
         "match" : "Pride and Prejudice"
      }
    }
}
```

The response to the previous query shows that the query is invalid:

```
{
  "valid" : false,
  "_shards" : {
    "total" : 1,
    "successful" : 1,
    "failed" : 0
  }
}
```

Error Diagnostics

In order to find out more details on why the query is invalid, you can use the **explain** parameter in the following manner:

```
curl -XGET 'localhost:9200/ws/play/_validate/query?explain&pretty'
{
    "query": {
      "play" : {
         "match" : "Pride and Prejudice"
      }
    }
}
```

Looks like there was a mixup between the type of query (**match**) and the name of the field (**play**):

```
{
  "valid" : false,
  "_shards" : { ... },
  "explanations" : [ {
    "index" : "gb",
    "valid" : false,
    "error" : "org.elasticsearch.index.query.QueryParsingException:
          [gb] No query registered for [play]"
  } ]
```

}

Summary

In this chapter you were taken through the different means to search data in Elasticsearch. An overview of simple searches using structured and full text queries was given. The search can be made more powerful using mult-index, multi-type queries. Large query results can be paged. Thereafter, Search Lite was used to search data by using query string which requires all the parameters to be passed in the query string. The Query DSL is more powerful mechanism which involves full body query with a JSON request body and use of rich search language. The integration of filters and queries was covered in dealt. In the end, different error diagnostic measures were explained.

CHAPTER 6

Mapping and Analysis

In this previous chapter an overview of different means to search data in Elasticsearch was given. Both simple searches and full text queries were covered. An overview of Search Lite and Query DSL was given. The goal of this chapter is to give a perspective of data mapping and analysis. It will cover different types of mapping and analyses techniques.

Data Mapping and Analysis

The exploration of data in the index populated in Chapter 5 amuses for more than one reason. It looks like something is broken. There are a total of 12 records - 2 records corresponding to two authors and then 5 records per author corresponding to plays. Only the author records have exact date **1870-06-09**, but just take a look at the hits for the following queries:

```
GET /_search?q=1870              # 1 result
GET /_search?q=1870-06-09        # 1 result
GET /_search?q=date:1870-06-09   # 0 result
GET /_search?q=date:1870         # 0 result
```

You can notice that querying the **_all** field for only the full date returns the correct entry. However, searching for partial date (in this case, partial year) draws a blank. Why is it so? Looks like Elasticsearch has indexed the _all field differently from the date type fields. Let's deep dive into how Elasticsearch has understood document structure by checking out the mapping for "**cd**" index.

```
curl -XGET 'localhost:9200/cd/_mapping/author?pretty'
{
  "cd" : {
    "mappings" : {
      "author" : {
        "properties" : {
          "born" : {
            "type" : "date",
            "format" : "strict_date_optional_time||epoch_millis"
          },
          "country" : {
            "type" : "string"
```

G. S. Sachdeva, *Applied ELK Stack*, ISBN 978-1545022146

```
    },
    "died" : {
      "type" : "date",
      "format" : "strict_date_optional_time||epoch_millis"
    },
    "name" : {
      "type" : "string"
    }
  }
},
"play" : {
  "properties" : {
    "author" : {
      "type" : "string"
    },
    "play" : {
      "type" : "string"
    },
    "published" : {
      "type" : "string"
    }
  }
}
}
}
}
```

Elasticsearch dynamically generates a mapping based on its estimation of the field types. The response indicates that both "born" and "died" fields have been recognized as of type date. You might be wondering that where the _all field is. It does not get displayed as it is a default field and has string type. Indexing for date type fields and string type fields is done differently allowing them to be searched differently. In fact, all the basic data types - strings, numbers, Booleans, and dates might be indexed in a different manner. The fields that represent exact values and fields representing full text are indexed in a completely different manner. This is a crucial aspect which distinguishes Elasticsearch from all other databases.

Exact Values and Full Text

Elasticsearch categorizes data into following two types:

- **Exact Values** - They are the specific value of a field. For e.g., income, age or date. They can also include exact strings like username or an email address. They are case sensitive. For e.g., the exact value "**Hello**" is not the same as the exact value "**hello**". Similarly, the exact value "**1870**" is not the same as the exact value "**1870-06-09**".

- **Full Text** - This is the textual data, more often than not written in some human language. For e.g., an email body, Facebook comments.

Exact values are easier to query. This is because of the binary nature of decision - a value would match the query or it won't. It can be expressed easily in SQL:

```
WHERE name = "Eric Anderson"
  AND id = 45796
```

AND date >= "2016-09-10"

Exploring full-text data requires much more finesse. Rather than asking "Does the document match specified query", we need to ask "How well does the document match the specified query". We need to figure out how relevant the document is to the specified query. Rarely would we go for matching the whole full-text field exactly. The common use case is to search within text fields. Besides this, we expect Elasticsearch to understand our intent.

- A search for play should also match played, playful, playing, plays.

- tom hanks should match Tom Hanks and mel gibson should match Mel Gibson.

- A search for UK should also return documents having reference to United Kingdom.

During the processing of queries on full-text fields, Elasticsearch initially analyzes the text and then uses the results to build an inverted index. Detailed treatment will be provided to the concept of Inverted Index and Analysis Process in the following sections.

Inverted Index

Elasticsearch perform fast full-text search by using an internal structure called as **inverted index**. This structure comprises of a list all unique words appearing in any document and correspondingly for each word a list of documents where it appears. Let's take example of two documents, each having content field containing the following text:

- Pack my box with five dozen liquor jugs

- Just pack my boxes with five dozen wine jugs

Let's see how an inverted index would get created for these two documents by splitting the content field of each document into separate words (terms or tokens). Thereafter, we will create a sorted list with all unique terms and then a list in which document does a term appear. The breakup would be as depicted in Table 6-1.

Table 6-1. Sorted Term List

Term	Document 1	Document 2
Just		X
Pack	X	
box	X	
boxes		X
dozen	X	X
five	X	X
jugs	X	X
liquor	X	
my	X	X
pack		X

wine		X
with	X	X

Now if we want to search for **pack my**, we only need to find the documents in which each of these terms appears as shown in Table 6-2.

Table 6-2. Matching Documents

Term	Document 1	Document 2
pack		X
my	X	X
Total	1	2

You can see that both the documents match, but the first document has more matching terms. A rudimentary algorithm which just counts the occurrence of matching terms will lead us to the conclusion that the second document is a better match. In other words, the second document is more relevant to our query than the first document. However, this approach is far from perfect:

- Pack can be changed to lowercase pack.

- boxes can be trimmed to its root form to become box.

- liquor and wine mean pretty much the same and probably one term - liquor can be used.

After applying these changes, the Term list would look like Table 6-3:

Table 6-3. Normalized Term List

Term	Document 1	Document 2
box	X	X
dozen	X	X
five	X	X
jugs	X	X
just		X
liquor	X	X
my	X	X
pack	X	X
with	X	X

You would be surprise to know that your search for **+Just +pack** would still not be successful. This is due to the fact that the exact term **Just** is not in the index. But if the normalization rules similar to the content field are applied to the query string also, it would reformat as a query for +**just** +**pack**. This would then match the first document.

▓ **Tip** Only terms that are part of index can be queried. Hence, necessitating normalization of both the indexed test and the query string.

Data Analysis

The next step after defining the mapping is to analyze the data using the following steps:

- **Tokenize** a group of text into separate terms appropriate for an inverted index.
- **Normalize** the terms into a standard form for them to be easily searched.

These tasks are performed by Analyzers. It is only a wrapper around the following three functions:

1. **Character Filters** - The first step is to pass the string through any character filters in turn. The aim is to spruce up the string before tokenization and to do away with any markup text.

2. **Tokenizer** - The next step is to break the strings into tokens based on individual terms. A straightforward way is to use whitespace or punctuation as delimiter for extracting tokens.

3. **Token Filters** - The last step is to route each term through a token filter. It can modify terms (for e.g., lowercasing Just), delete terms (for e.g., articles such as a, an, the) or supplement terms (for e.g., similar terms like liquor and wine)

There are different type of character filters, tokenizers and token filters available with Elasticsearch by default. These filters can be chained together to create novel analyzers serving unique purpose.

Prepackaged Analyzers

Elasticsearch comes with certain prepackaged analyzers that can be used straightway. You can find the details of some of the key analyzers. There is a subtle difference in their behavior. Let's see what outcome we get from each analyzer after applying on the following text:

If I were two-faced, would I be wearing this one(1)?

- **Standard Analyzer** - It is the default analyzer used by Elasticsearch. It works best for most of the scenarios for text in any language. The text is ripped on word boundaries. Most of the punctuation is done away with and all terms are lowercased. The output would be:

if, i, were, two, faced, would, be, wearing, this, one, 1

- **Simple Analyzer** - It fragments text whenever it encounters non-letters and converts the terms to lowercase. The output would be:

if, i, were, two, faced, would, be, wearing, this, one

- **Whitespace Analyzer** - The test is delimited on the basis of whitespace and is not lowercased. The output would be:

If, I, were, two-faced, would,, be, wearing, this, one(1)?

- **Language Analyzer** - This kind of analyzer is available for multiple languages. It takes care of language idiosyncrasies such as removing stop words (for e.g., words like **a an the** that don't impact relevance). It also trunks English words as it understands the rules of grammar. The output would be:

if, i, were, two, face, would, be, wear, this, one, 1

You might notice that **faced** and **wearing** have trunked to their root form.

When to Use Analyzers

On indexing a document, all the full-text fields are analyzed and converted to terms that can be used to form the inverted index. But when you want to search for a full-text field, the query string has to go through the same analysis process. This guarantees that the search terms are of the similar form as that exists in the index. Full text queries comprehend the significance of each field and take the correct action:

- On querying a *full-text* field, the same analyzer would be used to arrive at the correct list of terms which should be searched.

- On querying an *exact-value* field, rather than analyzing the query string, the exact specified value would be searched for.

You can Test Analyzers

There can be occasions when it is not obvious what is being tokenized and used in index. To get a clear picture, you can leverage the analyze API to figure out how the text has been analyzed. Just give the analyzer in the query-string parameters and the text to be analyzed in the body:

```
curl -XGET 'localhost:9200/_analyze?analyzer=simple&pretty' -d 'Be the change that you want to see in the world'
{
  "tokens": [ {
    "token": "be",
    "start_offset": 0,
    "end_offset": 2,
    "type": "word",
    "position": 0
  }, {
  "tokens": [ {
    "token": "the",
    "start_offset": 3,
    "end_offset": 6,
    "type": "word",
    "position": 1
  }, {
```

"tokens": [{
 "token": "change",
 "start_offset": 7,
 "end_offset": 13,
 "type": "word",
 "position": 2

}, {

"tokens": [{
 "token": "that",
 "start_offset": 14,
 "end_offset": 18,
 "type": "word",
 "position": 3

}, {

"tokens": [{
 "token": "you",
 "start_offset": 19,
 "end_offset": 22,
 "type": "word",
 "position": 4

}, {

"tokens": [{
 "token": "wish",
 "start_offset": 23,
 "end_offset": 27,
 "type": "word",
 "position": 5

}, {

"tokens": [{
 "token": "to",
 "start_offset": 28,
 "end_offset": 30,
 "type": "word",
 "position": 6

}, {

"tokens": [{
 "token": "see",
 "start_offset": 31,
 "end_offset": 34,
 "type": "word",
 "position": 7

```
}, {

  "tokens": [ {
    "token": "in",
    "start_offset": 35,
    "end_offset": 37,
    "type": "word",
    "position": 8

}, {

  "tokens": [ {
    "token": "the",
    "start_offset": 38,
    "end_offset": 41,
    "type": "word",
    "position": 9

}, {

  "tokens": [ {
    "token": "world",
    "start_offset": 42,
    "end_offset": 47,
    "type": "word",
    "position": 10

} ]

}
```

The actual entity to be stored in index is the **token**. Order of appearance of term in the original text is specified by **position**. Character positions occupied by the original word in the original string are specified by **start_offset** and **end_offset**. You can see that the analyze API is quite useful as it throws light on the internal functioning of Elasticsearch.

Assign Analyzer

On spotting a new string field in a document, Elasticsearch automatically treats it as a full-text string and assigns the standard analyzer. Now, depending on the situation, you may or may not want this. May be you want to assign some other analyzer that meets the peculiarities of the language of your data. There can be situations when you may want a string field to be treated just like a string field. In this case, the exact value is indexed without any analysis. To accomplish this you would have to manually configure these fields by specifying the mapping.

Data Mapping

Data mapping is essential to provide specific treatment to data fields. For e.g., we may want numeric fields to be treated as numbers, date fields to be treated as dates and string fields as exact-value or full-text strings. A short recap from earlier chapters - each document in an index consists of a type. Each type has its own mapping (schema definition). This mapping defines fields within a type, the datatype for each field and how Elasticsearch should handle the field. Mapping also configures metadata associated with the type.

Simple Field Types

The following simple field types are supported by Elasticsearch:

- Boolean: boolean
- Date: date
- Floating-point: float, double
- String: string
- Whole number: byte, short, integer, long

While indexing a document, if Elasticsearch encounters a new field, it uses the heuristic of **dynamic mapping** to guess the field type from the available basic data types in JSON. These rules are specified in Table 6-4.

Table 6-4. Dynamic Mapping Rules

JSON Type	Field Type
Boolean: true or false	boolean
Whole number: 701	long
Floating point: 70.58	double
String, valid date: 1870-06-09	date
String: foo bar	string

> ■ **Tip**   Indexing a number in quotes ("701"), maps it to as type **string** and not type **long**. On the other hand, if it the field already maps to type long, then the string value will be converted into a long. An exception would be thrown if the conversion to long cannot happen.

Observe the Mapping

Elasticsearch provides the facility to observe the mapping for multiple types in multiple indices by the use of **/_mapping endpoint**. Early in this chapter, the mapping for **cd** index was shown.

> ■ **Tip**   There may be chance that your mapping is not correct. **Income** field may be mapped to type **string** instead of **integer**. This can produce confusing results so you should go back and correct the mapping.

Mapping Customization

Elasticsearch provides for good enough basic field datatypes which are sufficient for most of the cases. But there may be a situation when you want to customize mapping for certain fields. Thankfully, Elasticsearch allows for mapping customization:

- Differentiate full-text string fields from exact value string fields.
- Use of analyzers specific to different languages
- Field optimization for limited matching

The type of a field is its most important attribute. For fields that are not **string**, you will not generally need to map anything but type:

```
{
  "cache_size": {
    "type": "integer"
  }
}
```

The default behavior for string fields is to consider them to contain full-text. This means, the field value will be processed by an analyzer before indexing it. Similarly, a full-text query on the field will require the query string to fist pass through an analyzer. The key mapping attributes for string fields are index and analyzer:

index

It influences indexing of string with possible values as following:

- **analyzed** - First the string is analyzed and then it is indexed. The string gets indexed as full text.
- **not_analyzed** - Index the field without analyzing. The value gets indexed exactly as specified.
- **no** - If you don't want the field to be searchable, you can specify it not to be indexed.

The default of index attrribute for a string field is **analyzed**. If however you want the field to be mapped as an exact value, specify the index mapping as **not_analyzed**:

```
{
  "label": {
    "type": "string",
    "index": "not_analyzed",
  }
}
```

analyzer

This attribute can be used to specify which analyzer to be used both at search time and at index time. The default behavior is to use **standard** analyzer but this can be modified by assigning one of the in-built analyzers, such as english, simple or whitespace.

```
{
  "play": {
    "type": "string",
    "analyzer": "english",
  }

}
```

Mapping Revision

You have seen that the mapping for a type can be specified when an index is created. Thereafter, mapping can be added for a new type or mapping for an existing type can be updated, using the /_**mapping** endpoint.

■ **Tip** Additions to an existing mapping can be done but it can't be changed. This is to ensure the sanctity of the already indexed data.

You can revise a mapping to add a new field but you can't modify an existing field from **analyzed** to **not_analyzed**. Let's take an example to demonstrate the different ways of specifying mappings. Let's create a new index, specifying that the string type fields should use the **english** analyzer:

```
curl -XPUT 'localhost:9200/sm' -d '
{
  "mappings": {
    "play": {
      "properties": {
        "play": {
          "type": "string",
          "analyzer": "english"
        },
        "author": {
          "type": "string",
          "analyzer": "english"
        },
        "published": {
          "type": "string",
          "analyzer": "english"
        }
      }
    }
  }
}'
```

The index would get created with the mappings specified in the body. Let's say at a later point you decide to update the mapping by adding a new **not_analyzed** text field called label to the play mapping, by using the _mapping endpoint:

```
curl -XPUT 'localhost:9200/sm/_mapping/play' -d '
{
  "properties": {
    "label" : {
      "type": "string",
      "index": "not_analyzed"
    }
  }
}'
```

You don't need to specify all the existing fields again, as they can't be changed anyways. The new field gets merged with the existing mapping.

Mapping Test

With the help of **analyze** API, you can test the mapping for string fields by name. Let's first check the mapping for play field:

```
curl -XGET 'localhost:9200/sm/_analyze?field=play' -d 'The Making of a Saint'
```

It gives the following output:

```
{
  "tokens" : [ {
    "token" : "make",
    "start_offset" : 4,
    "end_offset" : 10,
    "type" : "<ALPHANUM>",
    "position" : 1
  }, {
    "token" : "saint",
    "start_offset" : 16,
    "end_offset" : 21,
    "type" : "<ALPHANUM>",
    "position" : 4
  } ]
}
```

Now let's check the mapping for the label field:

```
curl -XGET 'localhost:9200/sm/_analyze?field=label' -d 'The Making of a Saint'
```

In this case, we get the following output:

```
{
  "tokens" : [ {
    "token" : "The Making of a Saint",
    "start_offset" : 0,
    "end_offset" : 21,
    "type" : "word",
    "position" : 0
  } ]
```

```
}
```

The play field fragments the text into different tokens, whereas the label field takes the complete text string as is. This demonstrates that the mapping is working is as intended.

Complex Field Types

Elasticsearch provides support for not only **simple** (scalar) datatypes but also **complex** data types like **arrays**, **objects** and **null values**.

Multi-value Fields

You may want to have more than one label in the label field. Rather than having a single string, you could have an array of labels:

```
{ "label" : [ "cache", "redis" ] }
```

Arrays don't need any specific mapping. Zero, one or more values can be present in a field, similar to how a full-text field is analyzed to produce multiple terms. Arrays do have a restriction in that all the values must be of the same datatype. You can't have both numbers and string in the same array. When you create a new field by indexing an array, the datatype of the first value in the array is used to determine the type of new field.

▩ **Tip**   Elasticsearch returns arrays in the same order as when they were indexed.

Empty Fields

You can have empty arrays also. This is same as zero value. You will be surprised to know that Elasticsearch has no way to store null values. So, fields with null values are also treated as empty fields. All the following fields would be treated as empty fields and would not be indexed:

```
"array_having_null_value" : [ null ] ,
"empty_array" : [],
"null_value" : null
```

Multi-level Objects

Another significant datatype is the object type. In other programming environments it is commonly referred to as **associative array**, **dictionary** or **hash map**. Inner objects typically insert an entity or object inside another. We can reformat the structure of documents with information about different plays (an earlier example):

```
{
  "author" : "William Shakespeare",
  "play" : {
```

```
    "name" : "Henry VI",
    "published": "1590"
  }
}
```

Elasticsearch figures out new object fields dynamically and maps them as type object and each inner field is listed under properties

Indexing Inner Objects

Elasticsearch considers all fields as a flat list of **key-value pairs**. While indexing inner objects, Elasticsearch transforms the document in the following manner:

```
{
  "author" : [william, shakespeare],
  "play.name" : [Henry, VI],
  "play.published": [1590]

}
```

You can refer to inner fields by their name. For e.g., you can directly refer to **name**. If two fields have the same first name, they you have to use the full path (for e.g., **play.name**).

Inner Object Arrays

Inner Objects can also have their own arrays. Let's say we have an employees' array with the following details:

```
{
  "employees" : [,
    { "name" : "Tom Hanks", "id" : 5712, "department" : "sales" },
    { "name" : "Mel Gibson", "id" : 6043, "department" : "operations" },
    { "name" : "Brad Pitt", "id" : 8954, "department" : "administration" }
  ]
}
```

As described earlier, the above specified document would be flattened and the result would look like following:

```
{
  "employees.name" : [brad, gibson, hanks, mel, pitt, tom],
  "employees.id" : [5712, 6043, 8954],
  "employees.department" : [administration, operations, sales]
}
```

You may have noticed that the correlation between different fields like name ("Tom Hanks") and id (5712) does not remain intact. Each of the multi-value fields is not an ordered array but only a bag of values. Correlated inner objects are also known as nested objects.

Summary

This chapter gave a perspective of data mapping and analysis. It covered different types of mapping and analyses techniques. Elasticsearch categorizes data either as exact value or full text. It performs fast full-text search by using an internal structure called as inverted index. There are various prepackaged analyzers available - standard, simple, whitespace and language. An overview of field type mapping was given and in the end the concept of multi-level objects was introduced.

## CHAPTER 7

鋤　鑭　簓

Data Exploration with Aggregates

The previous chapter gave a perspective of data mapping and analysis. Different types of mapping and analyses techniques were covered. This goal of this chapter is to figure out how to get an overview of data, rather than just doing search or query. An aggregation is the piece which converts raw data into actionable information. Insightful reports and dashboards can be made from the information received.

Aggregation Basics

Aggregations enable us to get an overview of data and have a plug-and-play syntax, i.e. separate functional blocks can be tied together to provide the desired behavior. A very few components make the foundation of Aggregates:

- **Buckets** - Group of documents meeting the criteria
- **Metrics** - Statistics computed on the documents in a bucket.

It is hard to believe but this is what all is need to work with Aggregates. Each aggregation is just an amalgamation of one or more buckets. It may or may not have associated metrics. A SQL based analogy can be seen below:

```
SELECT COUNT(sales)
FROM table
GROUP BY sales
```

In the example given above, *COUNT(sales)* is similar to a metric and *GROUP BY sales* is similar to a bucket. While, Grouping in SQL is similar to buckets, functions like *COUNT(), MAX(), SUM()* are similar to metrics. Let's deep dive into these concepts.

Buckets

As mentioned earlier, a bucket essentially is a group of documents meeting a certain criteria. Some sample criterion to arrive at buckets is as following:

- United States would land in *North America* continent bucket.
- A company can be either in *profitable* or *loss making* bucket.

G. S. Sachdeva, *Applied ELK Stack*, ISBN 978-1545022146

- A person would land either in *employed* or *unemployed* bucket.

When an aggregation is executed, the values inside each document are compared to figure out whether they match the criteria of the bucket. If the document(s) matches, it is considered as a part of bucket and the aggregation moves over to evaluate other documents. A bucket can be part of another bucket leading to hierarchical relationships. As an example, California can be part of USA country bucket and the entire USA can be part of North America continent bucket.

To help with data exploration, Elasticsearch contains different types of buckets - hourly, popularity, age ranges, geo-locations and many more. The central idea in each case is to compartmentalize documents on the basis of the specified criteria.

Metrics

While buckets facilitate compartmentalization of documents into small groups, but it is of not much help without some metrics. Bucketing is the first step which groups documents such that useful metrics can be computed.

Generally, metrics are straightforward mathematical operations (for e.g., min, max, mean, sum, etc.) that are computed using the document values. Some practical usage of Metrics could be to calculate the average sales, mean salary or the 99th percentile for query latency.

The Two Together

Aggregation comprises of buckets and metrics. It may have one or more bucket supported by zero or more metrics. There could even be buckets inside buckets. As an example, we can have different buckets for departments in an organization and then compute the average salary per group (metric).

Fun with Aggregation

In this section, we will start going through the concept of Aggregations by examples. As part of this exercise, we are going to build aggregations relevant to a mobile phone dealer. The data is about phone sales - phone model, color, sale price and date of sale.

To start with, bulk-upload the sample data in the following manner:

```
POST /phones/sales/_bulk
{ "index": {}}
{ "make" : "iPhone", "color" : "silver", "price" : 260, "sold" : "2016-01-16" }
{ "index": {}}
{ "make" : "iPhone", "color" : "gold", "price" : 400, "sold" : "2016-02-16" }
{ "index": {}}
{ "make" : "motorola", "color" : "white", "price" : 80, "sold" : "2016-03-06" }
{ "index": {}}
{ "make" : "htc", "color" : "silver", "price" : 140, "sold" : "2016-04-03" }
{ "index": {}}
{ "make" : "htc", "color" : "white", "price" : 80, "sold" : "2016-04-16" }
```

```
{ "index": {}}
{ "make" : "motorola", "color" : "black", "price" : 80, "sold" : "2016-07-18" }
{ "index": {}}
{ "make" : "samsung", "color" : "white", "price" : 70, "sold" : "2016-08-23" }
{ "index": {}}
{ "make" : "LG", "color" : "black", "price" : 40, "sold" : "2016-09-04" }
{ "index": {}}
{ "make" : "huawei", "color" : "black", "price" : 30, "sold" : "2016-10-05" }
{ "index": {}}
{ "make" : "huawei", "color" : "white", "price" : 30, "sold" : "2016-12-19" }
```

After inserting sample data, it is time to construct an aggregation. A phone dealer may be interested in knowing phones of which color sell the most. This can be easily found out using a simple aggregation. Let's do this using a terms bucket:

```
curl -XGET 'localhost:9200/phones/sales/_search?search_type=count&pretty' -d '
{
  "aggs" : {
   "colors" : {
     "terms" : {
       "field" : "color"
     }
    }
  }
}'
```

You can see that aggregations are placed at the top-level using the **aggs** parameter. Thereafter, the aggregation is named to **colors.** In the end, a single bucket of type **terms** is specified. The context of execution is that of search results, implying that it is similar to top-level parameter in a search request.

■ **Tip** Use of search_type implies that we are not interested in search results, but want the overall operation to be faster

---

The next step is to name the aggregation and then define it. In this case, only a single terms bucket is being defined. It will ensure that a new bucket is created for every unique term. As this example is specifying terms bucket to use the color field, so a new bucket will be created for each color. On executing the aggregation, we get the following results:

```
{
....
  "hits" : {
   "total" : 10,
   "max_score" : 0.0,
   "hits" : [ ]
  },
  "aggregations" : {
   "colors" : {
    "doc_count_error_upper_bound" : 0,
    "sum_other_doc_count" : 0,
```

```
    "buckets" : [ {
      "key" : "white",
      "doc_count" : 4
    }, {
      "key" : "black",
      "doc_count" : 3
    }, {
      "key" : "silver",
      "doc_count" : 2
    }, {
      "key" : "gold",
      "doc_count" : 1
    } ]
  }
 }
}
```

You can notice that there are no search hits in the output since the **search_type=count** parameter was used. The **colors** aggregation is part of the aggregations field. Unique terms found in color field (for e.g., gold, server) serve as **key** for each bucket. The number of documents is specified by the **doc_count** field. The number of documents with a particular color are represented by the corresponding count of each bucket. For e.g., there are two silver colored phones.

This example is executed in real time - any searchable document can be aggregated. This implies that the aggregation results can be fed into a graphing tool to create real-time dashboards. If you sell a gold colored phone, the graphs would get updated real-time to show increase in sales of gold colored phones.

Metrics to the Rescue

The previous example has demonstrated that plain vanilla aggregates are useful to tell us the number of documents in a bucket. But that turns out to be inadequate in many situations where more sophisticated statistics about the documents are required. For e.g., what is the maximum price of iPhone. You can get this information by indicating to Elasticsearch which all metrics are needed and on which fields. You can nest metrics inside buckets so that mathematical statistics are computed based on the values of documents in a bucket.

Let's go about understanding more of metrics by adding an average metric to the phones example:

```
curl -XGET 'localhost:9200/phones/sales/_search?search_type=count&pretty' -d '
{
  "aggs" : {
   "colors" : {
    "terms" : {
     "field" : "color"
    },
    "aggs" : {
     "mean_price" : {
      "avg" : {
       "field" : "price"
      }
```

```
        }
      }
    }
  }
}'
```

A new aggs level has been added for specifying the metric with the name **mean_price**. It is defined as **avg** metric over **price** field. The new aggregation level nests the avg metric inside the terms bucket resulting in an average for each color. You need to name the metric (mean_price in this case), so the values can be retrieved later. The metric (avg) needs to be bound to a field for which we want the average to be computed (price). Just see what the response is:

```
{
  ...
  "aggregations" : {
    "colors" : {
      "doc_count_error_upper_bound" : 0,
      "sum_other_doc_count" : 0,
      "buckets" : [ {
        "key" : "white",
        "doc_count" : 4,
        "mean_price" : {
          "value" : 65.0
        }
      }, {
        "key" : "black",
        "doc_count" : 3,
        "mean_price" : {
          "value" : 50.0
        }
      }, {
        "key" : "silver",
        "doc_count" : 2,
        "mean_price" : {
          "value" : 200.0
        }
      }, {
        "key" : "gold",
        "doc_count" : 1,
        "mean_price" : {
          "value" : 400.0
        }
      } ]
    }
  }
  ...
}
```

The information now returned is quite substantial. Earlier you knew that there are 3 black phones, but you can see that their mean price is 50. This information can be directly fed into graphs or dashboards.

Buckets within Buckets

The hierarchical nature of buckets adds a lot of power to aggregations. You already saw how to nest a metric within a bucket. Let's increase the fun element by nesting buckets within other buckets to find out the phone make count for each color:

```
curl -XGET 'localhost:9200/phones/sales/_search?search_type=count&pretty' -d '
{
  "aggs" : {
    "colors" : {
      "terms" : {
        "field" : "color"
      },
      "aggs" : {
        "mean_price" : {
          "avg" : {
            "field" : "price"
          }
        },
        "make" : {
          "terms" : {
            "field" : "make"
          }
        }
      }
    }
  }
}'
```

The **mean_price** metric can co-exist with the inner bucket. The inner bucket is an aggregation named **make**. It is also a terms bucket which will result in unique buckets for each phone make. There could be metrics or buckets at each level of aggregation. The mean_price metric indicates the mean price for each phone color and can exist independently of other buckets and metrics. This is crucial to build different metrics on the same set of documents. All of these metrics are collected by Elasticsearch in just one pass over the data.

You can see that the make aggregation is a bucket of type term, just like the outer colors terms bucket. This would result in (color, make) tuple for every unique combination of data. Let's see what the output of make bucket is:

```
{
...
  "aggregations" : {
    "colors" : {
      "doc_count_error_upper_bound" : 0,
      "sum_other_doc_count" : 0,
      "buckets" : [ {
        "key" : "white",
        "doc_count" : 4,
        "make" : {
          "doc_count_error_upper_bound" : 0,
          "sum_other_doc_count" : 0,
```

```
      "buckets" : [ {
        "key" : "htc",
        "doc_count" : 1
      }, {
        "key" : "huawei",
        "doc_count" : 1
      }, {
        "key" : "motorola",
        "doc_count" : 1
      }, {
        "key" : "samsung",
        "doc_count" : 1
      } ]
    },
    "mean_price" : {
      "value" : 65.0
    }
  },
  ...
}
```

The new aggregation is nested under each color bucket with a breakdown of phone makes for each color. The response indicates the following:

- There are four white colored phones.

- The mean price of a white colored phone is $65.

- Each of htc, huawei, motorola, samsung has one white colored phone.

Multiple Metrics

There could be multiple metrics associated with an aggregation. Let's add two more metrics to compute the min and max price for each phone make:

```
curl -XGET 'localhost:9200/phones/sales/_search?search_type=count&pretty' -d '
{
  "aggs" : {
    "colors" : {
      "terms" : {
        "field" : "color"
      },
      "aggs" : {
        "mean_price" : {
          "avg" : {
            "field" : "price"
          }
        },
        "make" : {
          "terms" : {
            "field" : "make"
          },
```

```
      "aggs" : {
       "min_price" : { "min" : {"field" : "price"} },
       "max_price" : { "max" : {"field" : "price" } }
      }
     }
    }
   }
  }
 }
}'
```

Another aggs level has been added for nesting. Thereafter, **min** and **max** metrics are added. Let's see what the outcome of executing this aggregate would be:

```
{
...
  "aggregations" : {
   "colors" : {
    "doc_count_error_upper_bound" : 0,
    "sum_other_doc_count" : 0,
    "buckets" : [ {
     "key" : "white",
     "doc_count" : 4,
     "make" : {
      "doc_count_error_upper_bound" : 0,
      "sum_other_doc_count" : 0,
      "buckets" : [ {
       "key" : "htc",
       "doc_count" : 1,
       "max_price" : {
        "value" : 80.0
       },
       "min_price" : {
        "value" : 80.0
       }
      }, {
       "key" : "huawei",
       "doc_count" : 1,
       "max_price" : {
        "value" : 30.0
       },
       "min_price" : {
        "value" : 30.0
       }
      }, {
       "key" : "motorola",
       "doc_count" : 1,
       "max_price" : {
        "value" : 80.0
       },
       "min_price" : {
```

```
      "value" : 80.0
    }
  }, {
    "key" : "samsung",
    "doc_count" : 1,
    "max_price" : {
      "value" : 70.0
    },
    "min_price" : {
      "value" : 70.0
    }
  } ]
  },
  "mean_price" : {
    "value" : 65.0
  }
...
}
```

The addition of another metric has increased the information available:

- There are four white colored phones.

- The mean price of a white colored phone is $65.

- Each of htc, huawei, motorola, samsung has one white colored phone

- The minimum and maximum price for a white colored htc phone is the same, i.e. $80.

Data Visualization with Bar Charts

Aggregations can be easily visualized using charts and graphs. This is one of the biggest advantages of aggregations. The most useful bucket is **histogram**, which is popularly known as bar chats. I am sure you would have bar charts in some context and would be familiar with them. You need to specify an interval for working with histogram. For example, while histogramming mobile phone price, you may specify an interval of $50. This creates a new bucket every $50. The relevant documents are sorted in corresponding buckets.

For our example, let's try to find out the number of phones sold in each price range. On top of it, we would like to figure out the total revenue generated in each price bracket. This is computed by summing the price of each phone in that interval. This can be done using a histogram and a nested sum metric:

```
curl -XGET 'localhost:9200/phones/sales/_search?search_type=count&pretty' -d '
{
  "aggs" : {
    "price" : {
      "histogram" : {
        "field" : "price",
        "interval" : 50
      },
      "aggs" : {
        "revenue" : {
          "sum" :{
```

```
        "field" : "price"
      }
    }
   }
  }
 }
}'
```

The query is built using price aggregation containing histogram bucket. There are two parameters required for histogram bucket - a **numeric field** and an **interval** to define the bucket size. The numeric parameter is the value to be used for computing buckets. The interval helps in defining the size of each bucket. An interval of 50 means, we will have the ranges [0-49, 50-99, ...].

The histogram bucket contains an associated metric. In our case, this is the sum metric which sums the price field from each document that fits in that price range. This would provide the total sales revenue for each range and can provide an insight on what kind of phones have better sales numbers. The response can be seen below:

```
{
...
  "aggregations" : {
   "price" : {
    "buckets" : [ {
      "key" : 0,
      "doc_count" : 3,
      "revenue" : {
       "value" : 100.0
      }
    }, {
      "key" : 50,
      "doc_count" : 4,
      "revenue" : {
       "value" : 310.0
      }
    }, {
      "key" : 100,
      "doc_count" : 1,
      "revenue" : {
       "value" : 140.0
      }
    }, {
      "key" : 150,
      "doc_count" : 0,
      "revenue" : {
       "value" : 0.0
      }
    }, {
      "key" : 200,
      "doc_count" : 0,
      "revenue" : {
       "value" : 0.0
      }
```

```
    }, {
      "key" : 250,
      "doc_count" : 1,
      "revenue" : {
       "value" : 260.0
      }
    }, {
      "key" : 300,
      "doc_count" : 0,
      "revenue" : {
       "value" : 0.0
      }
    }, {
      "key" : 350,
      "doc_count" : 0,
      "revenue" : {
       "value" : 0.0
      }
    }, {
      "key" : 400,
      "doc_count" : 1,
      "revenue" : {
       "value" : 400.0
      }
    } ]
  }
 }
}
```

Elasticsearch response is lucid with the histogram keys corresponding to the lower boundary of the interval. The key 0 means 0-49, the key 50 means 50-99, and so on. This data can be represented graphically as shown in Figure -1:

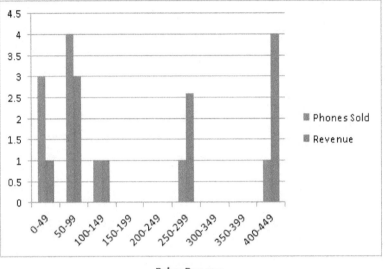

Figure 7-1. *Price Range Histograms*

■ **Tip** Microsoft-Excel has been used to make the histogram based on the raw data.

Bar charts can be built with other aggregations also as long as they can provide categories and statistics. Let's now build a bar chart for popular phones and their mean price. We will then calculate the **standard error** and add error bars on the chart. We will again use the terms bucket but this time with **extended_stats** metric:

```
curl -XGET 'localhost:9200/phones/sales/_search?search_type=count&pretty' -d '
{
  "aggs" : {
   "makes" : {
    "terms" : {
     "field" : "make",
     "size" : 10
    },
    "aggs" : {
     "stats" : {
      "extended_stats" : {
       "field" : "price"
      }
     }
    }
   }
  }
}
```

```
  }
}'
```

The result is a list of phone makes (sorted in order of popularity) along with different types of statistics:

```
{
...
  "aggregations" : {
    "makes" : {
      "doc_count_error_upper_bound" : 0,
      "sum_other_doc_count" : 0,
      "buckets" : [ {
        "key" : "htc",
        "doc_count" : 2,
        "stats" : {
          "count" : 2,
          "min" : 80.0,
          "max" : 140.0,
          "avg" : 110.0,
          "sum" : 220.0,
          "sum_of_squares" : 26000.0,
          "variance" : 900.0,
          "std_deviation" : 30.0,
          "std_deviation_bounds" : {
            "upper" : 170.0,
            "lower" : 50.0
          }
        }
      }, {
        "key" : "huawei",
        "doc_count" : 2,
        "stats" : {
          "count" : 2,
          "min" : 30.0,
          "max" : 30.0,
          "avg" : 30.0,
          "sum" : 60.0,
          "sum_of_squares" : 1800.0,
          "variance" : 0.0,
          "std_deviation" : 0.0,
          "std_deviation_bounds" : {
            "upper" : 30.0,
            "lower" : 30.0
          }
        }
      }, {
        "key" : "iphone",
        "doc_count" : 2,
        "stats" : {
          "count" : 2,
          "min" : 260.0,
          "max" : 400.0,
```

```
        "avg" : 330.0,
        "sum" : 660.0,
        "sum_of_squares" : 227600.0,
        "variance" : 4900.0,
        "std_deviation" : 70.0,
        "std_deviation_bounds" : {
          "upper" : 470.0,
          "lower" : 190.0
        }
      }
    }, {
      "key" : "motorola",
      "doc_count" : 2,
      "stats" : {
        "count" : 2,
        "min" : 80.0,
        "max" : 80.0,
        "avg" : 80.0,
        "sum" : 160.0,
        "sum_of_squares" : 12800.0,
        "variance" : 0.0,
        "std_deviation" : 0.0,
        "std_deviation_bounds" : {
          "upper" : 80.0,
          "lower" : 80.0
        }
      }
    }, {
      "key" : "lg",
      "doc_count" : 1,
      "stats" : {
        "count" : 1,
        "min" : 40.0,
        "max" : 40.0,
        "avg" : 40.0,
        "sum" : 40.0,
        "sum_of_squares" : 1600.0,
        "variance" : 0.0,
        "std_deviation" : 0.0,
        "std_deviation_bounds" : {
          "upper" : 40.0,
          "lower" : 40.0
        }
      }
    }, {
      "key" : "samsung",
      "doc_count" : 1,
      "stats" : {
        "count" : 1,
        "min" : 70.0,
```

```
    "max" : 70.0,
    "avg" : 70.0,
    "sum" : 70.0,
    "sum_of_squares" : 4900.0,
    "variance" : 0.0,
    "std_deviation" : 0.0,
    "std_deviation_bounds" : {
      "upper" : 70.0,
      "lower" : 70.0
    }
  }
}]
...
}
```

The statistics in which we are particularly interested are **stats.avg**, **stats.count** and **stats.std_deviation**. This information can be used to compute standard error by the following formula:

std_err = std_deviation / count

With this information we can make the bar chart as shown in Figure 7-2.

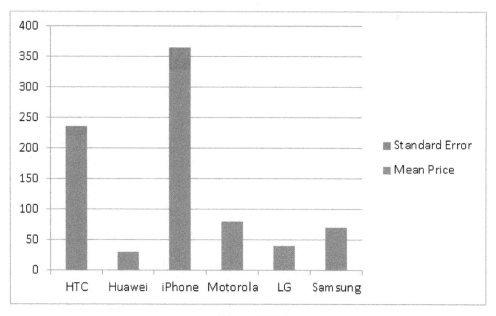

Figure 7-2. *Mean Price of Phone Makes with Standard Error*

■ **Tip** Microsoft-Excel has been used to make the histogram based on the raw data.

Time Series Aggregations

Search is the most popular activity in Elasticsearch and date histograms comes next in popularity. Use of date histograms serves many purposes. If your data has a timestamp then it can benefit tremendously from data histogram. It does not matter what kind of data you have - server logs, alarms, account transactions, etc. If you have data which consists of timestamp, it is natural to build metrics based on time:

- Number of phones sold each month in this year.
- Number of requests processed in last 1 hour by trading system.
- Average latency per week for Ecommerce site.

Data histograms are represented slightly different from regular histograms. Data histograms are best depicted by line graphs representing time series. One of the most popular uses of Elasticsearch is to plot analytics data over a time period. The **date_histogram** buckets is pretty similar to the regular histogram. Instead of building buckets based on a numeric field corresponding to numeric ranges, it builds buckets on the basis of time ranges. This necessitates each bucket to be of a certain calendar size (for e.g., 1 week or 2 months).

■ **Tip** A regular histogram can also work with dates. Since, it is not calendar aware it interprets dates as numbers and intervals have to be specified in milliseconds. On the other hand, date_histogram is aware of nuances of calendar system like number of days in February, leap year, etc.

Let's illustrate the advantages of date_histogram by building a simple line char to represent the number of mobile phones sold per month.

```
curl -XGET 'localhost:9200/phones/sales/_search?search_type=count&pretty' -d '
{
  "aggs" : {
   "sales" : {
    "date_histogram" : {
     "field" : "sold",
     "interval" : "month",
     "format" : "yyyy-MM-dd"
    }
   }
  }
}'
```

You can see that the interval is specified in terms óf calendar unit (month in this case). A date format is specified to make the bucket keys look nice. It is a relatively simple query having only a single aggregation that builds a bucket per month. This will provide the number of phones sold in each month. Dates are internally represented as numeric values only. The following is the response:

```
{
...
  "aggregations" : {
    "sales" : {
      "buckets" : [ {
        "key_as_string" : "2016-01-01",
        "key" : 1451606400000,
        "doc_count" : 1
      }, {
        "key_as_string" : "2016-02-01",
        "key" : 1454284800000,
        "doc_count" : 1
      }, {
        "key_as_string" : "2016-03-01",
        "key" : 1456790400000,
        "doc_count" : 1
      }, {
        "key_as_string" : "2016-04-01",
        "key" : 1459468800000,
        "doc_count" : 2
      }, {
        "key_as_string" : "2016-05-01",
        "key" : 1462060800000,
        "doc_count" : 0
      }, {
        "key_as_string" : "2016-06-01",
        "key" : 1464739200000,
        "doc_count" : 0
      }, {
        "key_as_string" : "2016-07-01",
        "key" : 1467331200000,
        "doc_count" : 1
      }, {
        "key_as_string" : "2016-08-01",
        "key" : 1470009600000,
        "doc_count" : 1
      }, {
        "key_as_string" : "2016-09-01",
        "key" : 1472688000000,
        "doc_count" : 1
      }, {
        "key_as_string" : "2016-10-01",
        "key" : 1475280000000,
        "doc_count" : 1
      }, {
        "key_as_string" : "2016-11-01",
        "key" : 1477958400000,
        "doc_count" : 0
      }, {
```

121

```
    "key_as_string" : "2016-12-01",
    "key" : 1480550400000,
    "doc_count" : 1
  }]
...
}
```

You can see that the buckets are corresponding to each month and a count of docs in each month is given. The **key_as_string** field represents the date in a pretty format. The Figure 7-3 shows the line graph corresponding to phone sales.

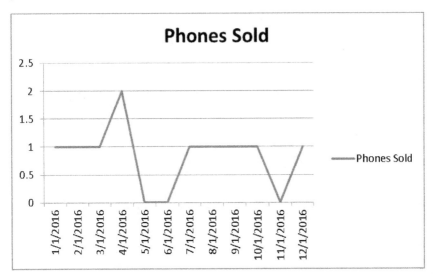

Figure 7-3. *Mobile Phones sold over time*

Multi-Tier Correlation

As mentioned in earlier sections, buckets can be nested in other buckets for more powerful experience. In order to show its advantage, let's create an aggregation that shows the total sum of prices for all phone makes, listed per quarter. Also we will compute the sum or prices per individual phone maker per quarter to indicate selling which phone is most profitable.

```
curl -XGET 'localhost:9200/phones/sales/_search?search_type=count&pretty' -d '
{
  "aggs" : {
  "sales" : {
    "date_histogram" : {
      "field" : "sold",
      "interval" : "quarter",
      "format": "yyyy-MM-dd",
      "min_doc_count" : 0,
```

```
        "extended_bounds" : {
         "min" : "2016-01-01",
         "max" : "2016-12-31"
        }
      },
     "aggs" : {
      "per_make_total" : {
        "terms" : {
         "field" : "make"
        },
        "aggs" : {
         "total_price" : {
           "sum" : {"field" : "price" }
         }
        }
      },
      "grand_total": {
        "sum": { "field": "price" }
      }
     }
    }
   }
  }
}'
```

The interval is now quarter instead of month. This aggregation would compute the sum per phone make and then the grand total of all makes combined together. Following is the response:

```
{
...
  "aggregations" : {
    "sales" : {
     "buckets" : [ {
      "key_as_string" : "2016-01-01",
      "key" : 1451606400000,
      "doc_count" : 3,
      "per_make_total" : {
        "doc_count_error_upper_bound" : 0,
        "sum_other_doc_count" : 0,
        "buckets" : [ {
         "key" : "iphone",
         "doc_count" : 2,
         "total_price" : {
           "value" : 660.0
         }
        }, {
         "key" : "motorola",
         "doc_count" : 1,
         "total_price" : {
           "value" : 80.0
         }
        } ]
      },
```

```
    "grand_total" : {
     "value" : 740.0
    }
  }, {
   "key_as_string" : "2016-04-01",
   "key" : 1459468800000,
   "doc_count" : 2,
   "per_make_total" : {
    "doc_count_error_upper_bound" : 0,
    "sum_other_doc_count" : 0,
    "buckets" : [ {
     "key" : "htc",
     "doc_count" : 2,
     "total_price" : {
       "value" : 220.0
     }
    } ]
   },
   "grand_total" : {
    "value" : 220.0
   }
  }, {
   "key_as_string" : "2016-07-01",
   "key" : 1467331200000,
   "doc_count" : 3,
   "per_make_total" : {
    "doc_count_error_upper_bound" : 0,
    "sum_other_doc_count" : 0,
    "buckets" : [ {
     "key" : "lg",
     "doc_count" : 1,
     "total_price" : {
       "value" : 40.0
     }
    }, {
     "key" : "motorola",
     "doc_count" : 1,
     "total_price" : {
       "value" : 80.0
     }
    }, {
     "key" : "samsung",
     "doc_count" : 1,
     "total_price" : {
       "value" : 70.0
     }
    } ]
   },
   "grand_total" : {
    "value" : 190.0
```

```
     }
   }, {
     "key_as_string" : "2016-10-01",
     "key" : 1475280000000,
     "doc_count" : 2,
     "per_make_total" : {
       "doc_count_error_upper_bound" : 0,
       "sum_other_doc_count" : 0,
       "buckets" : [ {
         "key" : "huawei",
         "doc_count" : 2,
         "total_price" : {
           "value" : 60.0
         }
       } ]
     },
     "grand_total" : {
       "value" : 60.0
     }
   } ]
   ...
 }
```

This response can be used to create bar charts for each individual phone make (per quarter). A line chart can be made for the total sales. The Figure 7-4 visually depicts the quarterly sales figures.

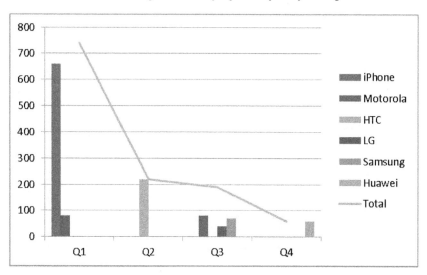

Figure 7-4. Quarterly Sales Figures

While the examples shown till now are simple in nature, but Elasticsearch aggregations can be used to handle much more complex real life scenarios.

Aggregation Scoping

You may have noticed that in all the examples given till now, there was no explicit query. The requests contained only aggregations. The beauty of aggregations is that they can be run along with the search requests. However, by use of **scope**, you can have much more directed aggregations. The default behavior is for aggregations to run in the same scope as the query. In simple terms, aggregations are computed on all the documents that match the query. Let's look at one of our initials examples, one more time:

```
curl -XGET 'localhost:9200/phones/sales/_search?search_type=count&pretty' -d '
{
  "aggs" : {
   "colors" : {
    "terms" : {
      "field" : "color"
    }
   }
  }
}'
```

You can very well see that the aggregation is specified in isolation, i.e. without any associated query. In such a scenario, Elasticsearch assumes that "*when no query is specified*", it should "*query all documents*". The query shown above is interpreted internally by Elasticsearch as following:

```
curl -XGET 'localhost:9200/phones/sales/_search?search_type=count&pretty' -d '
{
  "query" : {
   "match_all" : {}
  },
  "aggs" : {
   "colors" : {
    "terms" : {
      "field" : "color"
    }
   }
  }
}'
```

It may not be immediately obvious, but in reality, aggregations always operate within the scope of the query. This implies that an isolated aggregation operates within the scope of a **match_all** query, i.e. search all documents. The concept of scoping can help in customizing aggregations to a large extent. All the previous examples computed statistics for all the documents (data) - top-selling mobile phone, mean price of all phones, quarterly sales, etc.

Using scope, you can figure out "How many colors are iPhone available in?" This can be done by simply adding a query to the earlier requests (match query):

```
curl -XGET 'localhost:9200/phones/sales/_search?pretty' -d '
{
  "query" : {
   "match" : {
```

```
      "make" : "iphone"
    }
  },
  "aggs" : {
    "colors" : {
      "terms" : {
        "field" : "color"
      }
    }
  }
}
}'
```

You may notice that search_type=count has been omitted so as to ensure that both search results and aggregation results are visible:

```
{
...
  "hits" : {
    "total" : 2,
    "max_score" : 1.5108256,
    "hits" : [ {
      "_index" : "phones",
      "_type" : "sales",
      "_id" : "AVdB6RkFM4scS7EY9HVl",
      "_score" : 1.5108256,
      "_source" : {
        "make" : "iPhone",
        "color" : "silver",
        "price" : 260,
        "sold" : "2016-01-16"
      }
    }, {
      "_index" : "phones",
      "_type" : "sales",
      "_id" : "AVdB6RkFM4scS7EY9HVm",
      "_score" : 1.5108256,
      "_source" : {
        "make" : "iPhone",
        "color" : "gold",
        "price" : 400,
        "sold" : "2016-02-16"
      }
    } ]
  },
  "aggregations" : {
    "colors" : {
      "doc_count_error_upper_bound" : 0,
      "sum_other_doc_count" : 0,
      "buckets" : [ {
        "key" : "gold",
        "doc_count" : 1
      }, {
```

```
    "key" : "silver",
    "doc_count" : 1
  } ]
...
}
```

This seemingly simple scoping is stepping stone to potentially more advance dashboards. Any static dashboard can be turned into a real-time explorations service by adding a search bar. This would enable the user to search for terms and get related graphs updated dynamically.

Global Bucket

On many occasions, you may want to scope your aggregation on a subset rather than the complete data set. For e.g., comparing the average price of iPhone with the average price of all mobile phones. A regular expression scoped to the query can be used to find out the average price of iPhone. The average price of all mobile phones can be computed using a global bucket.

As it is apparent, the global bucket contains all the documents irrespective of the query scope. In other words, it does not consider scope. Being an aggregation, it can have nested (inner) buckets:

```
curl -XGET 'localhost:9200/phones/sales/_search?pretty' -d '
{
  "query" : {
   "match" : {
     "make" : "iphone"
    }
  },
  "aggs" : {
   "single_mean_price" : {
     "avg" : { "field" : "price" }
    },
   "all" : {
     "global" : {},
     "aggs" : {
      "mean_price" : {
        "avg" : { "field" : "price" }
       }
     }
    }
  }
}'
```

Notice that this aggregation runs in query scope and the global bucket takes no parameters. The **mean_avg_price** metric computation would be based on all documents falling under the query scope - all iPhones. This metric lies within a global bucket so it is not affected by scoping. The mean price computed for the aggregation corresponds to the average price of all phones.

Aggregations with Query Filters

The next logical step after aggregation scoping is filtering. As has been mentioned in earlier sections that aggregations operate in the context of the query scope, thereby any query filter would be applicable to the aggregation also.

Query with Filter

How would you find all phones whose prices is more than $100 and in the process compute the average price of such phones? Don't worry; **filtered** queries serve this very purpose:

```
curl -XGET 'localhost:9200/phones/sales/_search?search_type=count&pretty' -d '
{
  "query" : {
    "filtered" : {
      "filter" : {
        "range" : {
          "price" : {
            "gte" : 100
          }
        }
      }
    }
  },
  "aggs" : {
    "single_mean_price" : {
      "avg" : { "field" : "price" }
    }
  }
}'
```

It gives the following response:

```
{
...
  "hits" : {
    "total" : 3,
    "max_score" : 0.0,
    "hits" : [ ]
  },
  "aggregations" : {
    "single_mean_price" : {
      "value" : 266.6666666666667
    }
  }
}
```

The response indicates there are 3 phones with price greater than $100 and their average selling price is $267. In principle, **filtered** query is not different from a **match** query. Applying a filter on the query makes it return only a subset of document and then aggregation is applied only on those documents.

Filter Bucket

Consider a situation, wherein you want to filter just the aggregation results. This might be the case if let's say you are building the search page for mobile phone dealership. You may want to display search records based on what the user searches for. As a value addition, you may want to include the average price of phones sold in the last month (the base month is September).

Plain vanilla scoping won't help in this case as there are two different search criterions. Although the search results should match **iphone**, but the aggregations results have to match **iphone** and **sold > now - 1M**. You can solve this by the use of **filter**, which is actually a special bucket. Documents matching the filter criteria are added to the bucket:

```
curl -XGET 'localhost:9200/phones/sales/_search?search_type=count&pretty' -d '
{
  "query" : {
   "match" : {
    "make" : "LG"
   }
  },
  "aggs" : {
   "recent_sales" : {
    "filter" : {
      "range" : {
       "sold" : {
        "from" : "now-1M"
       }
      }
    },
    "aggs" : {
     "mean_price" : {
       "avg" : {
        "field" : "price"
       }
      }
     }
    }
   }
 }'
```

A **filter** bucket is used to apply filter in addition to the query scope. The **avg** metric will ensure that you get average for only those phones which are from LG and sold in last one month. It gives the following result:

```
{
...
  "aggregations" : {
```

```
  "recent_sales" : {
    "doc_count" : 1,
    "mean_price" : {
      "value" : 40.0
    }
  }
 }
}
```

You can see that filter bucket is like any other bucket and can therefore nest any other buckets or metrics. The filter is inherited by all nested components.

Post Filter

Till now we have used a filter to both search results and aggregations (**filtered query**), as well as filtering individual portions of the aggregation (**filter bucket**). There can be situation when you may want to filter just the search results but not the aggregations. This is made possible by use of a **post_filter**. It is a top-level search-request element and accepts a filter. The difference being that the filter is applied after the query execution. For this very reason, it does not affect either the query scope or aggregations.

This property can be used to apply additional filters to the search criteria, without affecting other aggregations or queries. Let's try to search for a phone and filter by color:

```
curl -XGET 'localhost:9200/phones/sales/_search?search_type=count&pretty' -d '
{
  "query" : {
    "match" : {
      "make" : "iphone"
    }
  },
  "post_filter" : {
    "term" : {
      "color" : "silver"
    }
  },
  "aggs" : {
    "all_colors" : {
      "terms" : { "field" : "color" }
    }
  }
}'
```

The post_filter element is at top-level and filters just the output of search. The output is following:

```
{
...
  "hits" : {
    "total" : 1,
    "max_score" : 0.0,
    "hits" : [ ]
  },
```

```
  "aggregations" : {
   "all_colors" : {
    "doc_count_error_upper_bound" : 0,
    "sum_other_doc_count" : 0,
    "buckets" : [ {
     "key" : "gold",
     "doc_count" : 1
    }, {
     "key" : "silver",
     "doc_count" : 1
    } ]
   }
  }
}
```

The query looks for all iphones. Thereafter, a list of colors is built with a terms aggregation. Since, aggregations operate in the query scope, the list of colors corresponds to the colors in which iphones are painted. In the end, the post_filter filters the search result to show only the silver colored iphones. This would happen after the query is executed so that the aggregations are not unaffected.

Multivalue Bucket Sorting

Have you ever wondered how does Elasticsearch decide the order of multi-value buckets like the terms, histogram and date_histogram? The default behavior is to sort buckets by **doc_count** in descending order. This serves well for majority of scenarios as generally we want to find the documents that maximize some criteria - income, population, price, etc. But there can be situations when you want to modify the sort order. Thankfully, Elasticsearch provides multiple ways to custom sort the buckets.

Intrinsic Sorts

These sort modes are intrinsic in nature and operate on data generated by bucket like **doc_count**. Their syntax differs on the basis of the bucket being used. Let's execute a terms aggregation which is sorted by doc_count in ascending order.

```
curl -XGET 'localhost:9200/phones/sales/_search?search_type=count&pretty' -d '
{
  "aggs" : {
   "colors" : {
    "terms" : {
     "field" : "color",
     "order" : {
      "_count" : "asc"
     }
    }
   }
  }
}'
```

The _count keyword can be used to sort on the basis of doc_count in ascending order.

```
{
...
  "aggregations" : {
   "colors" : {
    "doc_count_error_upper_bound" : 0,
    "sum_other_doc_count" : 0,
    "buckets" : [ {
      "key" : "gold",
      "doc_count" : 1
    }, {
      "key" : "silver",
      "doc_count" : 2
    }, {
      "key" : "black",
      "doc_count" : 3
    }, {
      "key" : "white",
      "doc_count" : 4
    } ]
    ...
}
```

The order object facilitates sorting on one of several values:

- **_count** - Sort by count of document. Best suited for terms, histograms and date_histogram.

- **_term** - Use the string value of a term to sort alphabetically. Best fit for terms.

- **_key** - Use numeric value of each bucket's key for sorting. Best fit for histogram and date_histogram.

Metric Based Sorting

There can be scenarios when you want to sort on the basis of a metric's computed value. For the mobile phones sales analysis, let's try to build a bar chart of sales by phone color sorting the bars by the average price in ascending order. This can be done by adding a metric to the bucket, and then refer the metric from the order parameter.

```
curl -XGET 'localhost:9200/phones/sales/_search?search_type=count&pretty' -d '
{
  "aggs" : {
   "colors" : {
    "terms" : {
      "field" : "color",
      "order" : {
       "mean_price" : "asc"
      }
    },
    "aggs" : {
     "mean_price" : {
       "avg" : {"field" : "price" }
     }
```

```
  }
  }
 }
}'
```

The mean price per bucket is computed. After that the buckets are sorted by the computed mean value in ascending order.

```
{
...
  "aggregations" : {
   "colors" : {
    "doc_count_error_upper_bound" : 0,
    "sum_other_doc_count" : 0,
    "buckets" : [ {
     "key" : "black",
     "doc_count" : 3,
     "mean_price" : {
      "value" : 50.0
     }
    }, {
     "key" : "white",
     "doc_count" : 4,
     "mean_price" : {
      "value" : 65.0
     }
    }, {
     "key" : "silver",
     "doc_count" : 2,
     "mean_price" : {
      "value" : 200.0
     }
    }, {
     "key" : "gold",
     "doc_count" : 1,
     "mean_price" : {
      "value" : 400.0
     }
    } ]
...
}
```

Just by referencing the metric name, you can override the sort order with any metric. Occasionally, metrics emit multiple values. Case in point being **extended_stats** metric as it provides half a dozen individual metrics. Sorting on a multi-value metric requires the use of the dot-path to metric of interest:

```
curl -XGET 'localhost:9200/phones/sales/_search?search_type=count&pretty' -d '
{
  "aggs" : {
   "colors" : {
    "terms" : {
```

```
    "field" : "color",
    "order" : {
     "stats.variance" : "asc"
    }
   },
   "aggs" : {
    "stats" : {
     "extended_stats" : {"field" : "price"}
    }
   }
  }
 }
}'
```

Use of dot notation facilitates sorting on the metric of interest and emits the following output:

```
{
...
  "aggregations" : {
   "colors" : {
    "doc_count_error_upper_bound" : 0,
    "sum_other_doc_count" : 0,
    "buckets" : [ {
     "key" : "gold",
     "doc_count" : 1,
     "stats" : {
      "count" : 1,
      "min" : 400.0,
      "max" : 400.0,
      "avg" : 400.0,
      "sum" : 400.0,
      "sum_of_squares" : 160000.0,
      "variance" : 0.0,
      "std_deviation" : 0.0,
      "std_deviation_bounds" : {
       "upper" : 400.0,
       "lower" : 400.0
      }
     }
    }, {
     "key" : "white",
     "doc_count" : 4,
     "stats" : {
      "count" : 4,
      "min" : 30.0,
      "max" : 80.0,
      "avg" : 65.0,
      "sum" : 260.0,
      "sum_of_squares" : 18600.0,
      "variance" : 425.0,
      "std_deviation" : 20.615528128088304,
      "std_deviation_bounds" : {
```

```
        "upper" : 106.2310562561766,
        "lower" : 23.768943743823392
      }
    }
  ...
}
```

In this case, sorting is being done on the variance of each bucket, so the colors with the least variance in price will appear earlier than those that have more variance.

Summary

This chapter covered a lot of ground by presenting lot of interesting topics. As a feature, aggregations are both powerful and flexible. Its ability to nest buckets and metrics and observe statistical anomalies in near real time provides insight in the data. The chapter started with introducing the concept of aggregation and use of buckets and metrics. Elasticsearch facilitates visualization of data by creating histograms and time series aggregations. It allows multi-tier correlation. More power can be added by use of scoping and filtering.

CHAPTER 8

Exploring Kibana

This previous chapter gave an overview of how to use aggregations to gather insightful information from data. The power of aggregations lies in nesting buckets and metrics to observe statistical insights in near real time. Scoping and filtering can be used to pack more power to aggregations. This chapter will introduce Kibana which is the third component of the ELK troika. Kibana is really the front-end of ELK stack and does a good job of hiding all data complexities. It can be used to present beautiful visualizations over data like charts and dashboards. Kibana visualizations are dynamic in nature as they change with change in data in real-time.

Introducing Kibana

Kibana is the front-end for Elasticsearch and provides delightful visualizations for data. Kibana is open source analytics engine which can be used to search, view and analyze data. Various kinds of visualizations are available to illustrate data in the form of tables, charts, histograms, maps, etc. There is a web based interface to handle large volume of data. Creating a dashboard is quite seamless and queries data in real time. Essentially, a dashboard is nothing but a way for analyzing JSON documents. You can save them, make them as templates or simply export them. The ease of setup and use will make you cut through the complexities of stored data in minutes.

Kibana comes as an Apache-licensed product. Its flexible interface comes out as a great combination for Elasticsearch's searching capabilities. You only need a web server and any modern web browser to start working with Kibana. It leverages REST APIs of Elasticsearch. Data can be visualized in real time by using dashboards. This helps in getting real-time insights.

Tip Kibana 4.5.1 is used as a reference for examples and snapshots in this Chapter.

Kibana Features

Kibana has the following key features:

- **Emphasis on Search Terms** - The list of documents returned as response to a search, contain the search terms as highlighted.

© Gurpreet S. Sachdeva 2017
G. S. Sachdeva, *Applied ELK Stack*, ISBN 978-1545022146

- **Aggregations** - In-depth use of Elasticsearch aggregations is done to facilitate visualizations. It has been covered in previous chapter that there two main types of aggregations - Buckets and Metrics. Buckets return a set of documents meeting criteria like terms, range, histogram, etc. Metrics, on the other hand, compute statistics like min, max, sum or average for a set of documents.

- **Scripted Fields** - Scripted fields help with computations real-time on indexed data. For e.g., for a certain field you want to add 500 before showing it. This can be saved as a scripted field. There is a caveat though - scripted fields cannot be searched.

- **Dynamic Dashboards** - Kibana Dashboards are flexible and dynamic allowing for individual visualizations to be conveniently arranged. Moreover, it enables automatic refreshing of data.

Kibana User Interface

The Kibana User interface consists of four main tabs:

1. **Discover** - This page is used for search based on free form text, fields or ranges.

2. **Visualize** - As the name suggests, this page provides the facility for creating multiple visualizations like bar charts, pie charts, line charts, etc. These charts can be saved for use in dashboards later.

3. **Dashboard** - This page is a set of collections of multiple visualizations and searches. It allows for easy application of filters based on click interaction which helps in drawing conclusions based on multiple data aggregations.

4. **Settings** - The settings page is used to configure Kibana operational parameters. Some of the examples are index patterns, scripted fields, data type of fields, etc.

Let's explore the Discover page in more detail in this chapter and we will cover the Visualize, Dashboard, and Settings pages in chapter 9.

Discover Page

The key function of Discover page is to execute interactive searches in your indexed data. You can perform ad hoc searches on the fields, filter data and view indexed documents. The Kibana default page is the Discover page and it looks like as shown in Figure 8-1:

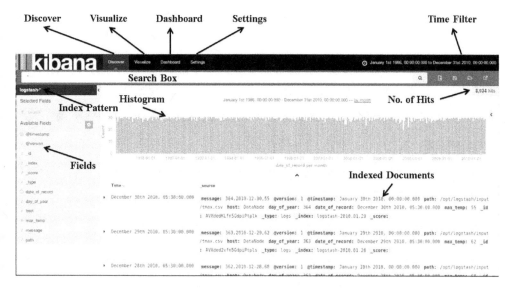

Figure 8-1. *Discover Page*

In the Discover page, all the indexed fields are shown in the **Index Pattern** on the left. The **Time Filter** is shown at the top and there is a **Search Box** to submit your search queries. A default **Histogram** is shown based on the **@timestamp** field in the documents. The **No. of Hits** in the document corresponding to the search is also displayed. The default value is **500** documents arranged on the basis of timestamp, with the latest at the top.

Time Filter

How many times it happens that you need to find some statistics corresponding to a time interval? No need to worry now as Kibana Discover page has a time filter. It enables you to filter data based on any specific time interval. The **absolute time interval** can be selected from the calendar or you can have it **relative** to the current time. There are some ready to use filters also available:

Quick Time Filter

A quick time filter helps filter quickly based on some already available time ranges: As shown in Figure 8-2, a quick time filter quickly filters documents based on some existing time ranges.

Figure 8-2. Time Filter - Quick

Relative Time Filter

If you want to filter relative to current time, then go for Relative Time Filter. The default value of time filter is set to last 15 minutes. Figure 8-3 depicts the Relative Time Filter:

Figure 8-3. Time Filter - Relative

Absolute Time Filter

If you want to filter between two dates, you can use Absolute Time Filter. It helps filtering based on a range of dates using From and To fields. Figure 8-4 illustrates this:

Figure 8-4. Time Filter - Absolute

Auto-Refresh Settings

You can choose an interval for performing auto-refresh as shown in Figure 8-5:

Figure 8-5. Auto-Refresh Setting

You can also specify time filter using click and drag on a stretch of a chart. See Figure 8-6 for an illustration:

Figure 8-6. Time Filter by Area Selection

Query and Search Data

Lucene query syntax is leveraged by Kibana for searching amongst indices stored in index patterns. As described in an earlier chapter, Elasticsearch query DSL can also be used. This helps in automatically refreshing the field list, indexed documents lists and the histograms.

■ **Tip** For string fields, both the analyzed and non-analyzed versions are saved in indices. The non-analyzed fields are shown with .raw extension in the Discover page.

Let us go through some examples of data search.

Free Text Search

The free text search filters documents containing the search term. It looks for the searched term in all the documents. For e.g., if you want to search for all the **Action** movies from an index pattern consisting of Hollywood movies, you just need to specify "**Action**" in the search box. Kibana would filter all documents containing the term **Action**.

Search keywords can be combined by use of different operators:

- **AND** - If you want to search for all documents corresponding to **Action** movies starring **Vin Diesel**, you can specify:

"Action" AND "Vin Diesel"

- **OR** - If you want to search for all documents corresponding to either an **Action** movie or starring **Vin Diesel**, you can specify:

"Action" OR "Vin Diesel"

- **NOT** - If you want to search for all documents corresponding to **Action** movies not starring **Vin Diesel**, you can specify:

"Action" NOT "Vin Diesel"

- **Groupings** - Different operators can be combined together. If you want to search for **Hollywood** movies which are either of **Comedy** or **Action** genre, you can specify:

("Action" OR " Comedy") AND "Hollywood"

- **Wildcard Searches** - You can perform wildcard searches in the following manner:

o   Trac* - This will enable search for documents having terms such as Trace, Track, Tracking, Tractor, etc.

o   Trac? - This will enable search for documents having term Trace or Tract.

Field Searches

You can use Field searches to look for specific values or ranges of values for fields in your indexed document, which is displayed on the left-hand side of the Discover page. You need to specify the field name, : separator and the value to be searched for:

\<field name\> : \<field value\>

Some examples of field search are as following:

Movie : "Action"
Movie : "Action" AND Actor : "Vin Diesel"

Range Searches

Range searches can be used to search for a range of values for a field. If you want to search for a range of values for the sales field:

sales : [100000 TO 200000]

You can combine Range and field searches using boolean operators:

sales : [100000 TO 200000] AND Movie : "Action"

▪ **Tip**   If special characters have to be searched for, then they have to be escaped using the \ operator. List of such special characters is as following:

+ - && | | ! ( ) { } [ ] ^ " ~ * ? : \

New Search

To initiate a new search, just click on the **New Search** button on the **Discover** toolbar. Figure 8-7 illustrates this.

Figure 8-7. New Search

Saving Search

You can save the search criteria using the **Save Search** option on the **Discover** toolbar. These saved searches can be used in visualizations later. They can also be used in dashboards for illustrating information in a traditional table format.

The **Load Saved Search** option on the **Discover** toolbar can be used to load the previously saved searches.

Field Search Using Field List

You can click on the positive or negative filter icon on certain values to the field to perform field search. Certain fields can be added on the right-hand side panel by using the **add button** on the field name in the field list. As shown in Figure8-8, this facilitates a comfortable view of fields as tables based on your searches.

Figure 8-8. Field Searches

This way can be used to quickly add fields and sort documents based on the fields. It is most helpful for building tables for a quick search.

Summary

This chapter presented a bird's eye view of Kibana. The Discover page was explored and different searching techniques were introduced. The Visualize, Dashboard, and Settings pages will be covered in detail in chapter 9.

Kibana - Data Visualization

The previous chapter gave an overview of Kibana and explored the Discover page. It covered execution of quick searches across indexed documents from Discover page. This chapter will take the exploration of Kibana further by covering the Visualization section. An overview will be given of the different techniques to build amazing charts and graphs which simplify comprehending complex data sets.

Visualize Page

The Visualize page is the most crucial page in Kibana and it helps in creating visualizations on top of data that has been analyzed using the Discover page. Different types of visualizations can be built from the data already present in Elasticsearch. This page plays a key role in analyses and understanding of data using the visualizations. You can create visualizations of different types, save them or combine them to form dashboards. The Visualize page enables creations of new visualization from a new search or saved search, as per requirements.

Visualization is the central component which makes Kibana feature rich and powerful. There are different types of visualizations like Vertical Bar Chart, Line Chart, Area Chart, Pie Chart, Tile Map and Data Table. These visualizations can be shared with other users having access to the Kibana instance. Visualizations leverage Elasticsearch for aggregation and visualization of data.

The Visualize page looks like the Figure 9-1.

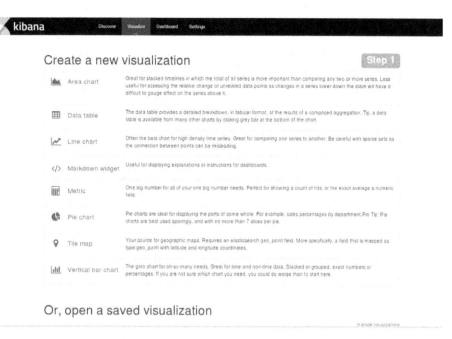

Figure 9-1. Visualization Page

In the Visualize page either you can create a new visualization or open an existing visualization from the saved list.

Metrics and Buckets Aggregations

Metrics and **Buckets** Aggregations are the foundation for making Kibana visualization. Aggregations enable us to get an overview of data and have a plug-and-play syntax, i.e. separate functional blocks can be tied together to provide the desired behavior. Buckets correspond to group of documents meeting the criteria and metrics are statistics computed on the documents in a bucket. A detailed treatment has been given to Aggregations in Chapter 7. Let's briefly revisit aggregations in the context of Kibana.

Buckets

In Kibana, the X-axis corresponds to the buckets. The following figure shows the buckets available in Kibana:

Figure 9-2. Buckets in Visualizations

The different buckets available in Kibana are as following:

- **Date Histogram** - Use it to group documents as per the specified field and time interval. It needs a field name of type date and interval for the configuration.

- **Histogram** - It is quite similar to Date Histogram, with a major difference being that it needs the field of type numbers and a numeric interval.

- **Range** - Very similar to Histogram but it enables configuring different ranges as per the requirements.

- **Date Range** - It needs a date field and a custom range corresponding to each bucket.

- **Terms** - Facilitate grouping of documents by the value of any field.

Metrics

Metrics are computations done on values of fields in each bucket. For e.g., calculating the average, count, maximum or minimum of a field in a document. In Kibana, the Y-axis is associated with metrics. The following figure shows the metrics available in Kibana:

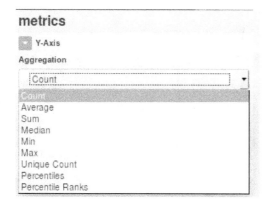

Figure 9-3. Visualization Metrics

The different metrics available in Kibana are as following:

- **Count** - The **Count** metric is used to calculate the count of the number of fields in each bucket in a bucket aggregation.

- **Min, Max, Sum, and Average** - Just like **Count** aggregation, **Min**, **Max**, **Sum** and **Average** calculate the minimum, maximum, sum and average, respectively, of all the values of a numeric field in the aggregation.

- **Unique Count** - Pretty similar to **Count** but counts only the unique values for a field.

Advanced Options

You can make use of **Advanced** options for buckets and metrics aggregations. You can give JSON input as scripted fields. The following snippet gives example of script:

```
{ "script" : "doc['income'].value * 200" }
```

The Figure 9-4 illustrates the Advanced option box:

Figure 9-4. JSON Input Advanced Options

The **New Visualization** page has the toolbar at top, metrics and buckets configuration on the left and preview pane on the right-hand side. This is illustrated with the following figure:

Figure 9-5. New Visualization Page

With the toolbar at the top, you can create new visualizations, save visualization, open a saved visualization, share visualization and refresh it. This is illustrated by the following figure:

Figure 9-6. Visualization Toolbar

For creating visualizations, you can use the following options:

- **From a saved search** - Leverages a search already saved from **Discover** page.
- **From a new search** - Create a new visualization based on a new search.

The different search source options are illustrated in the following figure:

Figure 9-7. Visualization Search Option

Choosing Search Data Source

Choosing the search source is essential to create the visualization which you want. You can either select a newly created search or an already saved search as data source for creating visualizations. All searches have an association with an index or a bunch of indices. You have the following options for choosing search data source:

- **From a saved search** - Leverages a search already saved from **Discover** page.
- **From a new search** - Create a new visualization based on a new search.

While selecting from a new search there are multiple indices to choose from, a drop-down menu is provided to select the particular index on which you want to visualize. It facilitates creation of visualizations based on stored data.

On the other hand, while selecting from a saved search, you can link the visualization with the search query saved on the **Discover** page. Since the search is associated with visualization, any change in the search dynamically updates the visualization.

Visualization Canvas

You can create, edit and configure **visualizations** through the visualization canvas. It has following key elements:

4. Toolbar

5. Aggregation Designer

6. Previewing Visualization

The following figure illustrates the different elements of the visualization canvas:

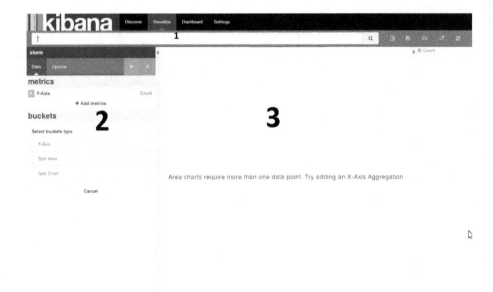

Figure 9-8. Visualization Canvas

Toolbar

Powerful analysis of data based on search queries and filters can be done using the toolbar. The search query can be specified on the basis of which visualization changes and updates dynamically. The search field can be used for interactive searching of data along with controls to create, save, or load visualizations. There is a search bar also along with main options like as **New Visualization**, **Save Visualization**, **Load Saved Visualization**, **Share Visualization** and **Refresh**.

New Visualization

You can create a fresh visualization using the **New Visualization**. The current visualization is erased and a new one is created. You can click on the **New Visualization** button, situated on the toolbar besides the search bar.

Figure 9-9. New Visualization

Save Visualization

You can save a visualization using the option of **Save Visualization**. The current visualization would get saved along with the selected index information. This option is available besides the **New Visualization** button on the toolbar.

Load Saved Visualization

You can load any previously created and saved visualizations by **Load Saved Visualization** option. It uses the specified index to load the visualization. If you try to load a saved visualization including a different index, then after loading it, the selected index would get updated. You can locate this option beside the **Save Visualization** button on the toolbar.

Share Visualization

You can share visualization by using the **Share Visualization** option. You can share both a freshly created visualization and an already saved one. This would help other people in your team in viewing it. There is also an option to either share the **link** to the visualization or **embedding** the visualization inside any HTML page. You can locate this option beside the **Save Visualization** button in the toolbar.

Refresh

You can use the Refresh button to refresh the page.

151

Aggregation Designer

This is the central component for creating visualizations. It is located on the left-hand side of the **Visualize** page. You can use it for configuring the metric and bucket aggregations. The **Aggregation Builder** consists of the following two tabs:

- **Data** - Use it to specify the metric and bucket aggregations.

- **Options** - Use it to display the various types of view options available with each type of visualization. For each visualization, there are specific view options to change the aspects. It adds a lot of flexibility to create different types of visualizations. The table 9-1 depicts some of the options associated with visualizations:

Table 9-1. Sample Table (Apply the Table Caption Style)

Visualization Type	View Options
Area Chart	Chart Mode (stacked, overlap, percentage, wiggle, silhouette), show tooltip, show legend
Data Table	Per page, show partial lines, show metrics for every bucket/level
Line Chart	Y-axis scale (linear, square root, log), smooth lines, show circles, show tooltip, show legend
Metric	Font size
Pie Chart	Donut, show tooltip, show legend
Tile Map	Map Type (scaled circle markers, shaded circle markers, heat map)
Vertical Bar Chart	Bar mode (stacked, percentage, grouped), show tooltip, show legend

For seeing the visualization of a preview canvas, use the green **Apply Changes** button at the top right of the aggregation builder, besides the two tabs - **Data** and **Options**.

Preview Canvas

Preview canvas can be used to review a visualization created using the aggregation designer. As soon as new changes are applied with different sets of metrics, options are automatically displayed dynamically on the preview canvas.

Building Visualization

To build a new visualization, you need to follow a step-by-step approach which can be triggered by clicking on the Visualize tab, which happens to be the second tab at the top of the page. The different steps are as following:

1. Chose a visualization type.

2. Chose a data source (either from a new search or an existing saved search).

3. Associate the aggregations (buckets and metrics) to be used for the visualization.

Let's look at each of these steps in detail.

Visualization Types

The different visualizations supported by Kibana are as following:

Area Chart

You can use Area Chart to create stacked timelines or distribute data. **Metrics** are used as **Y-axis** and **buckets** are used as **X-axis**. You can also have sub-aggregations in buckets to provide **Split Charts** functionality (multiple charts corresponding to different aggregations) or **Split Area** (Area chart splits on the corresponding to different aggregations).

We would like to create the chart based on hurricane data across continental United States from 1851 to 2015.

▦ **Tip**   The hurricane related data across the whole of United States can be found at:

http://www.aoml.noaa.gov/hrd/hurdat/All_U.S._Hurricanes.html

The sample data has the following fields:

- Year
- Month
- States Affected
- Category
- Central Pressure
- Maximum Wind
- Hurricane Name

For the purpose of our analysis, I have added the co-ordinates (latitude - longitude) of each state. A snippet of the data can be seen in Table 9-2:

Table 9-2. Continental United States Hurricanes

Year	States Affected	Category	Central Pressure	Max Wind	Name	Location
1851	Texas	1	974	80	NA	"31.1060,-97.6475"
1851	Florida	3	955	100	Great Middle Florida	"27.8333,-81.7170"
1851	Georgia	3	955	100	Great Middle Florida	"32.9866,-83.6487"
1852	Alabama	3	961	100	Great Middle Florida	"32.7990,-86.8073"
1852	Mississippi	3	961	100	Great Mobile	"43.3504,-84.5603"

153

1852	Louisiana	3	961	100	Great Mobile	"31.1801,-91.8749"
1852	Florida	3	961	100	Great Mobile	"27.8333,-81.7170"
1852	Florida	1	982	70	NA	"27.8333,-81.7170"
1852	Florida	2	965	90	Middle Florida	"27.8333,-81.7170"
1852	Georgia	2	965	90	Middle Florida	"32.9866,-83.6487"

In many cases, multiple states are affected by the same hurricane. I have kept separate rows for each state. This data has to be put in a format and location which is accessible to ELK stack. Let's see how the csv data looks like by using the UNIX **head** command:

```
$ head hurricane.csv
1851,Texas,1,974,80,NA,"31.1060,-97.6475"
1851,Florida,3,955,100,Great Middle Florida,"27.8333,-81.7170"
1851,Georgia,3,955,100,Great Middle Florida,"32.9866,-83.6487"
1852,Alabama,3,961,100,Great Mobile,"32.7990,-86.8073"
1852,Mississippi,3,961,100,Great Mobile,"43.3504,-84.5603"
1852,Louisiana,3,961,100,Great Mobile,"31.1801,-91.8749"
1852,Florida,3,961,100,Great Mobile,"27.8333,-81.7170"
1852,Florida,1,982,70,NA,"27.8333,-81.7170"
1852,Florida,2,965,90,Middle Florida,"27.8333,-81.7170"
1852,Georgia,2,965,90,Middle Florida,"32.9866,-83.6487"
```

Each row corresponds to the hurricane details for a particular state. This data is converted into json format which the ELK stack can understand. Let's see how the json data looks like by using the UNIX head command:

```
$ head hurricane.json
{ "create": { "_index": "storm", "_type": "hurricane" }}
{ "Year":1851, "State":"Texas", "Category":1, "Pressure":974, "Wind Speed":80, "Name":"NA",
"Location":"31.1060,-97.6475"}
{ "create": { "_index": "storm", "_type": "hurricane" }}
{ "Year":1851, "State":"Florida", "Category":3, "Pressure":955, "Wind Speed":100, "Name":"Great Middle
Florida", "Location":"27.8333,-81.7170"}
{ "create": { "_index": "storm", "_type": "hurricane" }}
{ "Year":1851, "State":"Georgia", "Category":3, "Pressure":955, "Wind Speed":100, "Name":"Great Middle
Florida", "Location":"32.9866,-83.6487"}
{ "create": { "_index": "storm", "_type": "hurricane" }}
{ "Year":1852, "State":"Alabama", "Category":3, "Pressure":961, "Wind Speed":100, "Name":"Great
Mobile", "Location":"32.7990,-86.8073"}
{ "create": { "_index": "storm", "_type": "hurricane" }}
{ "Year":1852, "State":"Mississippi", "Category":3, "Pressure":961, "Wind Speed":100, "Name":"Great
Mobile", "Location":"43.3504,-84.5603"}
```

Give the following command to load the bulk contents:

```
curl -XPOST 'localhost:9200/_bulk?pretty' --data-binary "@hurricane.json"; echo
```

The Area chart would show a comparison of states with highest occurrence of hurricanes along with category of hurricanes over a period of time. The chart will be split on the basis of states with highest occurrence of hurricanes and the area will be split on the basis of hurricane category. The X-axis indicates the period of time:

1. First of all specify the metrics on the Y-axis as **count**. You may use any other metric as per requirement.

2. Next add a **Split Chart** bucket type and add aggregation of **terms** specifying the field "**State**" with the top 5 size. By adding this, the chart is now split and shows the hurricanes in the top 5 states with largest number of occurrence of hurricanes.

3. Now let's add a Split Area sub-bucket and add sub-aggregation of terms specifying the top 5 values of field "**Category**". By doing this, the area has been split to show the distribution of hurricanes by their categories.

4. Since Area Charts display data over a period of time, let's add an X-axis sub-bucket, having the sub-aggregation as **Histogram** using the "**Year**" field with an interval of **10 years**.

5. Finally, we get a visualization that shows the category-wise distribution of hurricanes in top 5 states with largest number of occurrence over a period from 1850 to 2010 with an interval of 10 years.

■ **Tip** If while using Area Charts you come across the following error message: "**Area charts require more than one data point. Try adding an X-Axis aggregation.**" it indicates an error. An X-axis is needed as input for creating visualizations in the Area Chart. If the selected **Time Filter** does not fit into the visualization, it could also lead to error.

To display the visualization, click the **green Apply Changes button** to update the visualization or click the **grey Discard Changes button** to discard changes to the visualization. The output is as shown in the Figure 9-2:

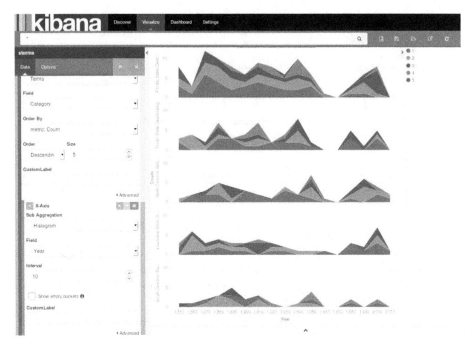

Figure 9-10. Area Chart

Save this visualization as **Area Chart** so that we can use it while creating dashboards.

■ **Tip** The default basis for split charts is rows, but it can be changed to columns by selecting columns just underneath the **Split Chart** bucket.

The default **Chart Mode** is set as **stacked** and it shows all the documents across the buckets from the height of the stacked elements. You can change the chart mode to any other mode by selecting the following chart modes:

- **Overlap** - In this mode, rather than stacking charts one upon each other, every area begins at the X-axis and is displayed in a **semi-transparent** way. This enables all the areas to be seen properly. It becomes easy to see the values of different buckets but little tedious to get a sum total of values of all the buckets.

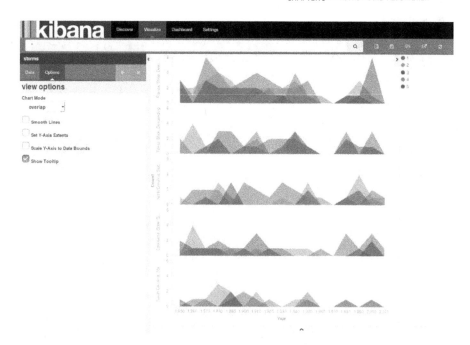

Figure 9-11. Overlap Area Chart

- **Percentage** - This chart mode has the height always as 100% and the count for each bucket is shown in terms of the percentage of the whole chart.

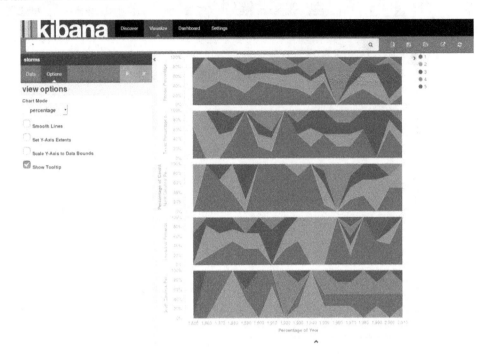

Figure 9-12. Percentage Area Chart

- **Wiggle** - Use this chart mode to display aggregation as a stream graph. It essentially is a stacked area graph displaced around a central axis resulting in a flowing shape:

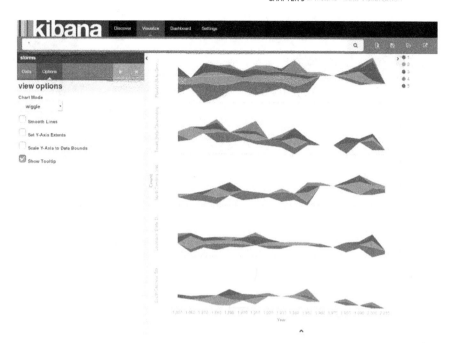

Figure 9-13. Wiggle Area Chart

- **Silhouette** - In this chart mode, aggregations are displayed as a variance from the central line from which the chart evolves in both directions:

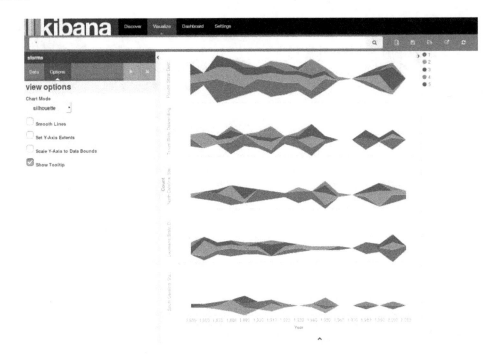

Figure 9-14. Silhouette Area Chart

The string fields specified in buckets, aggregations, or sub-aggregations, have options for customization, that can be edited/used by clicking on the **Advanced** button shown beneath **Order By**, and include the following options:

- ○ **Exclude Patterns** - Pattern to exclude from the results.

- ○ **Exclude Pattern Flags** - Set of java flags for exclusion pattern.

- ○ **Include Patterns** - Pattern to include in the results.

- ○ **Include Pattern Flags** - Set of java flags for inclusion pattern.

- ○ **JSON input** - Specific JSON properties to merge with aggregation.

There are quite a few **view** options that can alter the following behavior of **Area Charts**:

- • **Smooth Lines** - Use this option to curve the top boundary from point to point.

- • **Current Time Marker** - Draw a red line on current time data.

- • **Set Y-Axis Extents** - Set specific values for the Y-axis by providing y-max and y-min fields.

- • **Set Y-Axis to Data Bounds** - Modify upper and lower bounds to match values returned in data.

- • **Show Tooltip** - Enable rendering of information while hovering over visualization.

- • **Show Legend** - See the legend that is displayed besides the chart.

160

Data Table

You can use the Data table to show aggregated data in a tabular format. It helps identify **Top N** kinds of aggregations. Let's create a Data Table that shows the top 5 states with largest number of occurrence of hurricanes with a count of hurricanes in each state corresponding to **pressure range (mb)** from **961** to **1010** with an interval of **10mb**. This splits the rows on the basis of top states and rows are further split on the basis of hurricane pressure:

1. First of all, specify the metrics as **count**. You may choose any other metric as per requirement.

2. Next add a new **Split Rows** bucket and add aggregation of **terms** specifying the field "**State**" with top 5 size. This creates a **Data Table** showing a count of hurricanes in the top 5 states by the occurrence of hurricanes.

3. Now add a **Split Rows** sub-bucket and add **Range** sub-aggregation, specifying the field "**Pressure**" with ranges from 961 to 970 till 1001 to 1010.

4. In the end, click on the Apply Changes button to display the visualization. This would show the breakup of occurrence of hurricanes for the pressure ranges for the top 5 states.

You can see the output of Data Table in the Figure 9-15:

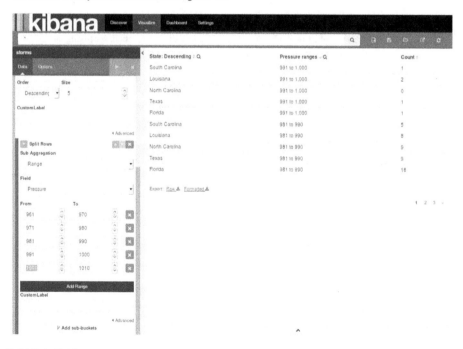

Figure 9-15. Data Table

There are certain options to alter the following behavior of **Data Table**:

- **Per Page** - Use this for pagination of the table. The default setting is 10 rows displayed per page. This setting can be changed as per convenience.

- **Show Metrics for Every Bucket** - Enables display of intermediate metrics result corresponding to each bucket aggregation.

- **Show Partial Rows** - Enable display of rows even if there is no result.

Line Chart

Line charts depict high density time series and are of great help while comparing one series with another. The lines can be displayed using different scales like **linear**, **log** or **square root**.

Let's create a chart that compares the top **5** states with largest number of occurrence of hurricanes with a breakup on the basis of wind speed from **1850 to 2010**. The chart is split on the basis of wind speed and the X-axis represent the period of time.

1. First of all, specify metrics on the Y-axis as **count**. You may choose any other metric as per requirement.

2. Next add a new **Split Chart** bucket and add aggregation of **terms** specifying the field "**State**" with top 5 size. By doing this we have effectively split the chart showing the occurrence of hurricanes in the top 5 states.

3. Now add a **Split Lines** sub-bucket and add **terms** sub-aggregation, specifying the field "**Wind Speed**" with top 5 size. This splits the area showing the top 5 categories in the top 5 states with the largest occurrence of hurricanes.

4. Since, Line Charts are better at displaying data over a period of time, let's add an X-axis sub-bucket, having sub-aggregation as **Histogram**, using the field "**Year**" with **10 years** as interval.

5. In the end, click on the Apply Changes button to display the visualization, which shows the top 5 categories for the top 5 states with largest occurrence of hurricanes.

You can see the output of Line Chart in the Figure 9-16:

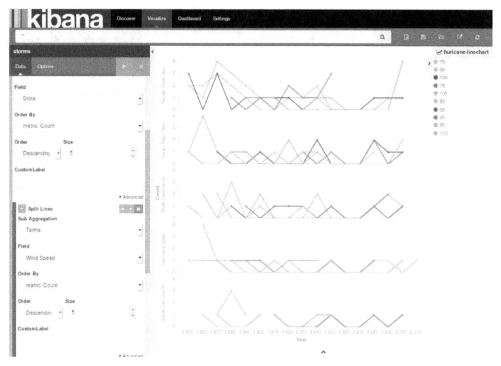

Figure 9-16. Line Chart

Let's save this visualization as LineChart, so that it can be used to create dashboards later in the chapter.

The default mode for Line Chart is **linear** and it is set in the **Options** tab. The mode can be changed to other scale by selecting any of the following scale options:

Square Root

Use this option to orient Y-axis scale on the basis of **square root** of the count value.

163

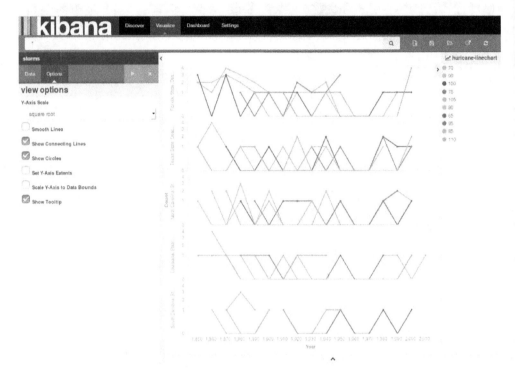

Figure 9-17. Line Chart with Square Root Scale

Log

This option orients Y-axis scale on the basis of **logarithm** of the count value. It is helpful in displaying data exponentially:

There are some more options to modify the behavior of **Line Charts**:

- **Smooth Lines** - Curve the top boundary from point to point.

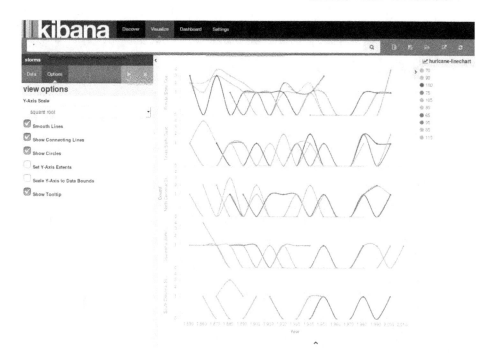

Figure 9-18. Line Chart with Smooth Lines

- **Show Connecting Lines** - Draw lines between points to points.

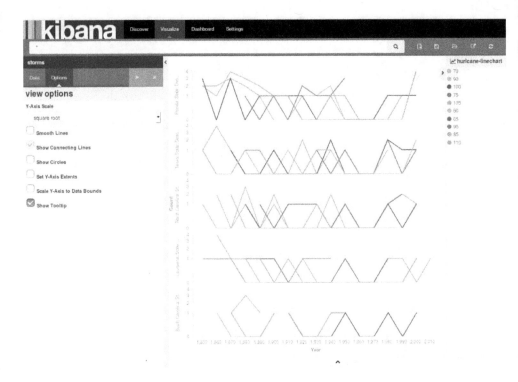

Figure 9-19. Line Chart Connecting Lines

- **Show Circles** - Draw each data point as a circle.

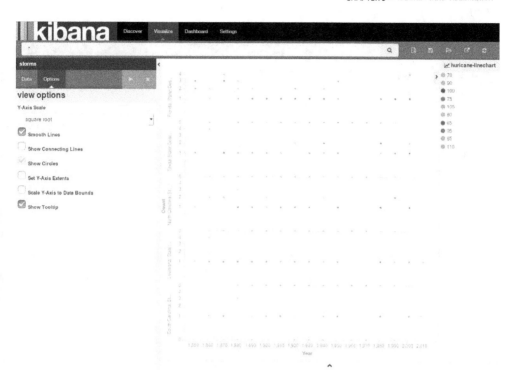

Figure 9-20. Line Chart with Circles

- **Current Time Marker** - Draw a red line on current time data.
- **Set Y-Axis Extents** - Specify y-max and y-min fields to set specific values for the Y-Axis.

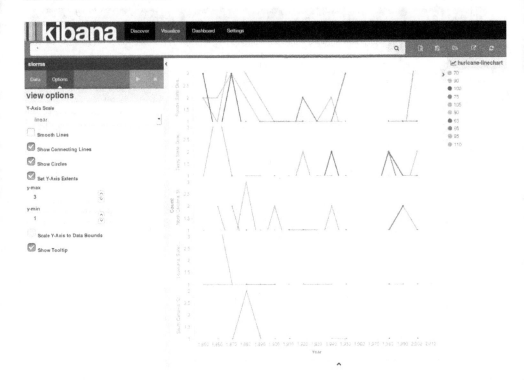

Figure 9-21. Line Chart with Y-Axis Extents

- **Set Y-Axis to Data Bounds** - Change upper and lower bounds to match values returned in data.

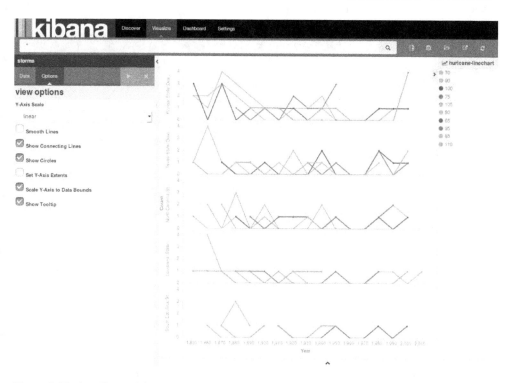

Figure 9-22. Line Chart with Y-Axis Data Bounds

- **Show Tooltip** - Enable information while hovering over the visualization.
- **Show Legend** - Display the legend that is shown besides the chart.

Bubble Charts is a variation to **Line Charts** and can be used to display data points as bubbles. A Line Chart can be converted into a Bubble Chart by using the following steps:

1. Create **Line Chart** visualization, or load an already created Line Chart visualization.

2. In **Data** tab, under **Metrics** heading, click on **Add Metrics** and select metrics type as **Dot Size** and specify **Dot Size Ratio** and **Aggregation** as **Count**.

3. In the **Options** tab, uncheck the **Show Connecting Lines** box and submit the changes by clicking on the **Apply Changes** button.

Save this visualization as **Line_Bubble**.

Figure 9-23. Bubble Chart

Markdown Widget

Markdown widget displays information or instructions on Dashboard and is useful for any requirements for text on Dashboard. It can display text, links, code, tables, etc. which is like supplementary information and sometimes quite useful. The text entered is displayed on the dashboard.

Metric

Metric condenses all the analysis for a field into one number. There is no bucketing done, i.e., the metrics aggregations get applied to the complete data set. This data set can be modified either by selecting another index or querying in the search bar.

You can start creating it by just clicking on the Add Metrics and select Metrics. Thereafter, select the aggregation followed by the field name. Metrics can help in calculating things like sum or average of a field.

Let's create Metric visualization related to hurricane data corresponding to different states from 1850 to 2010.

- Total number of hurricanes across United States of America from 1850 to 2010.

170

- Average Category for hurricanes.
- Average Hurricane Pressure
- Average Hurricane Wind Speed

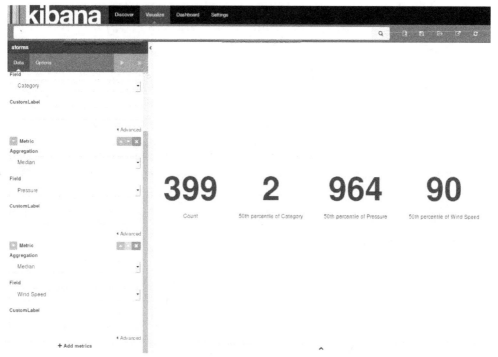

Figure 9-24. Metric

Pie Chart

Pie charts show parts of a whole or a percentage relationship. It depicts distribution of data over multiple slices in a pie chart. Each slice of the pie chart corresponds to a metric aggregation like **count, sum** or **unique count**. Type of data to be represented in one is determined by **Bucket aggregation**.

Let's create a pie chart that compares the **top 5 states** with largest number of occurrence of hurricanes with a breakup on the basis of **top 3 categories** from **1850 to 2010**. The chart is split on the basis of Year, split slices on the basis of top 5 states, and split splices on the basis of top 3 hurricane categories. While creating pie charts, split charts are generally used before split slices.

1. First of all, specify metrics on **Slice Size** as **count**. You may choose any other metric as per requirement.

2. Next add a new **Split Chart** bucket and add aggregation of **histogram** specifying the field "**Year**" with interval of **150 years**. By doing this we have effectively split the chart on the basis of years.

3. Now add a **Split Slices** sub-bucket and add **terms** sub-aggregation, specifying the field "**Category**" with top 3 size. This splits the slices in **Pie Chart** showing the top 5 states in two batches of 150 years and next 60 years.

4. To display the top hurricane categories for these states, let's add a **Split Slices** sub-bucket with sub-aggregation as **terms** specifying the field "**Category**" with top 3 size.

5. In the end, click on the Apply Changes button to display the visualization, which shows the top 3 categories for the top 5 states with largest occurrence of hurricanes in two batches of 150 years and next 60 years.

Figure 9-25 shows the Pie Chart illustrating the distribution of hurricane occurrences over states:

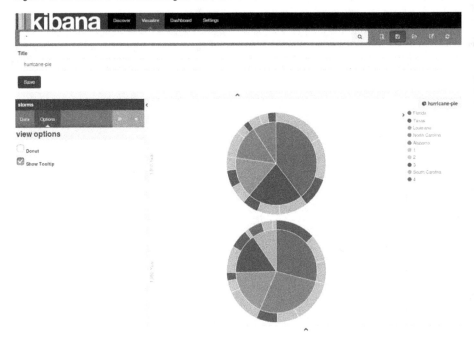

Figure 9-25. Pie Chart

Save this visualization as **PieChart**.

If you hover over a particular slice, it displays the percentage of occurrence of that event.

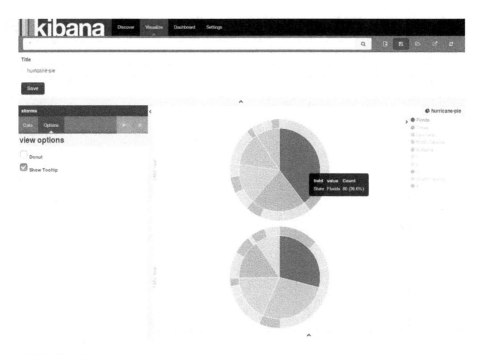

Figure 9-26. Pie Chart Percentage

The behavior of pie charts can be controlled by using the options provided in the **Options** tab:

- **Donut** - View pie chart in the shape of a donut.

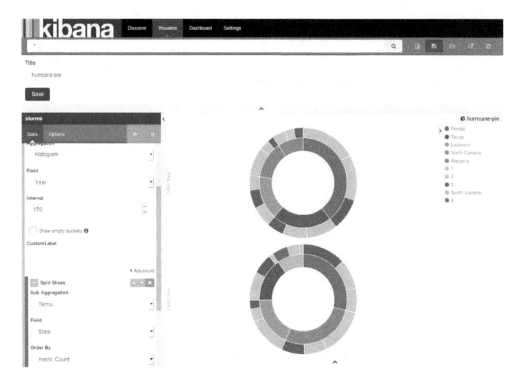

Figure 9-27. Pie Chart Donut

- **Show Tooltip** - Enable information when hovering over visualization.
- **Show Legend** - View the legend shown besides the chart.

Tile Map

You can use maps to locate geographic locations based on geographical coordinates. The **Geohash** bucket aggregation is used in Tile maps and it groups multiple coordinates into one bucket. A field with type as **geo_point** is required with inputs of **latitude** and **longitude**. The visualization displays the data points captured in the form of circles. The **size** is decided by the **precision** chosen and **color** signifies the **actual value** computed.

■ **Tip** In order to use Tile Maps, you have to upgrade to Kibana version **4.5.3** or later.

Let's map the **locations** of states where hurricanes have occurred from 1850 to 2010. This would require the use of **Geo Coordinates** in a bucket.

1. First of all, specify metrics on **Value Size** as **count**. You may choose any other metric as per requirement.

2. Next add a new **Geo Coordinates** bucket and add aggregation of **Geohash** specifying the field "**Location**". On doing this, you will see a map that has circles as data points captured by the location field.

3. In the end, click on the Apply Changes button to display the visualization, which shows the location on a map where hurricanes have occurred.

You can see the Map in the Figure 9-28:

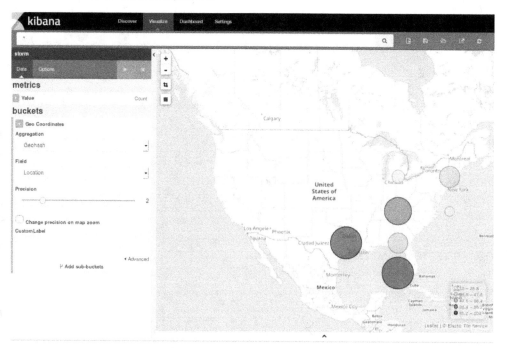

Figure 9-28. Tile Map

The default Map type is set as **Scaled Circle Markers** but can be changed from the **Options** tab.

Shaded Circle Markers

In this case, the size of each circle varies with the location of longitude and latitude. Being closer to the equator makes the circle size small. Similarly, being further from the equator makes the circle size large. You can use it to display the markers (data points) with different shades on the basis on the metric aggregations' value.

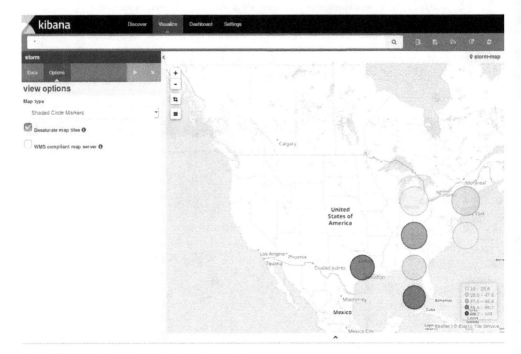

Figure 9-29. Tile Map with Shaded Circle Markers

Shaded GeoHash Grid

This option has markers displayed as rectangular cells of GeoHash grid instead of circles. You can use it to display the markers (data points) with different shades based on the metric aggregations' value.

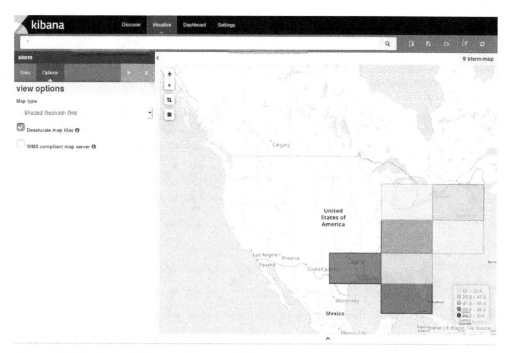

Figure 9-30. Tile Map with Shaded GeoHash Grid

Heat Map

Heat Map is a special type of tile map that is a two-dimensional graphical representation of data with values displayed using colors instead of text, numbers or markers (data points). It makes it easy to comprehend complex data sets. On the basis of total amount of overlap, blurring of markers and shading is done.

Heatmap contains following key properties:

- **Radius** - This sets the size of all Heatmap dots occurring on the map. A large radius signifies bigger size of overlap of dots. Similarly, a smaller radius signifies smaller size of overlap of dots. The default value is **25**.

- **Blur** - This sets the blurring amount for all Heatmap dots occurring on the map. Higher blur leads to fewer individual Heatmap dots shown on the map. Similarly, lower blur leads to more number of individual Heatmap dots. The default value is **15**.

- **Maximum Zoom** - This sets the zoom level of map at which all Heatmap dots will be displayed with full intensity. Higher zoom leads to increased intensity of dots. Similarly, lower zoom leads to reduced intensity of dots. The default value is **16**.

- **Minimum Opacity** - This sets the opacity for all Heatmap dots. The default value is **0.1**.

- **Show Tooltip** - If you check this box, then it enables information when hovering over visualization.

Desaturate Map Tiles

It desaturates the map color so that the colors appear more clearly. The Figure 9-31 shows Heatmap when the **Desaturate map tiles** checkbox is ticked.

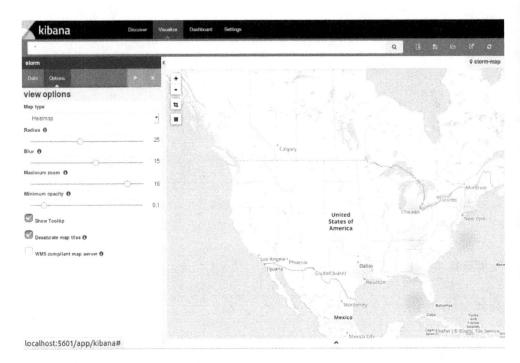

Figure 9-31. Heat Map with Desaturate Option Enabled

The Figure 9-32 shows Heatmap when the **Desaturate map tiles** checkbox is not ticked.

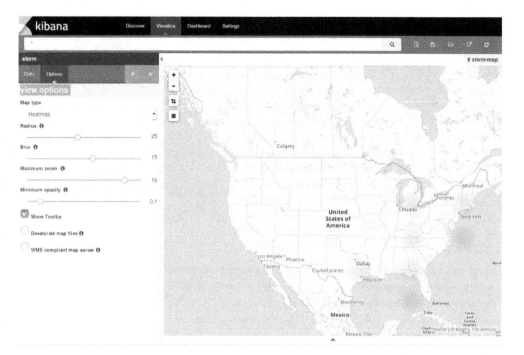

Figure 9-32. Heat Map with Desaturate Option Disabled

Tile Map can be explored in the following manner:

- Click-and-drag the **cursor** to move the **map center**.
- Change the **zoom level** by clicking on the **Zoom In/Out buttons**.
- Use the **Draw a Rectangle** button to make a filter for the box coordinates by drawing a rectangle box.
- Use the **Fit Data Bounds** button for automatically adjusting the map and displaying the map boundaries as per the GeoHash bucket that has at least a single result.

Vertical Bar Chart

This chart is used for multiple purposes and is suitable for both time and non-time based fields. You can use it as a single bar, stacked or grouped. **Y-axis** corresponds to **metrics** and **X-axis** corresponds to **buckets** aggregation.

Let's create a chart that would show a comparison of states with highest occurrence of hurricanes within a range of wind pressure. The bars will be split on the basis of states with highest occurrence of hurricanes and the chart will be split on the basis of **wind pressure** in two ranges: **926 to 950** and **951 to 975**. The X-axis indicates the period of time from 1850 to 2010 with 10 year intervals.

1. First of all, specify metrics on the Y-axis as **count**. You may choose any other metric as per requirement.

179

2. Next add a new X-axis bucket, with aggregation as **histogram** using the field "**Year**" with an interval of 10 years. This would result in a display of hurricanes statistics on a decade basis in terms of a histogram.

3. Now add a **Split Bars** sub-bucket and add **terms** sub-aggregation, specifying the field "**State**" with top 5 size. This splits the bar displaying the top 5 states having the largest occurrence of hurricanes.

4. To show hurricanes statistics on the basis of wind pressure, let's add a **Split Chart** sub-bucket having sub-aggregation as **Range** specifying the field "**Pressure**" with the ranges defined as from **926 to 950** and **951 to 975**.

5. In the end, click on Apply Changes button to display the visualization, which shows occurrence of hurricanes on a decade basis for the top 5 states with wind pressure in two ranges: **926 to 950** and **951 to 975**.

⬛ **Tip** If while using Bar Charts you come across the following error message: "**This container is too small to render the visualization.**" It indicates an error that the visualization created using the buckets cannot fit into the preview visualization canvas.

You can see the output of Bar Chart in the Figure 9-33:

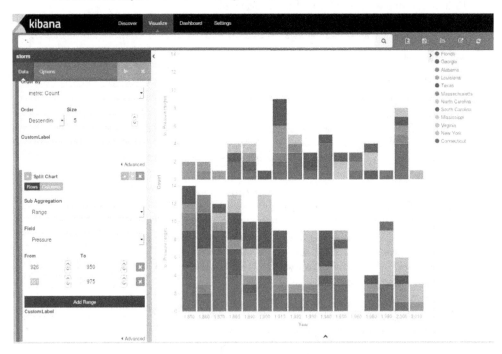

Figure 9-33. Bar Chart

The bar mode is **stacked** by default, which displays all the documents across the buckets from the height of the stacked elements. Save this visualization as **BarChart** so that it can be used later for creating dashboards. From the Options tab, you can change to other bar modes.

- **Percentage** - This bar mode results in the height of the bar shown as always 100% and the count for each bucket depicted in terms of percentage of the whole bar.

Figure 9-34. Bar Chart Percentage

- **Grouped** - The results of each bucket are grouped and displayed alongside each other.

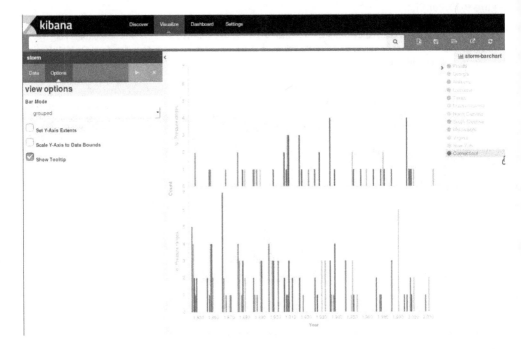

Figure 9-35. Bar Chart Grouped

There are few other options also available that can change the behavior of bar charts:

- **Current Time Marker** - Check this box to show a red line on current time data.

- **Set Y-Axis Extents** - Check this box to specify the **y-max** and **y-min** fields for setting a specific value for the Y-axis.

- **Scale Y-Axis to Data Bounds** - Check this box to modify upper and lower bounds to match values returned in data.

- **Show Tooltip** - Check this box in order to enable information display when hovering over visualization.

- **Show Legend** - Check this box to view legend shown next to the chart.

Summary

This chapter gave an overview of various data visualization mechanism available in Kibana. These visualization mechanisms not only present data in a user friendly manner, but also make it easier to comprehend complex data sets. Real-world data was used to create different visualizations like Area Charts, Line Charts, Pie Charts, Data Table, Tile Maps and Bar Graphs.

## CHAPTER 10

Kibana – Dashboard

The previous chapter gave an overview of different visualizations supported by Kibana and how it simplifies comprehending data. This chapter will cover the last piece in the Kibana armor - Dashboard. Various visualizations can be combined to give a holistic view using Dashboard. This serves single area for visualizing and analyzing data in real time. This chapter will cover the key topics - Associating visualizations with dashboard, Saving a dashboard, Customizing visualizations in dashboard, Embedding a dashboard into a web page and Explanation of debug panel.

Introduction to Dashboard Page

The **Dashboard** page enables you to arrange all the saved visualizations in a single page. Different types of visualizations created earlier can be displayed on a **single** page. User has freedom to arrange the visualizations in any manner on the dashboard. You can easily **move**, **resize**, **edit** or **remove** these visualizations. The arrangement of multiple visualizations on a single page facilitates understanding of data in an easy manner.

Some of the advantages of the **Dashboard** page are as following:

- Single page view for visualizations making it easier to interpret data.

- Straightforward to comprehend data visually rather than looking at raw data.

- Simple to use visualizations on multiple dashboards without coding.

- Making changes in any visualization automatically updates all the dashboards that use that particular visualization.

- Dashboards and visualizations updated in real time as more data streams in.

- Filtering dashboards based on search queries changes the visualizations in the dashboard as per the search results.

- Click on any visualization to create filters.

Tip In order to create a dashboard, there should be at least one saved visualization.

On opening the **Dashboard** page, you will see the empty Dashboard page as shown in Figure 10-1

© Gurpreet S. Sachdeva 2017
G. S. Sachdeva, *Applied ELK Stack*, ISBN 978-1545022146

Time Filter

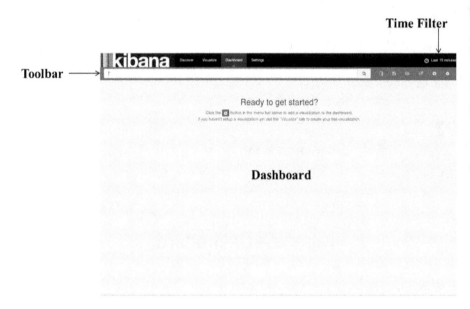

Toolbar ⟶

Dashboard

Figure 10-1. Dashboard Page

As shown in the Figure 10-1, the different areas of the Dashboard page are as following:

- **Time filter** which contains data for a particular time interval.

- **Toolbar** which consists of a search bar along with the options - **New** Dashboard, **Save** Dashboard, **Load Saved** Dashboard, and **Share and Add Visualization**.

- Dashboard **canvas** which displays the added visualizations. If the dashboard is empty, it simply states "**Click on the add button to add a visualization to the dashboard**".

▨ **Tip**   Default value for Time Filter is **15 minutes**. Make sure the appropriate value is specified for Time Filter.

Let's begin the journey to explore the **Dashboard** page.

Working with the Toolbar

The Toolbar is the central component of the Dashboard page since it provides different options to deal with visualizations. You can use the **search bar** to specify the search query or filters that can be used to analyze visualizations. When a search query is specified, it inspects all the documents and returns the results of the search query. The existing visualizations get updated according to the search query results obtained. The toolbar consists of a **search bar** along with buttons for options like **New Dashboard**, **Save Dashboard**, **Load Saved Dashboard**, and **Share and Add Visualization**.

Let's explore the usage of the different options of the toolbar.

New Dashboard Option

New Dashboard option facilitates start of addition of visualizations to an empty dashboard. It empties everything including visualizations created and added to the dashboard, along with the current dashboard. You can do this by clicking on the **New Dashboard button,** which is located on the toolbar, besides the search bar, as illustrated in the Figure 10-2.

Figure 10-2. New Dashboard

⊠ **Tip** Make sure to save visualizations after adding them. If you click on New Visualization, without saving first, the added visualizations would not be available.

Adding Visualizations

The Add Visualization facilitates adding visualizations to the dashboard. Any number of visualizations can be added. When starting with an empty dashboard, first click on the add button from the dashboard canvas or the add button situated at the end of the toolbar besides the share button.

Perform the following steps to add visualization:

1. Click on the Add Visualization button, as shown in Figure 10-3.

Figure 10-3. Add Visualization

2. Select the visualization which you want to add, as shown in Figure 10-4

Figure 10-4. Saved Visualizations

3. The selected visualization will appear on the dashboard canvas within a container.

Let's create a dashboard by adding saving visualizations which were created in Chapter 9. Following saved visualization would be used:

*   Hurricane
*   hurricane-linechart
*   storm-barchart
*   hurricane-datatable
*   hurricane-pie

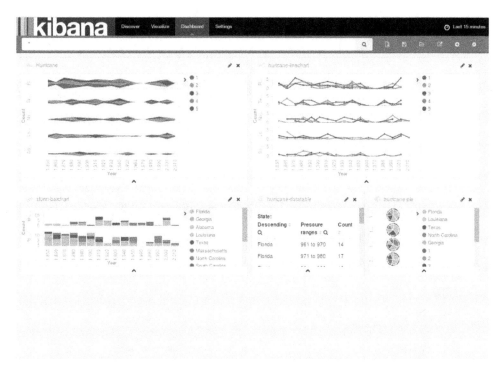

Figure 10-5. Create Dashboard

The dashboard illustrated by Figure 10-5 is not very appealing. It may not interest users to go through it at first glance. To make it more attractive, we need to customize it further.

■ **Tip** Dashboards can also contain saved searches. Just click on the add button and select a saved search from the searches tab, which is located beside the Visualizations tab.

Search Bar

Once visualizations have been added, you can query the dashboard similar to the Discover page. Based on the search query entered, all the relevant visualizations get updated with the result of the search query. This is an important feature which makes it easy to analyze data and monitor the trends for different aspects.

Save Dashboard

This option helps in saving the dashboard along with the added visualizations. This option can be found besides the New Dashboard button in the toolbar. Perform the following steps to save a dashboard:

1. Click on the **Save Dashboard** button present in the toolbar next to the **New Dashboard** button as illustrated in Figure 10-6.

Figure 10-6. Save Dashboard

2. Give a name to the dashboard so that it can be used for saving the dashboard. Let's use **MyDashboard** as the name to save to our dashboard. This is illustrated in Figure 10-7.

Figure 10-7. Save As Dashboard

3. Click on Save to save the dashboard. Anytime you do any changes to the dashboard, make it a point to save it.

Load Saved Dashboard

The **Load Saved Dashboard** option facilitates loading of saved dashboard. It can be used to load already saved dashboards which contain visualizations. This option is situated beside the **Save Dashboard** button on the toolbar.

Perform the following steps, to load a saved dashboard:

1. Click on the load saved dashboard button present on the toolbar, next to the **Save Dashboard** button as illustrated in Figure 10-8.

Figure 10-8. Load Saved Dashboard

2. Specify the saved dashboard name to load it. All saved dashboards can be seen below the displayed bar.

3. Select the dashboard to be loaded, as shown in Figure 10-9.

Figure 10-9. Select Saved Dashboard

Sharing the Saved Dashboard

You can share the saved dashboards among people who may wish to view it. There is also option to either share the link of saved dashboard or embed dashboard within any *HTML* page. This option is situated beside the **Load Saved Dashboard** button on the toolbar.

Perform the following steps, to share a saved dashboard:

1. Click on the share button present on the toolbar, next to the **Load Saved Dashboard** button as illustrated in Figure 10-10.

Figure 10-10. Share Dashboard

2. After clicking on it, you will find the link for embedding the dashboard and sharing it, as shown in Figure 10-11.

Figure 10-11. Share Dashboard Link

3. You can click on the copy to clipboard button beside **Share a Link** to copy the link and share it. You may also copy the clipboard button beside **Embed this dashboard** and paste the *iframe* source in an HTML page to display visualizations in a web page.

Working with Dashboard Canvas

The dashboard canvas can be used to display a preview of all saved visualizations added to the dashboard. Each visualization appears on the dashboard canvas within a container and these containers can be customized through various ways. This customization helps in making the visualization elegant.

Move Visualization

The visualizations within a dashboard can be moved as per user preference. The **container** having visualization can be moved anywhere in the dashboard. You can perform the following steps to move the visualizations:

1. First of all, click and drag the container title bar (heading) by using the mouse.

2. Once you decide the new location for the visualization, just release the mouse button.

■ **Tip** Bear in mind, the moving container will shift other containers also as per their size.

Resize Visualization

You can always resize the visualizations added in the dashboard. The container having visualization can be resized anywhere in the dashboard. You can perform the following steps to resize the container:

1. Move mouse pointer to the bottom-right corner of the container till the time the pointer does not change to indicate the resize option at the corner.

2. Click and drag for resizing the visualization.

3. Release the button at the point when you want to confirm the new size of the visualization.

Edit Visualization

You can even edit visualizations already added in the dashboard. You can perform the following steps to edit the visualization:

1. Initiate the editing process by clicking on the **Edit Visualization** button on the title bar of the container.

2. The **visualization canvas** page will be displayed and you can edit here.

3. Once you have completed editing, click on the **Save Visualization** button. The visualization changes would get saved and get updated automatically on the dashboard.

Remove Visualization

Existing visualizations can be removed from a dashboard. This makes it flexible to create dashboard as per your requirements and get rid of unnecessary visualizations.

⬛ **Tip** Removing a visualization from a dashboard just removes the link to the dashboard. However, the underlying visualization still remains intact.

In order to remove a container, just click on the **Remove Container** button present on the title bar of the container.

By doing some customizations the earlier dull looking dashboard with default settings get transformed into a visually appealing dashboard. This is illustrated in Figure 10-12.

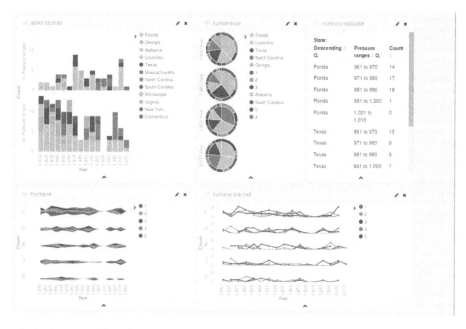

Figure 10-12. Elegant Dashboard

As you have seen that an elegant and beautiful visualization makes it quite simple to analyze and draw conclusions, rather than going through huge chunks of raw data. Various types of charts can help in forecasting trends.

> ■ **Tip** Default place for storing all dashboards is **.kibana** index. If this index gets deleted, then all the saved searches, visualizations and dashboards will get removed.

Embed Dashboard in Web Page

Let's use the saved dashboards and click on the copy to clipboard button beside the Embed this dashboard option to copy the link for embedding. We can have a simple HTML file and use this iframe source to embed a web page.

```
<html>
<head>
<title> Embed Kibana Dashboard</title>
</head>
<body>
<center><b>Fun with Embedded Dashboards </b></center>
<iframe
src="http://localhost:5601/#/dashboard/Kibana_Dashboard?embed&_a=(filters:!(),panels:!((col:1,id:AreaCh
art,row:1,size_x:6,size_y:3,type:visualization),(col:7,id:BarChart,row:5,size_x:6,size_y:3,type:visualization),
(col:1,id:Line_Bubble,row:8,size_x:12,size_y:5,type:visualization),(col:1,id:LineChart,row:5,size_x:6,size_y:
3,type:visualization),(col:7,id:PieChart,row:1,size_x:6,size_y:3,type:visualization)),query:(query_string:(anal
yze_wildcard:!t,query:'*')),title:Kibana_Dashboard)&_g=(refreshInterval:(display:Off,pause:!f,section:0,value
:0),time:(from:'2015-06-02T07:15:00.000Z',mode:absolute,to:'2015-06-02T08:03:00.000Z'))" height="600"
width="800"></iframe>
</body>
</html>
```

The previous **HTML** file contains an **iframe** source which contains different visualizations added to the dashboard. You can customize properties like **rows**, **x axis**, **y axis**, **height** and **width** for every visualization. Figure 10-13 shows the HTML page just described.

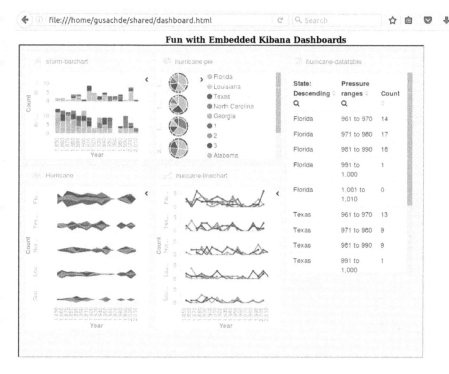

Figure 10-13. Dashboard HTML Page

■ **Tip** You can embedded visualization only if both Elasticsearch and Kibana are running.

Debug Panel

In case you wish to see the raw data of Elasticsearch behind any visualization, you can use the **Debug panel**. It gives detailed information for results of visualization and what the request of Elasticsearch was. It also showcases response from Elasticsearch.

In order to view the Debug panel, just click on **caret (^) button** at the bottom of any visualization. Let's examine the debug panel associated with Bar Chart created in previous Chapter, which shows the top five states with highest number of occurrences.

Table

Data behind the visualization can be represented in the form of a table. Data is displayed in the form of pages. This data can be sorted by clicking on any of the headers of the columns, as shown in the Figure 10-14.

| Table | Request | Response | Statistics |

Year ▾ Q	State: Descending ▾ Q	Pressure ranges ▾ Q	Count ▾
1,850	Florida	926 to 950	0
1,850	Florida	951 to 975	5
1,850	Georgia	926 to 950	0
1,850	Georgia	951 to 975	4
1,850	Alabama	926 to 950	0
1,850	Alabama	951 to 975	2
1,850	Louisiana	926 to 950	2
1,850	Louisiana	951 to 975	1
1,850	Texas	926 to 950	0
1,850	Texas	951 to 975	2

Export: Raw ▲ Formatted ▲

1 2 3 4 5 ...16 ▸   Page Size 10 ▾

Figure 10-14. Visualization Data Table

You can clearly see the raw data underlying the visualization. The **Page Size** can be changed as per preference. The table data can be exported in raw form or formatted form to a **CSV** file.

Request

The raw **request payload** sent to Elasticsearch can be viewed in **JSON** format from the **Request** tab. The Elasticsearch request body is shown which if required can be directly queried from Elasticsearch for the created visualization.

194

Table   Request   Response   Statistics

Elasticsearch request body

```
{
  "query": {
    "query_string": {
      "query": "*",
      "analyze_wildcard": true
    }
  },
  "size": 0,
  "aggs": {
    "2": {
      "histogram": {
        "field": "Year",
        "interval": 10
      },
      "aggs": {
        "3": {
          "terms": {
            "field": "State",
            "size": 5,
            "order": {
              "_count": "desc"
            }
          }
        },
```

Figure 10-15. Visualization Request

Response

The raw **response payload** received from Elasticsearch can be viewed in **JSON** format from the **Response** tab. The Elasticsearch response body is shown which returned as a result of the query used for creating visualization.

Figure 10-16. Visualization Response

Statistics

The Statistics tab displays the statistics used for the query in the tabular format like Query Duration, Request Duration, Hits (total number of records) and Index as shown in Figure 10-17.

Query Duration	36ms
Request Duration	1533ms
Hits	399
Index	"storm"

Figure 10-17. Visualization Statistics

Summary

This chapter highlighted the usefulness of dashboards in Kibana. Various components of the **Dashboard** page were explained. Thereafter, it was shown with example how to make beautiful dashboards from saved visualizations. Different visualizations can be combined together and customize to fit into a single panel. Dashboards can also be embedded within a web page.

CHAPTER 11

⌘ ⌘ ⌘

Designing for Scale

The previous chapter covered the wonders which Kibana dashboards can do to complex data sets. Dashboards provide a holistic view to represent data in different formats at the same time. We have come to a stage where most of the regular functions of ELK stack have been covered. Now with this chapter, our focus would be on how to scale. This enhances the capability to handle more data, index much more data sets and search data faster. In these days of Cloud computing and NoSql databases, scaling is very important as there can be situations when it is required to process millions or even billions of documents. It would not be possible always to support this kind of load with one instance of Elasticsearch. In this chapter we will cover the scaling capabilities of Elasticsearch.

Elasticsearch Cluster for Scale

Consider that you were using Elasticsearch to analyze documents related to medical records of a particular city. Now if you have to support many more cities, it will increase the number of documents manifolds. Even if your workload does not increase manifold, still there can be situations when you might be compelled to think of adding more horsepower to Elasticsearch.

You may want to search and index data faster with increased parallelization. With time you may run out of disk space on your machine. It might happen that Elasticsearch node is running out of memory while querying data. In all such situations, the easiest and fastest way is transform the single node Elasticsearch system to a cluster by adding more nodes. Elasticsearch can be horizontally scaled by addition of more nodes and this helps in sharing the indexing and searching workload.

Adding Nodes to Cluster

You can start creating Elasticsearch cluster by adding another node (or nodes) to the single node to make it a cluster of nodes. It is quite seamless to add a node to your environment by just extracting Elasticsearch distribution to a separate directory, entering the directory and running Elasticsearch from there. The following code snippet demonstrates this:

```
mkdir elasticsearch2
cd elasticsearch2
tar -zxvf elasticsearch-2.3.3.tar.gz
cd elasticsearch-2.3.3
bin/elasticsearch
```

© Gurpreet S. Sachdeva 2017
G. S. Sachdeva, *Applied ELK Stack*, ISBN 978-1545022146

Elasticsearch automatically picks the next available port to bind to - in this case, **9201** - and joins the existing node. For those of you who are more adventurous, you need not extract Elasticsearch distribution to another directory; multiple instances of Elasticsearch can also run from the same directory without interfering with one another. You can see the change in the status of Elasticsearch cluster by running the **health** command.

```
curl -XGET 'http://localhost:9200/_cluster/health?pretty'
{
  "cluster_name" : "elasticsearch",
  "status" : "green",
  "timed_out" : false,
  "number_of_nodes" : 2,
  "number_of_data_nodes" : 2,
  "active_primary_shards" : 3926,
  "active_shards" : 7852,
  "relocating_shards" : 0,
  "initializing_shards" : 0,
  "unassigned_shards" : 0,
  "delayed_unassigned_shards" : 0,
  "number_of_pending_tasks" : 0,
  "number_of_in_flight_fetch" : 0,
  "task_max_waiting_in_queue_millis" : 0,
  "active_shards_percent_as_number" : 100.0
}
```

You can see that the **unassigned_shards** count is **zero** which indicates that now there are no unassigned shards in the cluster. The shards get assigned to the new node. Figure 11-1 illustrates distribution of **foo** index before and after adding a node to the cluster. The left side demonstrates that the primary shards for the foo index have all been assigned to **Node1**, whereas the replica shards are still unassigned. The cluster state remains **yellow** as all the primary shards have a home whereas the replica shards don't. When a second node is added, the unassigned replica shards are assigned to the new node **Node2**, which makes the cluster state as **green**.

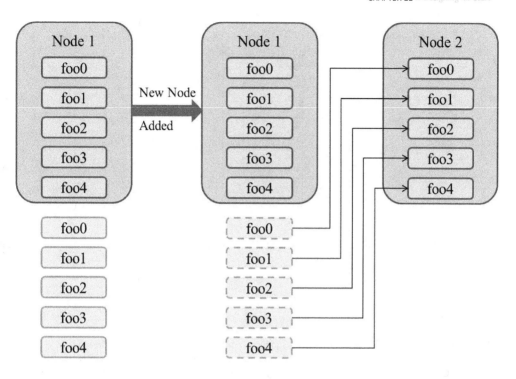

Figure 11-1. *Shard Allocation from one node to two nodes*

When a new node is added, Elasticsearch automatically balances out the shards among all nodes. Figure 11-2 illustrates the distribution of shards across three Elasticsearch nodes in the same cluster. It is pertinent to observe that there is no restriction on having primary and replica shards on the same node as long as the primary and replica shards for the same shard number are not on the same node. In case more nodes are added to the cluster, Elasticsearch tries to balance the number of shards evenly across all nodes because each node shares the burden by taking a portion of data (shards).

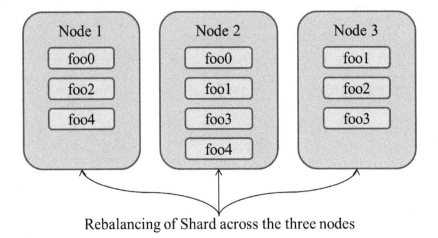

Rebalancing of Shard across the three nodes

Figure 11-2. Shard Allocation with three Elasticsearch Nodes

Adding nodes to Elasticsearch cluster has significant benefits like high availability and increased performance. Since replicas are enabled by default, Elasticsearch automatically promotes a replica shard to a **primary** in the event the primary shard can't be located. In case you lose the node hosting the primary shards for index, you can still access the data in your indices. The distribution of data amongst nodes leads to increase in performance as search and get requests can be handled by both primary and secondary shards. Horizontal scalability enhances memory of the cluster and could fasten memory intensive searches and aggregations.

Discovering Cluster Nodes

It might come as a surprise that how smoothly the additional node discovers the first node and automatically joins the cluster. Behind the scenes, Elasticsearch nodes can use multiple mechanisms to discover other nodes - **multicast** or **unicast**. Both these mechanisms can be used but the default configuration is to use only multicast as unicast requires a list of known nodes to connect to.

Multicast Discovery

At startup, Elasticsearch sends a **multicast** ping to the address **224.2.2.4** on port **54328**, which gets responded to by other Elasticsearch nodes with the same cluster name. In case there is a coworker's local copy of Elasticsearch running and joining your cluster, just change the **cluster.name** setting inside your **elasticsearch.yml** configuration file from the default **elasticsearch** to some specific name. Multicast discovery has the following configuration options which can be modified or disabled entirely by setting in elasticsearch.yml.

```
discovery.zen.ping.multicast:
  group: 224.2.2.4
  port: 54328
  ttl: 3
```

address: null
enabled: true

Multicast discovery mechanism is quite suitable for flexible clusters on the same network having nodes with IP addresses getting changed frequently. In simple terms, multicast discovery is akin to asking "Is there any other node out there running on Elasticsearch cluster?" Thereafter, simply wait for the response. Figure 11-3 illustrates this mechanism.

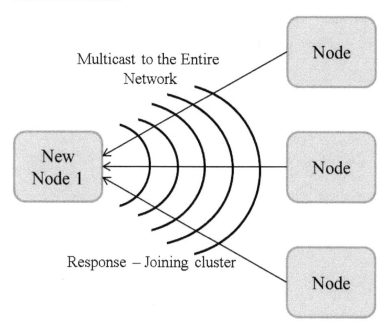

Figure 11-3. *Multicast Discovery Mechanism*

Multicast discovery is suitable for local development and quickly testing cluster configuration. A more stable mechanism is to have some or all of the nodes as "**gossip routers**" to discover more information about the cluster. This is well suited for situations wherein the IP address of the node will not change frequently. It helps in avoiding situations where nodes may get connected accidentally to cluster. This situation is avoided by unicast mechanism by not sending message to everyone on a network but connecting to a specific list of nodes.

Unicast Discovery

Unicast discovery utilizes a list of hosts for Elasticsearch to connect to and attempt to find out more information about the cluster. This is well suited for situations wherein the IP address of the node will not change frequently or in production systems where only specific nodes should be communicated with instead of the entire network. In this mechanism, IP address is specific and optionally the port or range of ports for other nodes is also mentioned. A sample unicast configuration would be setting **discovery.zen.ping.unicast.hosts: ["10.0.0.6", 10.0.0.7:9400",** **"10.0.0.8[9500-9600]"]** in elasticsearch.yml for all the Elasticsearch nodes. It is not required that all the nodes in the cluster need to be present in the unicast list to discover all the nodes, but sufficient address must be configured for each node to know about a gossip node that's available. For e.g., if the first node in the unicast list knows about four out of nine nodes in a cluster, and the second node in the unicast list knows about the other five out of nine nodes, the discover process triggered by a node will get to know about all the nodes in the cluster. Figure 11-4 illustrates the unicast discovery process.

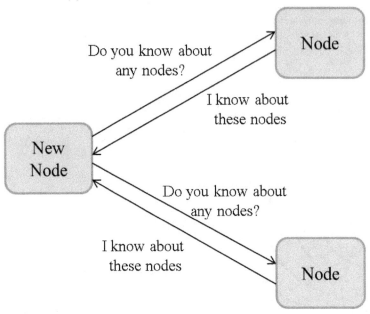

Figure 11-4. *Unicast Discovery Mechanism*

You need to explicitly disable unicast discovery. If you want to use only multicast discovery to find other Elasticsearch nodes, keep the list empty in the configuration file. Once all the nodes of the cluster are discovered, the Elasticsearch nodes hold a master election.

Master Node Election

After the nodes in the cluster have discovered each other, they will negotiate to elect the master. The master node is responsible for managing the state of the cluster, i.e. current settings and state of the shards, indices and nods in the cluster. After its election, the master node sets up a system of internal pings to ensure that each node stays alive and healthy while in the cluster. This helps in providing **fault detection**. All nodes are considered equally capable of being elected as master node unless the **node.master** setting is set to **false**. In case, the cluster has only a single node, that node itself becomes the master after a timeout period when it doesn't detect any other nodes in the cluster.

In production clusters with larger number of nodes, it is a best practice to set the minimum number of master nodes. Although this sound like Elasticsearch can have multiple master nodes, it actually determines how many nodes in a cluster are eligible to become a master before the cluster is in a healthy state. This setting helps in ensuring that the cluster doesn't try to perform potentially risky operations without first having a complete view of the state of the cluster. Either set the minimum number to the total number of nodes in cluster if the number of nodes is fixed or set it as per the best practice of number of **nodes in the cluster divided by 2, plus 1**. If you set the **minimum_master_nodes** setting to a number higher than 1, it can help prevent what is known as a **split brain** in the cluster. The best practice for a 3 node cluster is to set the value of minimum_master_nodes to 2 or for a 16-node cluster, you can set it to 9. This setting can be modified by changing **discovery.zen.minimum_master_nodes** in elastisearch.yml to the number that is appropriate for your cluster.

Tip Split brain is the scenario when one or more Elasticsearch nodes in the cluster, loose communication to the master node. They elect a new master and continue to process requests. At this point two Elasticsearch clusters are running independently of each other.

After the nodes are up and have discovered each other, you can see which node has been elected as master.

```
curl -XGET 'http://localhost:9200/_cluster/state/master_node,nodes?pretty'
{
  "cluster_name" : "elasticsearch",
  "master_node" : "4lqtTbfoQk6vS6BvwBqVug",
  "nodes" : {
   "MLOt_QcjSSqPnYpdDUN-NQ" : {
     "name" : "Alistaire Stuart",
     "transport_address" : "127.0.0.1:9301",
     "attributes" : { }
   },
   "4lqtTbfoQk6vS6BvwBqVug" : {
     "name" : "Hobgoblin II",
     "transport_address" : "127.0.0.1:9300",
     "attributes" : { }
   }
  }
}
```

Fault Detection

Now that the cluster has two nodes in it, as well as an elected master node, there is a need to communicate with all nodes in the cluster to make sure everything is in order within the cluster. This is referred to as the **fault detection** process. The master node does a **healthcheck** ping on all other nodes in the cluster and each node pings the master to make sure another election doesn't need to be held as illustrated in Figure 11-5.

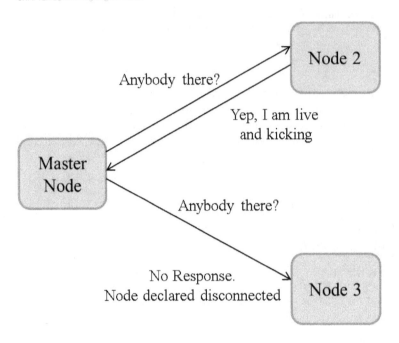

Figure 11-5. *Cluster Fault Detection*

You can see in the figure that each node sends a ping every **discovery.zen.fd.ping_interval** (default value is **1 sec**), waits for **discovery.zen.fd.ping_timeout** (default value is **30 sec**) and tries a maximum number of **discovery.zen.fd.ping_retries** (default value is **3**) before it declares a node as disconnected and routing shards or electing another master node. In case your environment has a higher latency, then change these values to reflect the ground reality.

Removal of Nodes from Cluster

We have seen till now, that adding nodes in the cluster can help scale easily. However, there can be situations when a node drops out of the Elasticsearch cluster or it stops working. Let's take example of a three node cluster to see removal of a node impacts the cluster.

Assume that power supply to Node1 gets disrupted. Obviously Node1 will become unavailable. There are three shards on Node1. First of all, Elasticsearch would do automatically is to turn the test0 and test3 replica shards that are on Node2 into primary shards as illustrated in Figure 11-6. Indexing first goes to the primary shards, therefore Elasticsearch tries to ensure that there are always primaries assigned for an index.

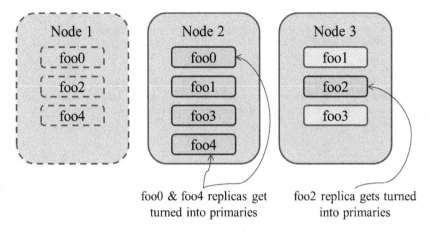

foo0 & foo4 replicas get   foo2 replica gets turned
turned into primaries   into primaries

Figure 11-6. Replica Shards turn into Primary Shards after Node loss

---

■ **Tip** Elasticsearch may choose any of the replicas to turn into a primary shard.

After the replicas for the missing primary shards are turned into primaries, the cluster looks like as illustrated in Figure 11-6. The cluster state changes to **yellow** indicating that some replica shards aren't allocated to a node. Elasticsearch would create more replica shards to maintain high-availability setup for the index. Since all the primaries are available, the data from the foo0 and foo4 primary shards on Node2 are replicated into replicas on Node3 and the data from the foo2 primary shard on Node3 will be replicated onto Node2, as illustrated in Figure 11-7.

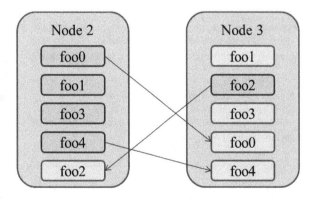

Figure 11-7. Recreating Replica Shards

After the replica shards get re-created to compensate for the node loss, the cluster comes back in **green** state with all the primary and replica shards assigned to a node. Bear in mind that all this while the entire cluster is available for searching and indexing as no data was actually lost. In case more than a single node is lost or a shard with no replicas is lost, the cluster comes into a **red** state. This implies that some amount of data has been lost permanently and you need to either reconnect the node with the data to the cluster or re-index the data which went missing.

You need to take a calculated risk while fixing the number of replica shards. If there is only a single replica, then even if one node disassociates from the cluster, there would be no data loss. Similarly, if there are replicas, two nodes can get disassociated without any loss of data. It becomes pertinent to choose the number of replicas with due consideration. It is a best practice to take a backup of your indices.

Decommissioning of Nodes

Elasticsearch does great job in automatically creating new replicas when a node goes down. However, in a cluster configuration, you may eventually face a situation where you want to shut down a node with some data on it, without the cluster state turning **yellow**. Some of the reasons for this could be degrading of hardware or lesser amount of request traffic. You can simply kill the **Java process** corresponding to the node and Elasticsearch would recover the data to the other nodes. But what about scenarios when you have a zero replica for an index? In such a situation, you would lose data if you shut down the node without moving the data first.

Fortunately, Elasticsearch has a mechanism for decommissioning a node by telling the cluster not to allocate any shards to a node or a set of nodes. In the three node example, let's assume the Node1, Node2 and Node3 have the IP address 192.168.1.5, 192.168.1.6 and 192.168.1.7, respectively. If you want to shut down Node1 while keeping the cluster in **green** state, you should decommission the node first so that all the shards move from Node1 to other nodes in the cluster. You can initiate decommissioning by making a transient change to cluster settings.

```
curl -XPUT "localhost:9200/_cluster/settings" -d '{
   "transient" : {
      "cluster.routing.allocation.exclude_ip" : "192.168.1.5"
   }
}'
```

On running this command, Elasticsearch starts moving all the shards from the decommissioned node to other nodes in the cluster. You can observe where shards are located in the cluster by first determining the ID of the nodes in the cluster with **_nodes** endpoint and then looking at the cluster state to check where each shard in the cluster is currently allocated.

Once you are sure that there are no shards on the node being decommissioned, you can safely stop Elasticsearch on that node without causing the cluster status to change from green state. This process can be safely repeated one at a time to decommission each node you don't want to run. You may also use a comma-separated IP addresses instead of 192.168.1.5 to decommission multiple nodes at once.

■ **Tip** Before decommissioning any node, make sure that the remaining nodes in the cluster would be able to handle allocating the shard in terms of disk and memory use.

Upgrading Elasticsearch Nodes

As your Elasticsearch cluster becomes stable, with time there may arise a need to upgrade to the latest version of Elasticsearch software. Depending on the situation at your cluster, upgrading may be simple or complex.

■ **Tip**   It is highly recommended to always run the latest version of Elasticsearch as there always new features being made available and bugs being fixed.

Certain key aspects should be considered before making the decision to upgrade Elasticsearch:

- After upgrading Elasticsearch, if you add any new documents, then you can't downgrade to the previous version.
- Before starting with upgrade, take a backup of all the data.
- Do not mix different JVM versions within the same Elasticsearch cluster.

The best way to upgrade an Elasticsearch cluster is to shut down all nodes and then upgrade each Elasticsearch installation with the method you originally used. For e.g. extracting the distribution if you used **.tar.gz** distribution or installing the **.deb** package using **dpkg** if you are using a Debian based system. After upgrading each node, simply restart the entire cluster and wait for Elasticsearch to be available with green status. See, it's that simple!

There can be many other tricky scenarios, for e.g. if downtime is not at all acceptable. For such situations you can perform a **rolling restart** to upgrade the Elasticsearch cluster while serving requests for indexing and searching data.

Rolling Restart

Rolling restart can help in restarting the cluster in order to upgrade a node or make a non-dynamic configuration change while still being available for requests. This is quite useful for production deployments of Elasticsearch. Rather than shutting down the whole cluster in one step, you just shut down the node one at a time. This process is slightly more tedious than full restart as it requires some additional steps.

4. Evaluate if you want Elasticsearch to automatically rebalance shards while each individual node is not running. In majority of cases, it is not preferred to have Elasticsearch start automatic recovery in case a node leaves the cluster for an upgrade as it would lead to rebalancing each and every node. Actually, the data is not lost, you just need to restart the node and rejoin the cluster.

5. In most cases, it is not necessary to shift data around the cluster while performing the upgrade. This can be accomplished by setting the **cluster.routing.allocation.enable** setting to node while performing the upgrade. Following steps need to be followed:

   a. Disable cluster allocation

   b. Shut down the node which is to be upgraded.

   c. Upgrade the node.

d. Start the upgraded node.

e. Wait for the upgraded node to join the cluster.

f. Enable cluster allocation.

g. Wait for cluster state to turn **green**.

■ **Tip** Repeat this process for every node that is to be upgraded.

You can disable cluster allocation by using the following cluster settings API:

```
curl -XPUT "localhost:9200/_cluster/settings" -d '{
  "transient" : {
    "cluster.routing.allocation.enable" : "none"
  }
}'
```

On running this command, Elasticsearch stops rebalancing shards around the cluster. For e.g. if a primary shard is lost for an index due to the corresponding node being shut down, Elasticsearch will still transform the replica shard into a new primary, but a new replica would not be created. In this state, you can simply shut down the single Elasticsearch node and perform the upgrade.

Once you are done with the upgrade, ensure that you re-enable allocation for the cluster. Till the time you don't re-enable allocation, Elasticsearch would not automatically replicate your data. The allocation can be re-enabled by setting the **cluster.routing.allocation.enable** setting to **all** instead of **none**. See the command below:

```
curl -XPUT "localhost:9200/_cluster/settings" -d '{
  "transient" : {
    "cluster.routing.allocation.enable" : "all"
  }
}'
```

The twin steps of disabling allocation and then re-enabling allocation need to be performed for each and every node in the cluster which is to be upgraded. In case you perform these steps once in the beginning and once in the end, Elasticsearch would not allocate the shards that exist on the upgraded node every time you upgraded a node and your cluster status would continue to be **red** after you have upgraded multiple nodes. By following the step-by-step process of re-enabling allocation and waiting for the cluster to come to the **green** state after each node is upgraded, your data is not lost and is available when you move to the next node that needs to be upgraded. You can repeat these steps for all the nodes that need to be upgraded.

The case of indices not having any replicas is a little peculiar. In case you have an index that has no replicas, you can decommission the node by following the steps covered in an earlier section. You need to move all the data off it before shutting down to upgrade.

Quick Restart

The disable and enable allocation steps can take quite a while for the cluster to return to a green state when upgrading a single node. This is due to the fact that Elasticsearch replicates shard segment rather than at the document level. This implies Elasticsearch node sending data for replication is actually asking peer node if it has data for a particular segment. If it doesn't have the corresponding file or the file is different, then the entire segment is copied. A large volume of data may be copied in case the documents are the same. Till the time, Elasticsearch comes out with a way of verifying the last document written in a segment file, it has to copy over any differing files while replicating data between the primary shard and the replica shard.

There can be two different ways to make segment files identical on the primary and replica shards:

- **Optimize API** - Use the optimize API to create a single, large segment for both the primary and the replica.

- **Toggling** - Toggle the number of replicas to **0** and then back to a higher number to ensure that all replica copies have the **same segment files** as the primary shard. In this case, for a short period, there would be only a single copy of the data, so you need to be **cautious** while performing this approach in production environment.

■ **Tip** To reduce recovery time, you may halt indexing data into the cluster while upgrading the node.

Cluster Information

Elasticsearch provides mechanism to fetch cluster information in a user friendly manner. The regular **_cluster** API can dump a ton of information for a big cluster which is difficult to comprehend. For such scenarios, the **_cat** API is quite suitable. The _cat API provides both helpful diagnostic and debugging tools that can print data in a more human-readable manner, rather than dumping a huge JSON response. Let's first revisit the standard _cluster APIs to fetch cluster information.

Checking cluster health using the cluster health API:

```
curl -XGET "localhost:9200/_cluster/health?pretty"
{
  "cluster_name" : "elasticsearch",
  "status" : "green",
  "timed_out" : false,
  "number_of_nodes" : 2,
  "number_of_data_nodes" : 2,
  "active_primary_shards" : 3926,
  "active_shards" : 7852,
  "relocating_shards" : 0,
  "initializing_shards" : 0,
  "unassigned_shards" : 0,
  "delayed_unassigned_shards" : 0,
  "number_of_pending_tasks" : 0,
```

```
"number_of_in_flight_fetch" : 0,
"task_max_waiting_in_queue_millis" : 0,
"active_shards_percent_as_number" : 100.0
}
```

Checking cluster health using the _cat API:

```
curl -XGET "localhost:9200/_cat/health?v"
epoch       timestamp    cluster      status node.total node.data shards  pri  relo  init
1479650899 19:38:19 elasticsearch yellow      2       2        5129 3921  0   2
```

Fetching the list of nods as well as master node details using _cluster API:

```
curl -XGET "localhost:9200/_cluster/state/master_node,nodes&pretty"
{
  "cluster_name" : "elasticsearch",
  "master_node" : "4lqtTbfoQk6vS6BvwBqVug"
}
```

Fetching the list of nods as well as master node details using _cat API:

```
curl -XGET "localhost:9200/_cat/nodes?v"
host       ip          heap.percent ram.percent load   node.role master name
127.0.0.1 127.0.0.1 25            96          2.56 d         m      Alistaire Stuart
127.0.0.1 127.0.0.1 64            96          2.56 d         *      Hobgoblin II
```

■ **Tip**   The node with "m" in the master column is the master node.

The _cat API comes with many other features, all of which are quite helpful in troubleshooting different scenarios. You can know the full list of options in _cat API by giving the following command:

```
curl -XGET "localhost:9200/_cat "
```

Some of the most popular and useful _cat APIs are listed below:

- **allocation** - Informs about the number of shards allocated to each node.
- **count** - Count of number of documents in the entire cluster or index.
- **health** - Information regarding health of the cluster.
- **indices** - Details about existing nodes.
- **master** - Indicates which node is currently elected master node.
- **nodes** - Different information regarding all the nodes in the cluster.
- **recovery** - Status of in-progress shard recoveries in the cluster.
- **shards** - Indicates count, size and names of shards in the cluster.
- **plugins** - Information about installed plugins.

It is quite interesting to see how the shards are distributed across each node using the _cat API. This way is much simpler than using the regular commands. See below to fetch out the count of shards across each node.

```
curl -XGET 'localhost:9200/_cat/allocation?v'
shards disk.indices disk.used disk.avail disk.total disk.percent host       ip        node
 1447    14.1mb      7.9gb     2.4gb      10.4gb          76       127.0.0.1 127.0.0.1 Alistaire Stuart
 3921    39.6mb      7.9gb     2.4gb      10.4gb          76       127.0.0.1 127.0.0.1 Hobgoblin II
```

Get detailed information about primary and replica shards.

```
curl -XGET 'localhost:9200/_cat/shards?v'
index   shard prirep state      docs  store ip         node
phones  2     r      STARTED 5  4.7kb 127.0.0.1 Alistaire Stuart
phones  2     p      STARTED 5  4.7kb 127.0.0.1 Hobgoblin II
phones  3     r      STARTED 2  4.1kb 127.0.0.1 Alistaire Stuart
phones  3     p      STARTED 2  4.1kb 127.0.0.1 Hobgoblin II
phones  4     r      STARTED 1  3.9kb 127.0.0.1 Alistaire Stuart
phones  4     p      STARTED 1  3.9kb 127.0.0.1 Hobgoblin II
phones  1     r      STARTED 1  3.9kb 127.0.0.1 Alistaire Stuart
phones  1     p      STARTED 1  3.9kb 127.0.0.1 Hobgoblin II
phones  0     r      STARTED 1  3.9kb 127.0.0.1 Alistaire Stuart
phones  0     p      STARTED 1  3.9kb 127.0.0.1 Hobgoblin II
```

Use of _cat/allocation and _cat/shards APIs is also helpful to determine when a node can be safely shut down after performing the decommissioning of a node.

Scaling Options

Although adding node to a cluster might seem to be an easy task, but in reality a little planning can go a long way in improving the performance of the cluster. Different configurations of Elasticsearch can be suitable for different kind of needs. You need to decide how you will index data and how you will search it. There are three key considerations for an Elasticsearch cluster in production environment - **over-sharding, data slicing, and maximizing throughput.**

Over-Sharding

Over-sharding is the name given to the approach wherein intentionally large number of shards is created for an index so that there is enough room to add nodes and grow in the future. The Figure 11-8 illustrates the over-sharding process.

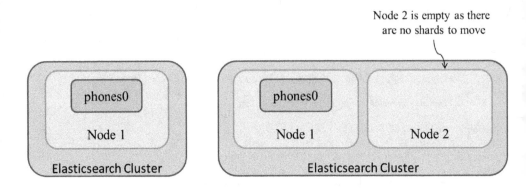

Figure 11-8. *Two Nodes Scaling a Single Shard*

You can see in the Figure 11-8 that the **phones** index has a single shard and no replicas. If you add another node, practically any benefit from adding nodes is removed. You may wonder but adding another node won't let you scale in this particular situation. This is because the entire indexing and querying load is still handled by the node with the single shard on it. Since, a shard is the smallest unit that Elasticsearch can move around; it is always better to make sure that there are at least as many primary shards in the cluster as you plan to have nodes. For e.g. if a cluster currently has **3-nodes** and **8 primary shards**, there is scope to add more nodes to handle additional requests. Now if you need more than 8 nodes, there is no possibility to distribute the primary shards across nodes because there will be more nodes than shards.

You might think it is an easy problem - you just need to probably create 100 primary shards. Although it seems like a good idea but there is hidden cost to each shard Elasticsearch has to manage. Each shard is actually a complete **Lucene index** and requires a number of file descriptors for each segment of the index. There is memory overhead too. A large number of shards for an index lead to increased memory use that could instead have been used to increase performance. You may hit the limit of machine's file descriptor or RAM limits. On top of this, while compressing data; you will end up splitting the data across 100 different things. This results in a lower compression ratio as compared to a reasonable number of shards.

There is no best or perfect **shard-to-index** ratio that can fit all situations. The default is **5 shards** but keep in mind how you plan on growing in the future.

■ **Tip** Once an index is created with certain number of shards, the number of primary shards can never be modified for that index.

Careful consideration for number of shards should be done as you would not like to re-index significant portion of data with the passage of time.

Data Slicing

Currently, there is no way to increase or decrease the number of primary shards in an index necessitating spanning of data into multiple indices, from the beginning. This is a reasonable way to split data. Let's use the data from the **phones** index described in **Chapter 7**. Just to recap that particular example, the phones index contains sales data of different smartphones and has details like **make, price, color and date of sale**. Segmenting data in this manner is helpful when searching as the segmentation is handled by putting the right data in the right place. If a user wants to search in a particular brand of phones, for e.g. HTC or Samsung, you will have to search only those particular indices rather than the entire phones index.

Use of **aliases** is another mechanism that can be used along with indices. An alias is nothing but a pointer to an index or a set of indices. It has provision for changing the indices that it points to at any time. This is immensely helpful for segmenting data in a semantic manner. You can create an alias called **htc-group** that points to only HTC phones. This technique is quite popular in situations where data-based information is indexed (for e.g. log files). Data can be segmented by date on a monthly, weekly or daily basis. You create an alias named "**recent**" which always points to the data that should be searched without having to change the name of the index being searched every time the segment rolls over. The biggest USP of aliases is the incredible level of flexibility and minimal overhead.

If you are creating indices, bear in mind that since each index has its own shard, there would be an overhead of creating a shard. Be careful not to make too many shards as a consequence of creating too many indices. Use the scarce resources for something better like handling requests. Once you gain familiarity with your data, you can always tweak the node configuration to get maximum performance.

Maximizing Throughput

We all want to maximize throughput from our system but more often than not, we have vague idea about the throughput. What exactly do you want to max out on - is it the indexing throughput or fast searches. Elasticsearch can be fine-tuned in multiple ways to suit different throughput considerations. Let's say you have to handle hundreds and thousands of new documents, how can you index them as fast as possible? A straightforward approach for a faster indexing is to temporarily reduce the number of replica shards in the cluster. While indexing data, the default approach is that the request won't get completed until the data exists on the primary shard as well as all the replicas. So, you can try to reduce the number of replicas to one while indexing and then increase to more than one, once all the data has been indexed.

You can tweak Elasticsearch to enable fast searches by adding more replicas since only a primary or a replica shard can be used for searching. Figure 11-9, illustrates a three node cluster where the third node can't participate in searches until it has a copy of the data.

■ **Tip** Having more shards has a small cost in terms of increase in file descriptors and memory.

If the request traffic is too high for the nodes in the cluster to handle, you can consider adding nodes with **node.data** and **node.master** both set to **false**. These nodes can then participate in handling incoming requests, distribute the requests amongst the data nodes and collate the results for the response. In this manner, the nodes searching the shards don't have to handle connections from search clients. They only have to search in shards.

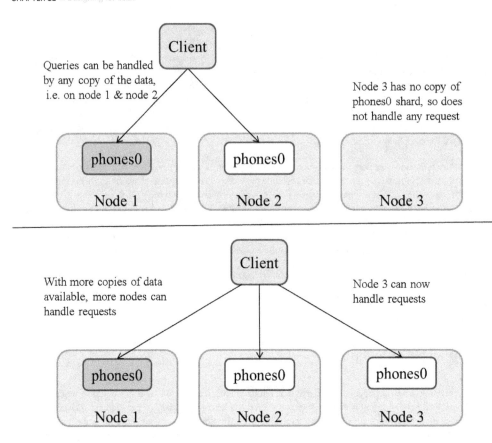

Figure 11-9. Request Traffic Distributed to Additional Replicas

Aliases

Aliases are one of the most useful features of Elasticsearch. Aliases are like pointers or name that can be used to correspond with one or more actual indices. This makes things simpler by providing the flexibility when scaling the cluster and managing how data is spread across indices. You can use alias even for a single index in an Elasticsearch cluster.

Working with Alias

Aliases are managed by maser node and have a small overhead associated with them. For e.g. if there is an alias by the name of **car** which points to an index named **Honda**, there is additional overhead of extra key in the cluster map that maps the name car to concrete index Honda. This implies that in comparison to additional indices, aliases tend to be much lighter. In fact thousands of them can be maintained without having a significant impact on the cluster.

Having said that, you need to be cautious against creating thousands or millions of aliases because at that level, even the minimal overhead of single entry in a map adds up to a significant value. This can cause the cluster state to grow to a large size. This results in increased time for creating cluster state as the entire cluster state is sent to each node every time it changes.

Benefits of Aliases

It is highly recommended to use Aliases for all Elasticsearch indices because it provides lot more flexibility at the time of future re-indexing. Let's assume you started by creating an index with a single primary shard and then later on decided that you need more capacity on your index. If you already have an alias for the original index, you can simply change the alias to point to the additionally created index without changing the name of the index to search for.

Another significant benefit is to create windows into different indices. For e.g. if you create periodic (daily, weekly, etc.) indices for you data, you can have a sliding window of the last period's (week or day) data by creating an alias for the last few periods. On a regular basis, you can continue adding new data to the alias while removing the old data.

Living with Aliases

You can use the **aliases** API to create Aliases. Each action is like a map consisting of either an add or remove action followed by the index and alias on which to apply the operation. See the below example for clarity.

```
curl -XPOST 'http://localhost:9200/_aliases' -d '
{
  "actions" : [
  {
   "add" : {
    "index" : "phones",
    "alias" : "ph-alias"
   }
  },
  {
   "remove" : {
    "index" : "old-phones",
    "alias" : "old-ph-alias"
   }
  }
  ]
}'
{"acknowledged":true}
```

As the above example shows, the **phones** index is added to an alias named **ph-alias**, and the made-up index **old-phones** is removed from the alias **old-ph-alias**. The very act of adding an index to an alias creates it. Similarly, removal of all indices, which an alias points to, removes the alias. Interestingly, there is no manual alias creation and deletion. However, the alias operations will fail if the index does not exist. There is no limit to the add or remove actions. All these actions are executed atomically. It is possible to perform individual actions on the Alias API by using the common HTTP methods that Elasticsearch uses. The following calls would have the same result:

```
curl -XPUT 'localhost:9200/phones/_alias/ph-alias'
curl -XDELETE 'localhost:9200/old-phones/_alias/old-ph-alias'
```

Creating Aliases

There are many options available for creating aliases. You may create aliases on a specific index, many indices, or a pattern that matches index names:

```
curl -XPUT 'http://localhost:9200/{index}/_alias/{alias}'
```

Create **bar** alias on **foo** index.

```
curl -XPUT 'http://localhost:9200/foo/_alias/bar'
```

Create **bar** alias on **foo** index.

```
curl -XPUT 'http://localhost:9200/_all/_alias/bar'
```

Create **bar** alias on both the indices **foo1** and **foo2**.

```
curl -XPUT 'http://localhost:9200/foo1,foo2/_alias/bar'
```

Create **bar** alias on all indices with the pattern **foo***.

```
curl -XPUT 'http://localhost:9200/foo*/_alias/bar'
```

Alias **deletion** can be done in a similar manner.

```
curl -XDELETE 'http://localhost:9200/{index}/_alias/{alias}'
```

All the aliases of a concrete index can be fetched by issuing a **GET** request on an index with **_alias**. You can also retrieve all indices and the associated aliases by not specifying the index name. You can retrieve alias for an index in the following manner.

```
curl 'localhost:9200/phones/_alias?pretty'
{
    "phones" : {
        "aliases" : {
            "ph-alias" : { }
        }
    }
}
```

There are other ways also to fetch alias information from an index. You can give a specific index, _all, comma-delimited list of index names, pattern to match or just leave it blank. Similarly, you can give the alias name, comma-delimited list or a pattern.

```
curl -XGET 'http://localhost:9200/{index}/_alias/{alias}'
```

Retrieve alias **bar** for index **foo**.

```
curl -XGET 'http://localhost:9200/foo/_alias/bar'
```

Retrieve all aliases for index **foo**.

```
curl -XGET 'http://localhost:9200/foo/_alias/*'
```

Retrieve all indices with alias **bar**.

```
curl -XGET 'http://localhost:9200/_alias/bar'
```

Retrieve all indices with aliases that match the pattern **bar***.

```
curl -XGET 'http://localhost:9200/_alias/bar*'
```

Camouflaging Documents with Filters

Aliases can also be used to automatically apply a filter to queries. For e.g. there can be an alias that points only to the groups that contain the Elasticsearch tag. This helps in creating an alias that does this filtering automatically as shown below:

```
curl -XPOST 'http://localhost:9200/_aliases' -d '
{
  "actions" : [
  {
   "add" : {
     "index" : "phones",
     "alias" : "htc-group",
     "filter" : {
      "term" : {"make" : "htc"}
     }
    }
   }
  ]
}'
{"acknowledged":true}

curl -XGET 'localhost:9200/phones/sales/_count' -d '
{
  "query" : {
   "match_all" : {}
  }
}'
{"count":10,"_shards":{"total":5,"successful":5,"failed":0}}

curl -XGET 'localhost:9200/htc-group/_count' -d '
{
  "query" : {
   "match_all" : {}
  }
}'
{"count":2,"_shards":{"total":5,"successful":5,"failed":0}}
```

As you can see the **htc-group** alias contains only two groups instead of ten. This is due to the process of automatically applying the **term** filter for groups that contain the tag elasticsearch. This can be leveraged for varied

219

needs. For e.g., while indexing sensitive data, you can create a filtered alias to make sure that anyone using that particular alias can't see data for which they don't have access.

Routing

It is the process of routing which places documents in a particular shard. Elasticsearch uses the **hash** of the **document Id**, either specified by you or generated by Elasticsearch, to select in which shard should the document be indexed into. There is also provision for manually specifying the routing of a document when indexing. This is typically what happens in **parent-child** relationships as the child document has to be in the same shard as the parent document.

Instead of the document Id, Elasticsearch can also use a **custom** value for hashing. You just need to specify the **routing query parameter** on the URL and the associated value will be used for hashing instead of the Id.

Significance of Routing

In the absence of any routing, Elasticsearch makes sure that all the documents are distributed in an even manner across all the different shards. This begs the question that why then we need routing? Customization of routing allows collection of multiple documents with a shared routing value into a single shard. After these documents land in the same index, it allows routing certain queries in a way that they are executed on a subset of the shards for an index.

Routing Strategies

Routing as a strategy requires the following:

- Pick good routing values while indexing documents
- Reuse those values while performing queries

In our phones example, first of all figure out a good way to separate each document. In this example, select the **phone make** to use as the routing value. This looks like a fair choice for a routing value as the phone makes vary widely enough that you have quite a few values to pick from. Each phone is associated with a brand (make) so it makes it easy to extract that from a document before indexing. Picking up something which has only few different values, can lead to unbalanced shards for the index. If there happen to be only four possible routing values for all documents, all documents will end up routed between a maximum of four shards. It is essential to pick a value that will have sufficient cardinality to spread data among shards in an index.

After picking up the desired routing value, make sure to specify this routing value when indexing documents. You can index document with a routing value of **Lenovo** in the following manner:

```
curl -XPOST 'localhost:9200/phones/sales/10?routing=Lenovo' -d '
{
  "make" : "Lenovo",
  "color" : "gold",
  "price" : 100,
  "sold" : "2016-11-03"
}'
```

```
{"_index":"phones","_type":"sales","_id":"10","_version":1,"_shards":{"total":2,"successful":2,"failed":0},"crea
ted":true}
```

You can index document with a routing value of **Sony** in the following manner:

```
curl -XPOST 'localhost:9200/phones/sales/11?routing=Sony' -d '
{
  "make" : "Sony",
  "color" : "black",
  "price" : 150,
  "sold" : "2016-12-15"
  }'
{"_index":"phones","_type":"sales","_id":"11","_version":1,"_shards":{"total":2,"successful":2,"failed":0},"crea
ted":true}
```

You can index document with a routing value of **Blackberry** in the following manner:

```
curl -XPOST 'localhost:9200/phones/sales/12?routing=Blackberry' -d '
{
  "make" : "Blackberry",
  "color" : "black",
  "price" : 120,
  "sold" : "2016-11-21"
}'
{"_index":"phones","_type":"sales","_id":"12","_version":1,"_shards":{"total":2,"successful":2,"failed":0},"crea
ted":true}
```

As you can see in the above example, three different routing values - **Lenovo, Sony, and Blackberry** have been used for three different documents. This implies that instead of hashing the IDs 10, 11 and 12 to determine which shard to put the documents in, the routing values are used. In the indexing process, this does not help much. The real benefit comes by combining routing on the query side. Multiple routing values can be combined using comma.

You can query with a routing value of Lenovo and Blackberry in the following manner:

```
curl -XPOST 'localhost:9200/phones/sales/_search?routing=Lenovo,Blackberry' -d '
{
  "query" : {
    "match" : {
      "color" : "black"
    }
  }
}'
{
  "hits" : {
    "total" : 2,
    "max_score" : 1.0,
    "hits" : [
      {
        "_index" : "phones",
        "_type" : "sales",
        "_id" : "AVdB6RkFM4scS7EY9HVt",
        "_score" : 1.0,
```

```
  "_source" : {
    "make" : "huawei",
    "color" : "black",
    "price" : 30,
    "sold" : "2016-10-05"
  }
},
{
  "_index" : "phones",
  "_type" : "sales",
  "_id" : "12",
  "_score" : 1.0,
  "_routing" : "Blackberry",
  "_source" : {
    "make" : "Blackberry",
    "color" : "black",
    "price" : 120,
    "sold" : "2016-11-21"
  }
 }
]
}
}
```

It is interesting to observe that instead of returning all three documents, only two are returned. When Elasticsearch receives such request, it hashes the value of the two specified routing values, **Lenovo** and **Blackberry**. The query is then on executed on all the shards they are hashed to. In this case Lenovo and Blackberry both get hashed to the same shard, and **Sony** gets hashed to a different shard.

Taking this strategy further to hundreds of thousands of documents, by specifying the routing while indexing and searching, you can limit the scope of where a search request is executed. This can phenomenally improve the performance for an index that might have 1000 shards. Rather than querying on all 1000 shards, it can be limited in scope. This makes it run faster with less impact to the Elasticsearch cluster.

In the examples shown till now, Lenovo and Blackberry route to the same shard value. They could also have been hashed to different shard values. Interestingly, there is a way to know which shard a request will be executed on? Elasticsearch provides an API to show the nodes and shards on which a search request will be executed.

Determining Shards

As mentioned earlier, it is possible to determine on which shard and node, a query gets executed on. You can use the search shards API to see which shards the request is going to be executed on. You need not specify the routing value.

```
curl -XGET 'localhost:9200/phones/_search_shards?pretty'
{
  "nodes" : {
    "MLOt_QcjSSqPnYpdDUN-NQ" : {
      "name" : "Alistaire Stuart",
      "transport_address" : "127.0.0.1:9301",
      "attributes" : { }
```

```json
  },
  "4IqtTbfoQk6vS6BvwBqVug" : {
    "name" : "Hobgoblin II",
    "transport_address" : "127.0.0.1:9300",
    "attributes" : { }
  }
},
"shards" : [ [ {
  "state" : "STARTED",
  "primary" : true,
  "node" : "4IqtTbfoQk6vS6BvwBqVug",
  "relocating_node" : null,
  "shard" : 0,
  "index" : "phones",
  "version" : 36,
  "allocation_id" : {
    "id" : "mcScD7QST2exi3_9LjZrXw"
  }
}, {
  "state" : "STARTED",
  "primary" : false,
  "node" : "MLOt_QcjSSqPnYpdDUN-NQ",
  "relocating_node" : null,
  "shard" : 0,
  "index" : "phones",
  "version" : 36,
  "allocation_id" : {
    "id" : "M6g5vZ8hROy-0rOW4lN1aA"
  }
} ], [ {
.....
  "state" : "STARTED",
  "primary" : false,
  "node" : "MLOt_QcjSSqPnYpdDUN-NQ",
  "relocating_node" : null,
  "shard" : 4,
  "index" : "phones",
  "version" : 36,
  "allocation_id" : {
    "id" : "TN7Myk0lQRWxg4WupVAMUA"
  }
}, {
  "state" : "STARTED",
  "primary" : true,
  "node" : "4IqtTbfoQk6vS6BvwBqVug",
  "relocating_node" : null,
  "shard" : 4,
  "index" : "phones",
  "version" : 36,
  "allocation_id" : {
    "id" : "Fxm1R2UKQaqZMbywgll98A"
  }
}
```

```
  }]]
}
```

You can specify the routing value also.

```
curl -XGET 'localhost:9200/phones/_search_shards?pretty&routing=Lenovo'
{
  "nodes" : {
    "MLOt_QcjSSqPnYpdDUN-NQ" : {
      "name" : "Alistaire Stuart",
      "transport_address" : "127.0.0.1:9301",
      "attributes" : { }
    },
    "4lqtTbfoQk6vS6BvwBqVug" : {
      "name" : "Hobgoblin II",
      "transport_address" : "127.0.0.1:9300",
      "attributes" : { }
    }
  },
  "shards" : [ [ {
    "state" : "STARTED",
    "primary" : true,
    "node" : "4lqtTbfoQk6vS6BvwBqVug",
    "relocating_node" : null,
    "shard" : 1,
    "index" : "phones",
    "version" : 40,
    "allocation_id" : {
      "id" : "LX29QZHLTayDlzEaclPJcg"
    }
  }, {
    "state" : "STARTED",
    "primary" : false,
    "node" : "MLOt_QcjSSqPnYpdDUN-NQ",
    "relocating_node" : null,
    "shard" : 1,
    "index" : "phones",
    "version" : 40,
    "allocation_id" : {
      "id" : "bA3JOpAnRoCwzP_w4cpE4w"
    }
  }]]
}
```

As you can see that even though the index consists of two shards, when the routing value is specified, only shard 1 is going to be searched. You just cut the amount of data the search query must sift through by half. Routing is certainly useful for indices having large number of shards, but for day-to-day regular usage, you can keep away from it.

Routing Configuration

It always helps if you specify that you intend custom routing for all documents and to stop you from indexing a document without a custom routing value. This can be configured through the mapping of a type. For e.g. you can create an index called **routed-phones** and corresponding routing in the following manner:

```
curl -XPOST 'localhost:9200/routed-phones' -d '
{
  "mappings" : {
    "sales" : {
      "_routing" : {
        "required" : "true"
      },
      "properties" : {
        "color" : {
          "type" : "string"
        },
        "make" : {
          "type" : "string"
        },
        "price" : {
          "type" : "long"
        },
        "sold" : {
          "type" : "date",
          "format" : "strict_date_optional_time||epoch_millis"
        }
      }
    }
  }
}'
{"acknowledged":true}
```

Now let's try to index a document without a routing value.

```
curl -XPOST 'localhost:9200/routed-phones/sales/13' -d '
{
  "make" : "Blackberry",
  "color" : "black",
  "price" : 140,
  "sold" : "2016-11-29"
}'
{"error":{"root_cause":[{"type":"routing_missing_exception","reason":"routing is required for [routed-phones]/[sales]/[13]","index":"routed-phones"}],"type":"routing_missing_exception","reason":"routing is required for [routed-phones]/[sales]/[13]","index":"routed-phones"},"status":400}
```

As you can see, Elasticsearch gives an error as the required routing value is missing.

Routing in Combination with Aliases

Till now we have seen that aliases provide a powerful and flexible abstraction on top of indices. They can also be leveraged along with routing to automatically apply routing values while querying or indexing. This is with an assumption that the alias points to a single index. Try indexing into an alias that point to a group of indices, and you will get an error. This is due to the fact that Elasticsearch doesn't know which concrete index the document should be indexed into.

You can go ahead and create an alias called **Lenovo-group** that automatically filters out phones with "**Lenovo**" in the make and adds "**Lenovo**" to the routing when searching and indexing to limit where queries are executed as shown below:

```
curl -XPOST 'localhost:9200/_aliases' -d '
{
  "actions" : [
  {
   "add" : {
    "index" : "phones",
    "alias" : "Lenovo-group",
    "filter" : {
     "term" : {"make" : "Lenovo"}
    },
    "routing" : "Lenovo"
   }
  }
  ]
}'
{"acknowledged":true}

curl -XPOST 'localhost:9200/Lenovo-group/_search?pretty' -d '
{
  "query" : {
   "match_all" : {}
  },
  "fields" : ["make"]
}'
{
  "took" : 462,
  "timed_out" : false,
  "_shards" : {
   "total" : 1,
   "successful" : 1,
   "failed" : 0
  },
  "hits" : {
   "total" : 0,
   "max_score" : null,
   "hits" : []
  }
```

}

You can use the alias while indexing also. Indexing with the **Lenovo-group** alias, is similar to document being indexed with **routing=Lenovo** query string parameter. Since aliases are lightweight, you have the luxury to create as many as required while using custom routing for scaling.

Summary

This chapter covered how multiple nodes, each containing multiple indices, which in turn are made up of a number of shards, come together to form Elasticsearch cluster. The process of node addition was covered along with maser node election. Different ways to remove and decommission nodes have been described. Alias provide a convenient way to address a subset of data in an index. The chapter ended with an overview of routing and how to use in combination with aliases to make a flexible and scalable cluster.

## CHAPTER 12

ELK Stack in Production

The previous chapter covered the different scaling strategies for Elasticsearch. An overview of node addition, decommissioning, alias and routing was provided. When running ELK stack in production environment, there could be multiple things which we need to take care of. Monitoring the different components and troubleshooting any problem is quite important. Custom configurations are required for specific scenarios. This chapter will address the key aspects of running ELK stack in production environment.

Deployment Considerations

There is a big difference between playing with Elasticsearch on your laptop as compared to real deployments on multi-node production environment. There are quite a few best practices which are worth considering. They are of course not the "**final word**" but they are certainly suitable for a wide range of deployments.

Memory

Memory is a resource which always seems scarce and with Elasticsearch your chances of running out of it are pretty high. Elasticsearch operations like **sorting** and **aggregations** are memory hungry so it is prudent to have enough heap space for these operations. Even if heap size is small, extra memory can be given to the OS filesystem cache. Since, Lucene uses many disk-based data structures, Elasticsearch utilizes OS cache significantly. Any ways memory prices have dropped these days so we should try to allocate as high memory as possible.

 Tip   Although it is quite common to see machines with 32 GB or 16 GB of RAM size, the ideal memory size is 64 GB of RAM. There could be challenges with if RAM size is less than 8 GB or more than 64 GB.

Disks

Disks are quite essential for cluster configurations and more for indexing-heavy clusters. Disks being the slowest subsystem in a server, it is very easy for write-heavy clusters to saturate the disks. This creates bottleneck for the entire cluster. If your budget allows, you should always go for **SSDs**. Having a SSD gives a good enough boost for query and indexing performance.

■ **Tip** While using SSD, ensure that the OS I/O scheduler is configured correctly. The default scheduler is **cfq** which is more suitable for spinning media. In case of SSD, it is better to go for **deadline** or **noop** scheduler.

Another efficient way to increase disk speed is to use **RAID 0**, for both spinning disks and SSDs. It is best to avoid **Network-Attached-Storage (NAS)** as it is generally found to be slow leading to large latencies.

Network

Distributed systems work best with fast and reliable networks. This holds true for Elasticsearch clusters also. Nodes can communicate easily if latency is low. High bandwidth facilitates seamless shard movement and recovery. The modern data center networks (1 GbE, 10 GbE) are suitable for clusters in most of the scenarios.

■ **Tip** While Elasticsearch clusters should not span across multiple data centers even if these data centers are in close geographical proximity.

We are living in interesting times. On the one hand it is possible to procure big machines with hundreds of gigabytes of RAM with multi-core CPUs. On the other hand, it is quite easy to spin up hundreds or thousands of small virtual machines in cloud platforms such as AWS. What should one do? Well, the answer as in most such situations is - "It Depends!" There is no prominent advantage of small machines as there would be additional overhead of managing a cluster with thousands of nodes. Similarly, gigantic machines are best avoided as they can lead to imbalanced resource usage and logistical complexity in case running multiple nodes per machine. As a rule of thumb, go for **medium-to-large** machines.

Java Virtual Machine

As a best practice, always run the most recent version of the Java Virtual Machine (JVM), unless otherwise mentioned on the Elasticsearch documentation. Both Elasticsearch and Lucene are quite demanding and often expose weaknesses in JVM.

■ **Tip** Java 8 is preferred over Java 7 / Java 6 for ELK stack installations.

JVM comes with dozens of settings, parameters and configurations. They virtually give you the freedom to tweak every aspect of the JVM. Elasticsearch is a complex piece of software, so unless you are very sure, do not change any of the JVM settings.

Data Management

Elasticsearch is generally believed to perform with good speed the operations like **indexing**, **searching** and **aggregations**. However, there are many aspects to consider while deciding how fast we want these operations to be.

- **Request Complexity** - Multiple operations like index, update, delete, search and get can be clubbed together in a single HTTP call. This can give phenomenal boost to performance.

- **Tradeoff between Indexing Speed and Searching Speed** - Internally, Elasticsearch uses Lucene segments for data storage. A better understanding of Lucene segments can help in taking an informed decision.

- **Memory** - Elasticsearch relies on caching for faster data access. Large caches require significant memory.

    The subsequent sections will provide more details of the above listed factors.

Request Grouping

One of the easiest things to do for faster indexing is to send multiple documents to be indexed at once using the **bulk** API. This not only saves network round-trips but also allows for more indexing throughput. You can include different types of operations in a single bulk request. In the same bulk request, you can include operations for **creating documents** or **overwriting** them. Not only that, you can also include **update** or **delete** operations in a bulk request. For performing multiple **get** or **search** operations you can use **multiget** and **multisearch** APIs.

Bulk Indexing, Updating and Deleting

If you index documents one at a time, there are some overheads which have to be incurred every time.

- Application must wait for response from Elasticsearch before moving on to the next task.
- Elasticsearch needs to process all request data for every indexed document.

    In order to boost indexing speed, it is best to use bulk API, which can help in indexing multiple documents at the same time. As illustrated in Figure 12-1, when you send a HTTP request with multiple indexing operations, you get single HTTP response for all the operations.

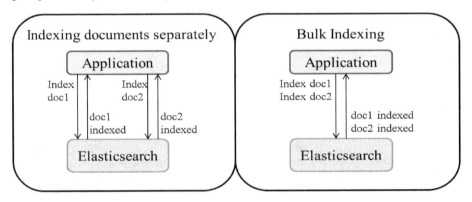

Figure 12-1. *Bulk Indexing can process multiple documents*

Bulk request for indexing documents can be given in the following manner.

curl -XPOST 'localhost:9200/{index}/_bulk --data-binary @$REQUESTS_FILE

Or

curl -XPOST 'localhost:9200/{index}/{type}/_bulk --data-binary @$REQUESTS_FILE

Let's refresh from the example regarding authors, first introduced in Chapter 5. The request file can be specified in the following manner:

```
{ "create": { "_index": "ws", "_type": "author", "_id": "1" }}
{ "name": "William Shakespeare", "born": "1564-04-26", "died": "1616-04-23", "country": "United Kingdom" }
{ "create": { "_index": "cd", "_type": "author", "_id": "2" }}
{ "name": "Charles Dickens", "born": "1812-02-07", "died": "1870-06-09", "country": "United Kingdom" }
{ "create": { "_index": "ws", "_type": "play", "_id": "3" }}
{ "author": "William Shakespeare", "play": "Comedy of Errors", "published": "1589" }
{ "create": { "_index": "cd", "_type": "play", "_id": "4" }}
{ "author": "Charles Dickens", "play": "The Pickwick Papers", "published": "1836" }
{ "create": { "_index": "ws", "_type": "play", "_id": "5" }}
{ "author": "William Shakespeare", "play": "Henry VI", "published": "1590" }
{ "create": { "_index": "cd", "_type": "play", "_id": "6" }}
{ "author": "Charles Dickens", "play": "Oliver Twist", "published": "1837" }
{ "create": { "_index": "ws", "_type": "play", "_id": "7" }}
{ "author": "William Shakespeare", "play": "Richard III", "published": "1592" }
{ "create": { "_index": "cd", "_type": "play", "_id": "8" }}
{ "author": "Charles Dickens", "play": "Nicholas Nickleby", "published": "1838" }
{ "create": { "_index": "ws", "_type": "play", "_id": "9" }}
{ "author": "William Shakespeare", "play": "Taming of the Shrew", "published": "1593" }
{ "create": { "_index": "cd", "_type": "play", "_id": "10" }}
{ "author": "Charles Dickens", "play": "The Old Curiosity", "published": "1840" }
{ "create": { "_index": "ws", "_type": "play", "_id": "11" }}
{ "author": "William Shakespeare", "play": "Romeo and Juliet", "published": "1594" }
{ "create": { "_index": "cd", "_type": "play", "_id": "12" }}
{ "author": "Charles Dickens", "play": "David Copperfield", "published": "1849" }
```

The **_index** and **_type** fields indicate where to index each document. The **_id** field indicates the ID of the document being indexed.

■ **Tip** If the index **"author"** and type **"play"** already exists, it is suggested to DELETE the associated data before proceeding ahead. Otherwise, you will get **"Document already exists"** error message.

---

curl -XPOST 'localhost:9200/_bulk?pretty' --data-binary "@plays.json"; echo

On running the above mentioned command, you will get a JSON containing the time it took to index the bulk request and the responses for each operation. An errors flag indicates if any operation failed. The response would look like this:

```
{
  "took" : 4343,
  "errors" : false,
  "items" : [ {
    "create" : {
      "_index" : "ws",
      "_type" : "author",
      "_id" : "1",
      "_version" : 1,
      "_shards" : {
        "total" : 2,
        "successful" : 1,
        "failed" : 0
      },
      "status" : 201
    }
  }, {
    "create" : {
      "_index" : "cd",
      "_type" : "author",
      "_id" : "2",
      "_version" : 1,
      "_shards" : {
        "total" : 2,
        "successful" : 1,
        "failed" : 0
      },
      "status" : 201
    }
  }, {
............................
  } ]
}
```

Just in case one (or more) document fails to be indexed, it does not mean the whole bulk request has failed. Items in the same bulk request are independent of each other.

■ **Tip** The size of bulk request influences the performance.

Just like performing indexing operation in bulk, similarly you can perform **update** or **delete** operations also in bulk. The update operation looks similar to the index operation with a notable exception that the **document ID** has to be specified. The document content can contain doc or script similar to performing individual update operation. The delete operations are specified differently as there is no document content. There is just the metadata line with document ID.

Multisearch and Multiget APIs

Use of **multisearch** and **multiget** provide similar benefits as bulk APIs. Grouping multiple search or get requests saves time and avoids network latency. A typical use of sending multiple search requests at the same time is while searching different types of documents. The multisearch API is similar to the bulk API in the following manner:

- You need to hit the **_msearch** endpoint and it is optional to specify the index or type in the URL.

- Request contains two single-lines JSON strings - the first line contains parameters like **index, type, routing value**, or **search type**. The second line contains the query body consisting of the request payload.

    Let's put the contents of the multisearch request in a csv file (**bulksearch.json**).

```
{"index" : "phones", "type" : "sales"}
{"query" : {"match" : {"make" : "iPhone"}}}
{"index" : "phones", "type" : "sales"}
{"query" : {"match" : {"make" : "htc"}}}
```

You can invoke the multisearch request in the following manner:

```
curl 'localhost:9200/_msearch?pretty' --data-binary @bulksearch.json
```

The following snippet shows the result of the multisearch request.

```
{

  "responses" : [ {

    "took" : 51,

    "timed_out" : false,

    "_shards" : {

      "total" : 5,

      "successful" : 5,

      "failed" : 0

    },

    "hits" : {

      "total" : 2,

      "max_score" : 1.5108256,

      "hits" : [ {

        "_index" : "phones",

        "_type" : "sales",
```

```
    "_id" : "AVdB6RkFM4scS7EY9HVl",

    "_score" : 1.5108256,

    "_source" : {

      "make" : "iPhone",

      "color" : "silver",

      "price" : 260,

      "sold" : "2016-01-16"

     }

   }, { … }

    ]

   }

 }, {

  "took" : 38,

  "timed_out" : false,

  "_shards" : {

   "total" : 5,

   "successful" : 5,

   "failed" : 0

  },

  "hits" : {

   "total" : 2,

   "max_score" : 1.9162908,

   "hits" : [ {

    "_index" : "phones",

    "_type" : "sales",

    "_id" : "AVdB6RkFM4scS7EY9HVo",

    "_score" : 1.9162908,
```

```
        "_source" : {

            "make" : "htc",

            "color" : "silver",

            "price" : 140,

            "sold" : "2016-04-03"

        }

    }, { ... }

    ]

    }

    } ]

}
```

Multiget is apt for situations where an external application needs to fetch a set of documents without doing any initial search. For example, if you are storing system properties at regular time intervals, the ID can be the timestamp. In such a scenario, if you want to fetch specific system properties belonging to a specific duration, you don't need to do any filtering. You can simply call **_mget** endpoint and send a docs array with the index type, and ID of the documents you want to fetch. Refer to the Employee example mentioned in **Chapter 4**. If you want to fetch details of multiple Employees, you can do in the following manner.

```
curl -XGET "http://localhost:9200/_mget" -d '{
    "docs" : [
        {
            "_index" : "foo",
            "type" : "eis",
            "_id" : "33124"
        },
        {
            "_index" : "foo",
            "type": "eis",
            "_id" : "AVbA4WNg7uqRWQFJiJSn",
            "_source" : "department"
        }
    ]
}'
```

A docs array is returned in the response body. This docs array contains response per document and it is in the same order as specified with the request. You can see that each of these responses is same that is expected from an individual get request. Since, we had specified only one particular field, i.e. "**department**" for the second document; you can see that for the second document only this particular field is present in the response body.

```
{
"docs":[{"_index":"foo","_type":"eis","_id":"33124","_version":1,"found":true,"_source":
{
    "name": "Tom Smith",
```

```
    "id": 33124,
    "manager": "Rob Stewart",
    "department": "sales",
    "contact details": {
    "mobile phone": "+12072553130",
    "email": "tom.smith@foo.com" }}
},
{"_index":"foo","_type":"eis","_id":"AVbA4WNg7uqRWQFJiJSn","_version":1,"found":true,"_source":
{
    "department": "hr",
}
}]}
```

In case the documents you want to retrieve have the same _index value, you can just specify the default _index in the URL.

```
curl -XGET "http://localhost:9200/foo/_mget" -d '{
    "docs" : [
        {
            "type" : "eis",
            "_id" : "33124"
        },
        {
            "type": "eis",
            "_id" : "AVbA4WNg7uqRWQFJiJSn",
            "_source" : "department"
        }
    ]
}'
```

Similarly, if the documents have the same _index and _type value, you can specify the _index and _type values in the URL.

```
curl -XGET "http://localhost:9200/foo/eis/_mget" -d '{
    "ids" : [ "33124", "AVbA4WNg7uqRWQFJiJSn" ]
}'
```

Clubbing multiple operations in the same request with multiget API may appear to introduce additional complexity, but the requests become fast without any additional cost. Same is the case with multisearch and bulk APIs. You can try out different request sizes to figure out what works best your documents and environment.

Elasticsearch Tuning

Elasticsearch stores documents in disk in **segment**. But before that it saves documents intermittently in **cache**. Both the segment handling and cache management can be tuned based on the scenario for optimal functioning of Elasticsearch.

Lucene Segment Optimization

One receiving documents, Elasticsearch indexes them in memory in inverted indices called segments. These segments are written to disk from time to time. Bear in mind that these segments can't be modified but only deleted. This makes it easier for the operating system to cache them. Besides this, bigger segments are formed from smaller segments to consolidate the inverted indices in order to make searching faster. There are different means to configure how Elasticsearch manages these segments. Detailed description of these options will be given in subsequent sections.

Thresholds for Refresh and Flush

By **refreshing**, Elasticsearch's views get reopened and newly indexed documents are made available for searching. The indexed data is committed from memory to disk in **flushing**. Both these operations have significant cost so it is important to configure them optimally. Elasticsearch offers near-real time searching capability as its operations are not carried on the very latest indexed data but on an earlier snapshot. A point-in-time view of the index is kept opened so that multiple searches hit the same files and reuse the same caches. This has a related consequence that each refresh has a performance penalty as caches are invalidated leading to slow down of search operations. The reopening process also requires cpu cycles which could otherwise be used for indexing.

The default value for the refreshing interval is **1 second**. However, you can change this value as per your requirement. The following command would set the refresh interval to **3 seconds**:

```
curl -XPUT 'localhost:9200/{index}/_settings' -d '{
  "index.refresh_interval" : "3s"
}'
```

You can verify that your changes have been applied by giving the following command:

```
curl -XGET 'localhost:9200/{index}/_settings?pretty'
```

Increasing the value of **refresh_interval** leaves cpu cycles for indexing.

Tip You can disable automatic refreshing by setting **refresh_interval** to **-1**.

Disabling automatic refreshing can be suitable for situations where indices change in batches and not frequently, such as warehouse where goods are stocked every night. In this case, indexing throughput is preferable than data freshness. You can manually refresh using the following command:

```
curl -XGET 'localhost:9200/{index}/_refresh'
```

Elasticsearch periodically persists the in-memory segments to the actual Lucene index on the disk and this process is called **flushing**. In order to ensure data is not lost when a node goes down, Elasticsearch keeps track of indexing operations that are still in the transaction log. During the process of flushing, the transaction log is also cleared. Flushing happens in one of the following conditions:

- Memory buffer becomes full.
- Certain period of time has passed since the last flush.
- Transaction log hits a certain threshold.

You can control how often flushing happens by configuring the settings for the above mentioned conditions. The **memory buffer size** can be controlled through the **indices.memory.index_buffer_size** setting in the **elasticsearch.yml** configuration file. This setting controls the entire buffer for a node and can be specified either as a percent of overall JVM heap like **15%** or an absolute value like **50 MB**. Transaction log has index specific settings which control both the size at which a flush should occur (through **index.translog.flush_threshold_size**) and the time since the last flush (through **index.translog.flush_threshold_period**). You can change these settings in the following manner:

```
curl -XPUT 'localhost:9200/{index}/_settings' -d '
{
  "index.translog" : {
    "flush_threshold_size" : "250mb",
    "flush_threshold_period" : "20m"
  }
}'
```

One or more segments get created in disk after a flush is done. While servicing a query, Elasticsearch would look in all the segments and then merges the results as an overall result. More the number of segments to search through, the slower would be the search. It is best to keep segments at a minimum by merging smaller segments into bigger segments.

Merge Policies

Segments are cached to make searches fast. Changing the dataset, such as addition of a document does not require rebuilding the index for data stored in existing segments. A direct consequence of creating mode indices is an increase in number of segments. This makes indexing faster but it has an overhead. When you update a document, the earlier version is not changed. Rather the existing version is deleted and a new version is indexed. Similarly, when you delete a document, it does not remove the document from the segment. It's only marked as deleted in a separate **.del** file. Documents can be removed only during segment merging.

For these reasons in the background smaller segments are merged to form larger segments to keep their number manageable. The merging process also removes deleted documents. However, the merge process is performance intensive, especially in terms of I/O. You can tune the merge policy to control how often merges happen and how big the segments grow to. The default merge policy is **tiered**, whereby the segments are divided into tiers. If there are more than the maximum numbers of segments in a tier, a merge is triggered for that tier. There are some configuration options to control the merge policies:

- **index.merge.policy.segments_per_tier** - A high value leads to more segments in a tier leading to less merging and better performance. If you don't need to index often and want better search performance, you should lower this value.

- **index.merge.policy.max_merge_at_once** - This configuration setting specifies how many segments can be merged at the same time. Having a lower value leads to lesser merging.

- **index.merge.policy.max_merged_segment** - This setting specifies the maximum segment size. If you want less merging and faster merging, you should lower this value as bigger segments are difficult to merge.

- **index.merge.scheduler.max_thread_count** - This configuration setting specifies how many threads are working in background for merging segments. This actually sets a limit on the number of merges that can happen simultaneously.

The configuration options specified above are specific to index. They can be changed at runtime also in the following manner:

```
curl -XPUT 'localhost:9200/{index}/_settings' -d '
{
  "index.merge" : {
    "policy" : {
      "segments_per_tier" : 3,
      "max_merge_at_once" : 3,
      "max_merged_segment" : "1gb",
    }
    "scheduler.max_thread_count" : 1
  }
}'
```

It is possible to trigger merge manually also. A manual merge is also known as **optimize**. You consider running manual merge for indices which are not expected to change later. Optimizing is I/O intensive and invalidates lot of caches. If after optimizing, you continue to index, update, or delete documents, the advantage would be lost. Optimizing is most suitable for static indices. You can rigger optimizing in the following manner:

```
curl -XPUT 'localhost:9200/{index}/_optimize?max_num_segments=1'
```

The optimizing operation can take a long time for a large index. For such scenarios, you can run it in the background by setting **wait_for_merge** to **false**.

Store Throttling

Since, merges have a big impact on I/O throughput, Elasticsearch limits the amount of I/O throughput that merges can use through store throttling. This is controlled at the node level by the **indices.store.throttle.max_bytes_per_sec** having a default value of **20mb**. This limit is suitable for a wide range of scenarios but in certain situations it might need to be tweaked.

In systems with fast disk where more I/O throughput is required for merging, the throttle limit can be raised. You can in fact remove the limit by setting the value as **none**. The following command would raise the throttling limit to **250MB/s**.

```
curl -XPUT 'localhost:9200/_cluster/settings' -d '
{
  "persistent" : {
    "indices.store.throttle" : {
      "type" : "all",
      "max_bytes_per_sec" : "250mb"
    }
  }
}'
```

■ **Tip** You can check cluster settings to see if the configuration changes have been applied.

Cache Management

Elasticsearch utilizes caching for serving huge amount of request traffic on a large number of documents, and that too on commodity hardware. You might have wondered once indexing is done, the second query is often quite faster than the first one. This is due to caching. This section elaborates on the different kinds of caches used by Elasticsearch and how to keep them in optimal running condition.

Filter Caches

Lots of queries utilize filters as they provide good performance. Elasticsearch, by default, caches frequently used filters on bigger segments. This avoids caching too aggressively but catches frequent filters and optimizes them. The results of a cached filter are stored in the **filter cache**. This cache is a node level cache. The default value is **10%** but can be changed by modifying the following setting in **elasticsearch.yml**.

indices.cache.filter.size : 20%

You will have to monitor your actual usage over a period of time to decide on the desired filter cache size. There are situations when filter cache entries have a short lifespan. This happens typically if no more searches are happening which can utilize the cached filter query. The cache entry will remain for some time before it eventually gets evicted. A full cache having many evictions has a performance challenge because every search operation will consume CPU cycles to fit in new cache entries by evicting old ones. In order to prevent evictions from happening at the same time when queries are run, you can introduce a **TTL** (time to live) on cache entries. This can be done on a per-index basis in the following manner:

```
curl -XPUT 'localhost:9200/{index}/_settings' -d '
{
  "index.cache.filter.expire" : "30m"
}'
```

Tip Just having room for filter caches is not enough, you need to ensure that filters take advantage of the cached entries.

Shard Query Cache

The filter cache is segment specific and its primary purpose is to make filters run faster. Shard query cache, on the other hand, maintains a mapping between the **whole request** and its **result** on the **shard level**. This is illustrated in Figure 12-2.

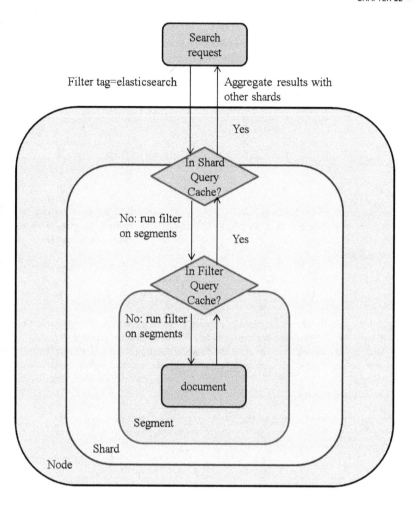

Figure 12-2. Shard Query Cache and Filter Cache

Shards will try to service identical requests from the cache. Results cached at the shard level are limited by the total number of hits, aggregations and suggestions. For this very reason, shard query cache works only when the query has **search_type** set to **count**.

■ **Tip**   By setting the **search_type** to **count** in the URI parameters, Elasticsearch gets the hint that real interest is not in query results, but only in the number.

Since the shard query cache entries differ from one request to another, so they serve a narrow set of requests. If the search is for a different term or slightly different aggregation, then the cache would not be able to service. When a refresh happens, the shard's contents get modified and all the shard query cache entries get invalidated. This narrow nature of cache entries makes shard query cache useful in situations where shards rarely

241

change and there are many identical requests. For e.g. if you have indexed logs and the indices are time-based, you may be fine running aggregations on older indices that would remain unchanged until they are deleted. These older indices are fit to be cached in shard query cache. You can enable the shard query cache by default at the index level by the following command:

curl -XPUT 'localhost:9200/{index}/_settings' -d '

{

  "index.cache.query.enable" : true

}'

You can enable or disable the shard query cache on a per query basis, overriding the index-level setting. You just need to add the **query_cache** parameter to the URL. Similar to the filter cache, the shard query cache has a **size** configuration parameter. If there is limited memory, then you should lower the cache size to provision for memory used by index and search requests.

JVM Heap and OS Cache

Just like all JVM processes, if Elasticsearch does not have enough memory for servicing requests, it throws an **out-of-memory** exception. This will make the node crash and become unavailable. As a side effect, there would be extra load on other nodes as they replicate and relocate shards in order to get back to the original state. You should be cautious of JVM heap as even if there is no out-of-memory exception in the logs, the node may become unresponsive. This happens due to the **garbage collector** (GC) taking more CPU cycles to free up memory, which already is scarce. Less CPU cycles are available for actual operations.

If the JVM heap is constantly under pressure, you can use one (or more) of the following steps:

- Decrease the filter cache and/or shard query cache.
- Decrease the **index buffer size**.
- Decrease the **size** value of searches and aggregations
- Add some non-data and non-master nodes to act as clients. They will take the load of aggregating per-shard results of searches and aggregations.

All the JVM collectors are generational collectors, which implies that they have a **young generation** area for newly allocated objects and an **old generation** area for objects which have been around for quite some time. Objects in young generation are promoted to old generation if they are needed for longer duration or if lots of new objects are to be allocated. The second case occurs typically for **aggregations**, which need to iterate through large sets of documents and create lots of objects that may be reutilized in the next aggregation.

You would prefer that the potentially reusable objects get promoted to the old generation instead of some random temporary objects. To accomplish this Elasticsearch implements a **PageCacheRecycler** where big arrays used by aggregations are prevented from being garbage-collected. The default value of page cache is **10%** of the total heap. In some cases, this may be unnecessarily high, for e.g. for a 30 GB heap size, the cache would be 3 GB. You can change the size of the cache from elasticsearch.yml by modifying the parameter **cache.recycler.page.limit.heap**.

There can be times when you would need to take other measures to tune the JVM settings. For e.g., you don't want long GC pauses. There are some options to trigger the GC frequently so as to reduce the **STW** (Stop the World) pause time.

- Increase the **survivor space** (lower -XX:SurvivorRatio) or the **whole young generation** (lower -XX:NewRatio) compared to the total heap.

- Use **G1 GC** (-XX:+UseG1GC) garbage collector. It has better allocation and collection algorithms and works best for large heap sizes requiring low-latency.

Tip Rule of thumb is to allocate half of the node's RAM to Elasticsearch JVM heap, but not more than 32 GB.

OS level caches are dependent on the RAM of servers. You can redesign your indices in a way that works best with the operating system's caching. For e.g. while indexing application logs, you expect that most of the indexing and searching will require the recent data. For time-based indices, the latest index is likely to fit in the OS cache rather than the whole dataset, making the operations faster. Searches for older data would hit the disk, but users would not mind little higher time for past and infrequently accessed data. Typically, if you put "hot" data in the same set of indices or shards by using time-series based indices, user based indices or routing, you will leverage the OS cache in an efficient manner.

Warmers for Caches

All the different types of caches - filter caches, shard query caches and OS caches start getting built when a query first runs. The first query is inevitably slower as the caches have to be loaded and there is more slowness in case of large amount of data or a complex query. If this slowdown is giving headache, then you can **warm up** the caches in advances by using **index warmers**. A warmer facilitates defining any kind of search request containing queries, filters, sort criteria or aggregations. After it is defined, Elasticsearch runs the query with every operation. This will certainly slow down the refresh process but the user queries will always get handled through "**warm caches**".

Warmers are quite useful for situations when the first time query is too slow and you would rather want the refresh operation to take a hit rather than the user. In case there are millions of documents and consistent search performance was essential, warmers tend to be quite useful. You can have more than warmers, but bear in mind the more warmers you have, the slower the refreshes would be. Generally, you would like to use a few popular queries as your warmers. You can define warmer by using the PUT request in the following manner:

```
curl -XPUT 'localhost:9200/phones/sales/_warmer/_search?search_type=count&pretty' -d '
{
  "aggs" : {
   "colors" : {
    "terms" : {
     "field" : "color",
     "order" : {
      "_count" : "asc"
     }
    }
   }
  }
}'
```

You can get the list of warmers on an index by doing a GET request on the _warmer type.

```
curl -XGET 'localhost:9200/phones/sales/_warmer/?pretty'
```

You can delete warmers by using the DELETE request

```
curl -XDELETE 'localhost:9200/phones/sales/_warmer/?pretty'
```

■ **Tip** In case you are using multiple indices, it is better to register warmers at index creation.

Configuration Management

In this section we will see the different tuning options available under the hood. With a smart use of these configuration options, you can get the maximum performance from your Elasticsearch cluster.

Better than Defaults

Although the default configuration settings of Elasticsearch suffice for a large number of scenarios, Elasticsearch is a highly flexible system that can be further tuned for maximum performance. Most uses of Elasticsearch could be for just search queries, however, in the recent past there have been deployments which are pushing the boundaries. Elasticsearch is being used now logging aggregator, source of data and also in some cases used in hybrid storage architecture in conjunction with other databases.

Index Templates

Creating of new indices and associated mappings is not a difficult task. There can be some scenarios when the future indices should also have the same settings and mappings as the previous ones. Some such scenarios are as following:

- **Multi-tenancy** - Systems with dynamic tenants need to store tenant-specific data in silos.
- **Log Aggregation** - Frequent log indexing might be required for fast querying and storage. In cloud based systems, different systems push their logs onto a central Elasticsearch server.
- **Regulations** - Blocks of data may have to be either kept or removed after a certain period of timer as per the regulatory compliance.

Templates are quite helpful when a mature and deterministic pattern is needed for homogenous data storage.

Template Creation

Index templates are applied to any newly created index. Indices with a matching predefined naming pattern get the template applied to them. The index creation event should match the template pattern for the template to be applied. You can apply templates either using **REST API** or through a **configuration file**. The former requires a running cluster.

244

Let's look at a simple index template used for log aggregation so that the log aggregation tool would have a new index created per day. The default behavior of Logstash is to make API calls using the daily timestamp prefixed to the index name, for e.g. logstash-11-10-2016. Let's assume that you are using Elasticsearch default settings, which allow for automatic index creation. When Logstash makes a call to the Elasticsearch cluster with a new event, the new index will get created with the name of **logstash-12-10-2016** and the document type gets auto mapped. Let's first use REST APIs for template creation:

```
curl -XPUT 'localhost:9200/_template/logging_index' -d '
{
  "template" : "logstash-*",
  "settings" : {
   "number_of_shards" : 2,
   "number_of_replicas" : 1
  },
  "mappings" : {
   "logs" : {
    "properties" : {
     "@timestamp" : {
      "type" : "date",
      "format" : "strict_date_optional_time||epoch_millis"
     },
     "@version" : {
      "type" : "string",
      "index" : "not_analyzed"
     },
     "date_of_record" : {
      "type" : "date",
      "format" : "strict_date_optional_time||epoch_millis"
     },
     "day_of_year" : {
      "type" : "string",
      "norms" : {
       "enabled" : false
      },
      "fielddata" : {
       "format" : "disabled"
      },
      "fields" : {
       "raw" : {
        "type" : "string",
        "index" : "not_analyzed",
        "ignore_above" : 256
       }
      }
     }
    }
   }
  }, "aliases" : { "december" : {} }
}'
```

The **PUT** command tells Elasticsearch to apply this template whenever indexes request matching the **logstash-*** pattern is received. The template applies an alias so that all indices for a given month can be grouped together.

Templates Configured on the Filesystem

You can even have templates configured on the file system if you follow these rules:

- **JSON** format should be used for template configuration. For ease of use, name with a **.json** extension

- Template definitions should be placed in Elasticsearch configuration location under a **templates** directory.

- Template definitions should be kept in the directories of nodes that are eligible to be elected as master.

For the previous example, the **template.json** file will look like this:

```
{
  "template" : "logstash-*",
  "settings" : {
   "number_of_shards" : 2,
   "number_of_replicas" : 1
  },
  "mappings" : { .... },
  "aliases" : { "december" : {} }

}'
```

The result would be similar to that when using REST APIs.

Merging of Multiple Templates

Elasticsearch facilitates configuration of multiple templates with different settings. We can extend the previous example by configuring a template to handle log events by month and another will store log events in one index as shown below:

```
curl -XPUT 'localhost:9200/_template/logging_index_all' -d '

{

  "template" : "logstash-12-*",

  "order" : 1,

  "settings" : {

   "number_of_shards" : 2,

   "number_of_replicas" : 1

  },
```

```
 "mappings" : {

  "date" : { "store" : false }

 },

 "alias" : { "december" : {} }

}'
```

The above template would be applied to any index beginning with "**logstash-12-**".

```
curl -XPUT 'localhost:9200/_template/logging_index' -d '

{

 "template" : "logstash-*",

 "order" : 0,

 "settings" : {

  "number_of_shards" : 2,

  "number_of_replicas" : 1

 },

 "mappings" : {

  "date" : { "store" : true }

 }

}'
```

The above template would be applied to any index beginning with "**logstash-***" and the date filed would be stored. The topmost template would take care of December specific logs as it matches the pattern of index names beginning with "**logstash-12-**". The second template is a superset and aggregates all log stash indices. The order attribute makes sure that the lowest order number is applied first and then the higher order number overrides it. Due to this the two template settings get merged with all December log events not having the date field stored.

Retrieving Index Templates

To fetch the list of all templates, you can give the following command:

```
curl -XGET 'localhost:9200/_template'
```

You can also fetch one or many individual templates by name:

```
curl -XGET 'localhost:9200/_template/log_index'
curl -XGET 'localhost:9200/_template/log_index_1,log_index_2'
```

You can fetch template names by pattern also:

```
curl -XGET 'localhost:9200/_template/log_*'
```

Deleting Index Templates

You can delete a template name easily in the following manner:

```
curl -XDELETE 'localhost:9200/_template/log_index'
```

Monitoring and Troubleshooting

Elasticsearch provides mechanism to gauge the health and performance of the cluster. An understanding of diagnostic data and regular monitoring of overall cluster status can provide an early warning for any performance bottlenecks. There is a wide range of APIs that helps in monitoring the cluster without interacting with the actual stored data.

Health of the Cluster

As you are aware an Elasticsearch cluster can contain one or more nodes. It can be a modest cluster with 2-3 nodes or a big cluster with hundreds of nodes and few master nodes accessing thousands of indices. Thankfully the cluster health API scales up quite well to provide health information for any size of the cluster. It provides a high level view of the cluster and can alert in case of a problem somewhere in the cluster. You can run the cluster health API in the following manner:

```
curl -XGET 'http://localhost:9200/_cluster/health?pretty'
```

It will return the response in the JSON format. The response contains important information for the cluster.

```
{
  "cluster_name" : "elasticsearch",
  "status" : "green",
  "timed_out" : false,
  "number_of_nodes" : 2,
  "number_of_data_nodes" : 2,
  "active_primary_shards" : 3926,
  "active_shards" : 7852,
  "relocating_shards" : 0,
  "initializing_shards" : 0,
  "unassigned_shards" : 0,
  "delayed_unassigned_shards" : 0,
  "number_of_pending_tasks" : 0,
  "number_of_in_flight_fetch" : 0,
  "task_max_waiting_in_queue_millis" : 0,
  "active_shards_percent_as_number" : 100.0
}
```

The crucial piece of information is **status** value which can be one of three values:

- **green** - Cluster is fully operational with all the primary and replica shards allocated.

- **yellow** - The primary shards are allocated but at least one replica is missing. There is no data loss so no impact on search operations. Cluster high-availability can be a challenge. For a single node deployment, normal status is yellow.

- **red** - There is at least one missing primary shard (and its replicas). This implies that there is a data loss which can impact search operations.

The cluster status gives a general assessment of the cluster. Other fields also convey significant information:

- **number_of_nodes** and **number_of_data_nodes** are self-descriptive.

- **active_primary_shards** gives the number of primary shards in cluster. This is an aggregate across all indices.

- **active_shards** is sum total of all the shards across all indices, including replica shards.

- **relocating_shards** gives the number of shards currently moving from one node to another.

- **initializing_shards** indicates the shards currently being allocated.

- **unassigned_shards** are those shards that exist in the cluster state but not found in the cluster itself.

Detect Index Problem

What will you do if your cluster status turns **red**? Let's say you do a health check and it shows the following status:

```
{
  "cluster_name" : "elasticsearch",
  "status" : "red",
  "timed_out" : false,
  "number_of_nodes" : 5,
  "number_of_data_nodes" : 5,
  "active_primary_shards" : 125,
  "active_shards" : 250,
  "relocating_shards" : 0,
  "initializing_shards" : 0,
  "unassigned_shards" : 30,
  "delayed_unassigned_shards" : 0,
  "number_of_pending_tasks" : 0,
  "number_of_in_flight_fetch" : 0,
  "task_max_waiting_in_queue_millis" : 0,
  "active_shards_percent_as_number" : 100.0
}
```

What do you infer from this kind of status? Of course the cluster is red indicating missing data (primary & replicas). There were 7 nodes in the cluster but the status only shows 5 nodes. Looks like two nodes have gone missing. Also, there are 30 unassigned shards. What else do you know about the missing shards? Is it 30 indices with 1 primary shard each or 1 index with 30 primary shards? Is it 15 indices with 1 primary + 1 replica? Which is the missing index? Let's try to get some more information by checking cluster health with some more information using the **level** parameter.

```
curl -XGET 'http://localhost:9200/_cluster/health?level=indices&pretty'
```

The level parameter facilitates the cluster health API to provide list of indices in the cluster and details about each of these indices.

```
{
  "cluster_name" : "elasticsearch",
  "status" : "red",
  "timed_out" : false,
  "number_of_nodes" : 5,
  "number_of_data_nodes" : 5,
  "active_primary_shards" : 125,
  "active_shards" : 250,
  "relocating_shards" : 0,
  "initializing_shards" : 0,
  "unassigned_shards" : 30,
  "delayed_unassigned_shards" : 0,
  "number_of_pending_tasks" : 0,
  "number_of_in_flight_fetch" : 0,
  "task_max_waiting_in_queue_millis" : 0,
  "active_shards_percent_as_number" : 100.0,
  "indices" : {
      ...
    "phone" : {
      "status" : "red",
      "number_of_shards" : 5,
      "number_of_replicas" : 1,
      "active_primary_shards" : 0,
      "active_shards" : 5,
      "relocating_shards" : 0,
      "initializing_shards" : 0,
```

```
"unassigned_shards" : 30

  },

    …

  }

}
```

You can see that the **phone** index has made the cluster red and all the 30 missing shards are from this index. We clearly get to know which the problematic index is. Most probably the 30 shards are from the two nodes that are missing from the cluster. The level parameter has one more variant for shard related information.

curl -XGET 'http://localhost:9200/_cluster/health?level=shards&pretty'

The shards option provides a verbose dump which gives the status and location of every shard inside every index.

Examining Individual Nodes

For cluster level diagnostic information you can rely on cluster health API. Similarly, for node specific information, you can leverage **node-stats** API. This API provides a comprehensive set of statistics for each node in the cluster. You can use this API in the following manner:

curl -XGET 'localhost:9200/_nodes/stats'

Following is the output which has the cluster name and first node details at the top:

```
{
  "cluster_name" : "elasticsearch",
  "nodes" : {
    "QmO3WzTfR_StlFSiplCi2A" : {
      "timestamp" : 1480318094408,
      "name" : "Lorvex",
      "transport_address" : "127.0.0.1:9301",
      "host" : "127.0.0.1",
      "ip" : [ "127.0.0.1:9301", "NONE" ],
```

The nodes are specified in a hash with **UUID** of the node serving as the key. There is information about the node's network properties like transport address, host, etc. There is a wealth of information which can help in diagnosing node related issues during discovery or normal operations.

indices Section

The **indices** section provides the aggregate statistics for all the indices that are present on this particular node:

```
"indices" : {
  "docs" : {
    "count" : 9782,
    "deleted" : 0
```

```
    },
    "store" : {
      "size_in_bytes" : 41592264,
      "throttle_time_in_millis" : 0
    },
```

The statistics can be combined into the following groups:

- **docs** - Number of documents residing on the node. Also the number of deleted docs that haven't been purged from segments yet.

- **store** - Physical storage consumed by the node. It gives the number of shards currently moving from one node to another.

```
    "indexing" : {
      "index_total" : 1,
      "index_time_in_millis" : 122,
      "index_current" : 0,
      "index_failed" : 0,
      "delete_total" : 0,
      "delete_time_in_millis" : 0,
      "delete_current" : 0,
      "noop_update_total" : 0,
      "is_throttled" : false,
      "throttle_time_in_millis" : 0
    },
    "get" : {
      "total" : 0,
      "time_in_millis" : 0,
      "exists_total" : 0,
      "exists_time_in_millis" : 0,
      "missing_total" : 0,
      "missing_time_in_millis" : 0,
      "current" : 0
    },
    "search" : {
      "open_contexts" : 0,
      "query_total" : 20,
      "query_time_in_millis" : 190,
      "query_current" : 0,
      "fetch_total" : 6,
      "fetch_time_in_millis" : 51,
      "fetch_current" : 0,
      "scroll_total" : 0,
      "scroll_time_in_millis" : 0,
      "scroll_current" : 0
    },
    "merges" : {
      "current" : 0,
      "current_docs" : 0,
      "current_size_in_bytes" : 0,
      "total" : 0,
```

```
    "total_time_in_millis" : 0,
    "total_docs" : 0,
    "total_size_in_bytes" : 0,
    "total_stopped_time_in_millis" : 0,
    "total_throttled_time_in_millis" : 0,
    "total_auto_throttle_in_bytes" : 82334187520
},
```

- **indexing** - Number of docs that have been indexed. It gets incremented anytime an index operation happens, including updates.

- **get** - Details of get-by_ID statistics, including GET and HEAD request for a single document.

- **search** - Number of active searches (**open_contexts**), number of queries total. Additionally it also informs about the amount of time spent on queries since the node was started. The ratio between **query_time_in_millis** / **query_total** is a good indicator for query efficiency. A large value indicates more time being taken by each query.

- **merges** - Details of Lucene segment merges. It gives information like number of active merges, number of docs involved, cumulative size of merges being merged and the amount of time spent on merges.

- **filter_cache** - Amount of memory utilized by cached filter bitsets and the number of times a filter is evicted. A large number hints at looking at filters to ensure that they are caching properly.

- **id_cache** - Memory usage of parent/child mappings.

- **field_data** - Memory used by fielddata, which is utilized for aggregations and sorting.

- **segments** - Number of Lucene segments the node is currently serving. A large number can indicate problem with merging.

OS and Process Sections

This section provides resource statistics such as CPU and load.

```
"os" : {
  "timestamp" : 1480318109825,
  "cpu_percent" : 27,
  "load_average" : 4.69,
  "mem" : {
    "total_in_bytes" : 2097577984,
    "free_in_bytes" : 74170368,
    "used_in_bytes" : 2023407616,
    "free_percent" : 4,
    "used_percent" : 96
  },
  "swap" : {
    "total_in_bytes" : 1071640576,
    "free_in_bytes" : 668672000,
    "used_in_bytes" : 402968576
  }
},
"process" : {
```

```
"timestamp" : 1480318109838,
"open_file_descriptors" : 18566,
"max_file_descriptors" : 65535,
"cpu" : {
  "percent" : 10,
  "total_in_millis" : 9481560
},
"mem" : {
  "total_virtual_in_bytes" : 3204153344
}
},
```

The OS section illustrates for the entire OS while the Process section displays statistics related to the Elasticsearch process. These metrics are quite useful and some of them have been mentioned below:

- CPU
- Memory usage
- Open file descriptors
- System Load
- Usage of swap

JVM Section

The jvm section contains essential information about the JVM running Elasticsearch. Most important is garbage collection details which reflects on the stability of Elasticsearch cluster.

```
"jvm" : {
  "timestamp" : 1480318110038,
  "uptime_in_millis" : 142723571,
  "mem" : {
    "heap_used_in_bytes" : 775873376,
    "heap_used_percent" : 72,
    "heap_committed_in_bytes" : 1065025536,
    "heap_max_in_bytes" : 1065025536,
    "non_heap_used_in_bytes" : 79743032,
    "non_heap_committed_in_bytes" : 81043456,
```

- **jvm section** - This section gives general stats about heap memory usage. You can clearly see the heap usage, allocated memory, max heap size, etc. Typically, **heap_committed_in_bytes** should be identical to **heap_max_in_bytes**. If the commit size happens to be smaller, the JVM will resize the heap appropriately. Another important metric is **heap_used_percent_metric** which is configured to trigger GC when the heap reaches **75%** full. If this value is consistently >= **75%**, it indicate some serious memory related trouble.

```
  "pools" : {
    "young" : {
      "used_in_bytes" : 15291432,
      "max_in_bytes" : 69795840,
```

```
      "peak_used_in_bytes" : 69795840,
      "peak_max_in_bytes" : 69795840
    },
    "survivor" : {
     "used_in_bytes" : 8716288,
     "max_in_bytes" : 8716288,
     "peak_used_in_bytes" : 8716288,
     "peak_max_in_bytes" : 8716288
    },
    "old" : {
     "used_in_bytes" : 751865656,
     "max_in_bytes" : 986513408,
     "peak_used_in_bytes" : 813325376,
     "peak_max_in_bytes" : 986513408
    }
   }
  }
},
```

- The different heap areas like **young, survivor** and **old** sections represent how memory is being used. Excessive usage of a particular section indicates problem.

```
"gc" : {
 "collectors" : {
  "young" : {
   "collection_count" : 8805,
   "collection_time_in_millis" : 511285
  },
  "old" : {
   "collection_count" : 261,
   "collection_time_in_millis" : 14579
  }
 }
},
```

- **gc section** - This section displays the garbage collection counts and cumulative time for both young and old generations. You need to keep an eye for old generation count as they should remain small. The time spent doing garbage collection is quite crucial. If the JVM is doing more of GC, then less cpu cycles would be spent in performing actual computing.

Threadpool Section

Elasticsearch has a pool of threads which collaborate to perform computing for all operations. There are cases when a task is passed from one thread to another. The default configuration of threadpool suffices for most situations. It is still worthwhile to explore these statistics to see how the cluster is working. There are around a dozen threadpools and they all share the same format:

```
"index" : {
 "threads" : 1,
 "queue" : 0,
 "active" : 0,
 "rejected" : 0,
 "largest" : 1,
```

```
    "completed" : 1
  },
```

Each threadpool displays the number of configured **threads**, how many of these threads are **active** and how many tasks are waiting a **queue**. A queue filled up to its limit leads to tasks being rejected. This indicates that the Elasticsearch cluster is facing a resource constraint. The important threadpools to monitor are as following:

- **index** - Normal indexing requests
- **get** - Get-by-ID operations
- **merging** - Threadpool for Lucene merges
- **bulk** - Bulk requests
- **search** - Search and query operations

F5 and Network Sections

Towards the later part of node-stats API, you can see a group of statistics related to the filesystem - **disk I/O stats**, **free space, data path**, etc. You don't have to monitor free disk space separately as you can see its value in this section. There are two sections related to network statistics also:

```
"transport" : {
  "server_open" : 13,
  "rx_count" : 2793,
  "rx_size_in_bytes" : 3383451,
  "tx_count" : 3973,
  "tx_size_in_bytes" : 1906214
},
"http" : {
  "current_open" : 1,
  "total_opened" : 30
},
```

- **transport** - Basic statistics related to the **transport address**. This is related to inter-node communication and associated transport client or node client connections. Elasticsearch maintains a large number of inter-node connections so don't get scared by a big value.

- **http** - Statistics related to the **HTTP port** (most of the times **9200**). In case the **total_opened** metric is constantly increasing, then it is a indication that a HTTP client is not using **keep-alive** connections.

Circuit Breaker

The last section is for statistics related to **fielddata circuit breaker**.

```
"breakers" : {
  "fielddata" : {
    "limit_size_in_bytes" : 639015321,
    "limit_size" : "609.4mb",
    "estimated_size_in_bytes" : 0,
```

```
    "estimated_size" : "0b",
    "overhead" : 1.03,
    "tripped" : 0
  },
  ...
}
```

This section throws light on the maximum circuit-breaker size. It also indicates the number of times the circuit breaker has been **tripped** and what is the current value of overhead. This **overhead** value pads estimates as some queries are harder to estimate than others. The key item to watch for is the **tripped** metric. In case the number is too high or gradually increasing, it is a sign that your queries need to be optimized or there should be more memory allocated.

Cluster Statistics

You can get an output similar to **node-stats** API using the **cluster-stats** API. Of course there is a key difference that node stats displays statistics per node, whereas cluster-stats API displays the summation of all nodes in a single metric. There are quite a few useful statistics. You can get to know how much heap your cluster is using or whether filter cache is evicting properly. This API provides a quick summary which is more elaborate than cluster-health but less comprehensive than the detailed node-stats.

You can invoke this API in the following manner:

```
curl -XGET 'localhost:9200/_cluster/stats'
```

Index Statistics

Till now we have looked at only **node-centric** statistics. Sometimes it is helpful to look at statistics from an **index-centric** perspective. This could throw light on the number of search requests being received by an index or the amount of time spent fetching docs in a particular index. You can select the index of your choice and get corresponding statistics in the following manner:

```
curl -XGET 'localhost:9200/{index}/_stats'
```

You can get the statistics for multiple indices in the following manner:

```
curl -XGET 'localhost:9200/{index1},{index2}/_stats'
```

The node-centric statistics are useful for identifying hot indices inside the cluster. They can also help in knowing why some indices are faster or slower than others.

Pending Tasks

Some tasks are performed only by the master node such as creating a new index or transferring shards around the cluster. As you know, a cluster can have only one master, so only one node can perform **cluster-level metadata changes**. For most of the times, this is not an issue as the queue of metadata changes remains practically zero. In some exceptional scenarios, the number of metadata changes occurs faster than the master can process them. This can result in sizeable number of pending actions, which are queued.

The pending-tasks API displays the pending cluster-level metadata changes:

```
curl -XGET 'localhost:9200/_cluster/pending_tasks'
```

Most of the times, the response is something like the following:

```
{
  "tasks" : []
}
```

This indicates that there are no pending tasks. If there are an exceptionally high number of fields required to be kept in the cluster state, the master has to process if any one of them changes. This requires significant CPU overhead in addition to the network overhead of informing other nodes about the cluster state. This kind of clusters can have cluster-state actions pending and queued up. There are a few options to circumvent this situation:

- Increase the horsepower of master node.

- Try to limit the dynamic nature of documents which will help in limiting the cluster-state size.

- Have another cluster if a certain threshold has been crossed.

Logging

Elasticsearch dumps a lot of logs which are placed in **ES_HOME/logs**. The default logging level is **INFO** and it provides a moderate amount of information. It is structured to be lightweight so that logs in a production setup are not huge.

While debugging problems you may want to increase the log level to **DEBUG**. You can modify the **logging.yml** file and restart all the nodes. This is tedious process and involves unnecessary downtime. There is a smarter way to update logging levels by using the **cluster-settings** API. You can dynamically change the log level in the following manner:

```
curl -XPUT 'localhost:9200/_cluster/settings' -d '
{
  "transient" : {
    "logger.discovery" : "DEBUG"
  }
}'
```

Elasticsearch will start dumping DEBUG level logs while the setting is being applied.

▪ **Tip** The **TRACE** log level is quite verbose and it is best to be avoided in production environment.

Slowlog

There is another log known as the **slowlog**. It catches queries and indexes requests that take over a certain threshold of time. It is of great help in finding out queries that are slow. The slowlog is **disabled** by default. You can **enable** it by defining the **action** (**query**, **fetch**, or **index**), the **level** at which you want the event logged (**WARN**, **DEBUG**, etc.) and a **time threshold**.

As it is an **index-level** setting, it is applied to individual indices:

```
curl -XPUT 'localhost:9200/{index}/settings' -d '
{
  "index.search.slowlog.threshold.query.warn" : "15s",
  "index.search.slowlog.threshold.fetch.debug" : "400ms",
  "index.indexing.slowlog.threshold.index.info" : "5s",
}'
```

The above settings instruct Elasticsearch to do the following:

- Dump a **WARN** log when queries are slower than 15 seconds.
- Dump a **DEBUG** log when fetches are slower than 400 milli-seconds.
- Dump an **INFO** log when indexing takes longer than 5 seconds.

You can even define these thresholds in your elasticsearch.yml configuration file. If no threshold is configured, then indices will inherit the static configuration. After the thresholds are set, you can switch the logging level just like any other logger:

```
curl -XPUT 'localhost:9200/_cluster/settings' -d '
{
  "transient" : {
    "logger.index.search.slowlog" : "DEBUG",
    "logger.index.indexing.slowlog" : "WARN"
  }
}'
```

The above settings would do the following:

- **Search** slowlog is set to **DEBUG** level.
- **Indexing** slowlog is set to **WARN** level.

Rolling Restarts

There can be a situation when you are in need of performing a rolling restart of your cluster - keeping the cluster online and operational, but nodes are taken offline one at a time. This may be required in situations like a **version upgrade** of Elasticsearch or some **maintenance** on the server. In all these cases, there is a specific method to perform a rolling restart.

Elasticsearch strives to fully replicate the data and evenly balance it. If a single node is shut down for maintenance, the cluster immediately recognizes the loss of the node and begins rebalancing. You may want to stop the automatic rebalancing as you may have more knowledge of external factors. This can be achieved in the following manner:

6. Stop indexing new data, if possible.

7. Shard allocation should be disabled. This does not let Elasticsearch rebalance missing shards until it is specifically enabled again. You can disable allocation as follows:

```
curl -XPUT 'localhost:9200/_cluster/settings' -d '
{
  "transient" : {
    "cluster.routing.allocation.enable" : "none"
  }
}'
```

8. Shut down the node, by killing the Elasticsearch process:

9. Perform the maintenance upgrade.

10. Restart the node and confirm it becomes part of the cluster.

11. Re-enable shard allocation in the following manner:

```
curl -XPUT 'localhost:9200/_cluster/settings' -d '
{
  "transient" : {
    "cluster.routing.allocation.enable" : "all"
  }
}'
```

Rebalancing of shard may take some time and you should wait till the cluster has returned to status **green** before continuing.

12. Now it is safe to resume indexing. It will be better that you wait till the time cluster is fully balanced before resuming indexing.

Backup and Restore

Elasticsearch stores crucial piece of data in many cases. This necessitates routine backup of data and restoring an earlier snapshot in case of a crash. Elasticsearch replicas provide high availability and in case of a node loss also, the service is largely available. However, replicas can't provide from catastrophic failure. You need to back up your cluster to safeguard against catastrophic failures.

Cluster Backup

You can use the **snapshot** API to back up the cluster. The current state and data in the cluster are saved in a shared repository. The first snapshot is a complete copy of day, but all subsequent snapshots are incremental backups. The delta between the existing snapshots and new data are saved. Data gets incrementally added and deleted over time. This makes the subsequent backups pretty fast.

In order to take a backup, you first need to create a repository to save the data. There are several options to choose from for a repository:

- Shared filesystem such as NAS.

- Azure Cloud.

- Amazon S3.

- Hadoop Distributed File System (HDFS).

Creating the Repository

Let's use a shared filesystem repository:

```
curl -XPUT 'localhost:9200/foo_backup'
{
  "type" : "fs",
  "settings" : {
   "location" : "/mount/backups/foo_backup"
  }
}
```

A name is provided to the repository. In this case it is foo_backup. The repository type is specified as filesystem and a mounted drive is provided as destination.

■ **Tip** The shared filesystem path must be accessible from all nodes in the cluster.

A name is provided to the repository. In this case it is **foo_backup**. The repository type is specified as **filesystem** and a mounted drive is provided as destination. This creates the repository and required metadata. You may want to configure some other options also:

- **max_snapshot_bytes_per_sec** - This option regulates the speed of snapshotting data into the repo. The default value is **20mb per second**.

- **max_restore_bytes_per_sec** - This option regulates the speed of restoring data from the repo. The default value is **20mb per second**.

You can change these default settings in the following manner:

```
curl -XPOST 'localhost:9200/_snapshot/foo_backup' -d '
{
  "type" : "fs"
  "settings" : {
   "location" : "/mount/backups/foo_backup",
   "max_snapshot_bytes_per_sec" : "30mb",
   "max_restore_bytes_per_sec" : "30mb"
  }
}
```

}'

Note the use of **POST** operation instead of **PUT**. This will update the settings.

Snapshot of All Open Indices

There can be multiple snapshots for a repository. Each snapshot has an associated set of indices (for e.g. all indices, some subset or a single index). While creating a snapshot you need to specify which index you are interested in and give a unique name for the snapshot. You can create a snapshot with a basic command:

```
curl -XPUT 'localhost/9200/_snapshot/foo_backup/snapshot_1'
```

This will take a backup of all open indices into a snapshot named **snapshot_1** in the foo_backup repository. The snapshot happens in the background and the call returns immediately.

Snapshot of Particular Index

The default behavior is to take a backup of all open indices. But let's say there is not enough space to back up everything, you can take backup of selective indices.

```
curl -XPUT 'localhost/9200/_snapshot/foo_backup/snapshot_2' -d '
{
  "indices" : "index_1,index_2"
}
```

Now a backup of only **index_1** and **index_2** will be taken.

Listing Snapshot of Information

After a while of taking snapshots, you may not remember details related to each other. In particular, if the snapshots are named based on time boundaries (for e.g. backup_2016_11_27), this problem aggravates. To avoid this frustration, Elasticsearch provides API to obtain snapshot related information. To fetch information for a single snapshot, submit a GET request against the repo and snapshot name:

```
curl -XGET 'localhost:9200/_snapshot/foo_backup/snapshot_2'
```

The response will contain containing different pieces of information related to the snapshot. You can fetch the entire listing of all the snapshots in the repository in the following manner:

```
curl -XGET 'localhost:9200/_snapshot/foo_backup/_all'
```

Snapshot Deletion

Elasticsearch provides API to delete old snapshots which are no longer required. You just need to give a **DELETE HTTP** request to with the repository/snapshot name:

```
curl -XDELETE 'localhost:9200/_snapshot/foo_backup/snapshot_2'
```

Removing the snapshots through the **DELETE** request is the safest mechanism. Since snapshots are incremental in nature, they may be relying on old segments. The **delete** API can take care of this and will delete only that old data which is no longer in use. There is a risk of corruption if you do manual file deletion.

Monitoring Snapshot Progress

Although the **wait_for_completion** flag provides a basic form of monitoring, but it is not sufficient enough. Elasticsearch provides APIs for a more detailed status of the snapshot process in progress. First of all you fetch snapshot information using the GET request by specifying the snapshot ID:

```
curl -XGET 'localhost:9200/_snapshot/foo_backup/snapshot_2'
```

If at the time of this request, the snapshot is still in progress, you will get information like when the snapshot started, how long it has been running and so forth. This API uses the same threadpool as the snapshot mechanism. If you are taking snapshot of a large shard, there can be significant time delay between status updates. A better way is to poll the **_status** API.

```
curl -XGET 'localhost:9200/_snapshot/foo_backup/snapshot_2/_status'
```

The _status API return immediately and gives a detailed response.

Cancelling Snapshot

In case you want to cancel a snapshot, you can simply delete a snapshot in progress:

```
curl -XDELETE 'localhost:9200/_snapshot/foo_backup/snapshot_2'
```

If the snapshot is in progress, it will be first halted and then deleted.

Restore from Snapshot

After you have taken up a snapshot, it is quite easy to **restore** it. Just add **_restore** to the ID of the snapshot from which you wish to restore into the cluster.

```
curl -XPOST 'localhost:9200/_snapshot/foo_backup/snapshot_2/_restore'
```

The default action is to restore all the indices present in the snapshot. If **snapshot_1** contains three indices, all three will be restored into the cluster. It is possible to specifically select which indices to restore. If the snapshot is in progress, it will be first halted and then deleted.

There is an option to rename indices. This enables matching of index names with a pattern and then providing a new name during the restore process. This is quite handy for restoring old data to verify its contents without replacing existing data. Let's try to restore a single index from the snapshot and give a replacement name:

```
curl -XPOST 'localhost:9200/_snapshot/foo_backup/snapshot_2/_restore' -d '
{
  "indices" : "index_1",
  "rename_pattern" : ."index_(.+)",
  "rename_replacement" : "restored_index_$1"
}'
```

The above operation would restore **index_1** into your cluster but rename it to **restored_index_1**.

Monitor Restore Operations

The restoration of data from a repository relies on the recovery mechanism of Elasticsearch. You can monitor the process of restore using the **recovery** API. You can invoke the API by specifying the indices which are being recovered:

```
curl -XGET 'localhost:9200/_recovery/restored_index_2'
```

You can determine the recovery status of all the indices in the following manner:

```
curl -XGET 'localhost:9200/_recovery'
```

This will dump the list of all indices currently being recovered and then list all shards in each of those indices. Each shard will be associated with start/stop time, recover percentage, bytes transferred, etc.

Cancelling Restore

If you want to cancel a restore, just delete the indices being restored. Since a restore process is just shard recovery, invoking the **delete-index** API modifies the cluster state and halts recovery process. You can trigger cancellation in the following manner:

```
curl -XDELETE 'localhost:9200/restored_index_4'
```

In case **restored_index_4** was being restored, the delete command would suspend the restoration and delete any data that was restored into the cluster.

Summary

This chapter covered key aspects of running an Elasticsearch cluster like monitoring, configuration changes, logging, troubleshooting, back and restore. Elasticsearch has inbuilt mechanism to run clusters in a self-sufficient manner but every now and then you need to peek into the working of the cluster. Elasticsearch comes out with defect fixes regularly and it is important to understand the process of upgrades. In order to be fail-safe, it is important to have a disaster recovery plan and taking regular snapshots helps in that.

INDEX

A

Absolute Time Filter, 140

Aggregation Scoping, 126

Aliases, 216

    add/remove action, 217

    benefits of, 217

    creation, 218

    filters, 219

    routing combination, 226

    working process, 216

Amazon Web Services, 2, 49

Analyzer attribute, 99

Analyzing events, 31

Apache Lucene, 2

Area chart, visualization, 153

    chart modes

        overlap, 156

        percentage, 157

        silhouette, 159

        wiggle, 158

    fields, 153

    hurricanes, 154

    output, 156

    string fields options, 160

    UNIX head command, 154

    view options, 160

    X-axis, 155

B

Binary operators, 23

Bool filter, 84

Boolean logic, 23

Bubble chart, 169

Buckets, 146

Bulk information

© Gurpreet S. Sachdeva 2017

G. S. Sachdeva, *Applied ELK Stack*, ISBN 978-1545022146

indexing process, 231

operations, 66

request size, 69

updating and deleting, 230

C

Carbon Dioxide Information Analysis
   Center (CDIAC), 17

Cluster health and configuration, 54

Codec plugin, 43

Complex field types, 102

Compund clauses, 80

Conflict management, 69

D

D

Dashboard

  edit visualization, 190
Dasboard

  creation, 186

Dashboard, 183

  button, 185

  button option, 185

  debug panel

   request, 194
   response, 195
   statistics, 196
   table, 193

elegant and beautiful visualization,
   191

HTML page, 193

load option, 188

move option, 190

remove, 191

resize, 190

save button, 188

search bar, 187

share button, 189

web page, 192

window page, 217

Data exploration

  buckets, 105

  colors, 107

  components, 105

  metrics, 106

  multiple metrics, 111

  visualization (bar charts), 113

Data histograms, 120

Data management

  bulk indexing, update and delete,
   230

  multisearch and multiget, 233

operations, 230

request group, 230

Data mapping

analysis, 97

types, 98

Data node, 50

Data slicing, 215

date_histogram buckets, 120

Default logging configuration, 31

Desaturate map tiles

checkbox, 178

option disabled, 179

tile map, 179

Discover page, 15

Document information

creation, 65

deletion, 66

existence, 60

retrieval, 59

storage, 52

updates, 62

Dynamic dashboards, 138

Dynamic mapping rules, 98

E

Elasticsearch, 1, 91, 99

API, 53

configuration and settings, 7

fault detection, 205

health status, 55

index and type, 52

indices, 52

installation, 5

key features, 3

multicast discovery

mechanism, 202

object and document, 51

output configuration, 27

plugin configuration, 27

components, 27

response, 115

running, 6

shard allocation, 201

storage ecosystem, 50

Elasticsearch cluster, 199

aliases. *See* Aliases

cluster information, 211

custom Id, 57

document, 50

master node election, 204

node, 50

production environment, 228

removal nodes

decommission, 208
primary shards, 206
replica shards, 207
shard, 53

unicast discovery, 203

upgrade nodes, 209

key aspects, 209
quick restart, 211
rolling restart, 209
Elasticsearch, Logstash and Kibana, 2

data pipeline, 4

stack installation, 5

Environment variables, 7

Error Diagnostics, 88

Exact-value field, 95

Exists and missing filters, 83

F

Fault detection process, 205

Field referencs, 22

Field searches, 142, 143

Filter

bucket, 130

events, 25

free text search, 141

query combination, 86

via query, 87

Full-text

field, 92

query, 84

G

GitHub repository, 40

Global bucket, 128

Grok filter, 31

H

Heat map, 177

Histogram, 113

bucket, 114

HTTP HEAD method, 60

I

Impedance mismatch, 49

Index management, 53

Indexing inner objects, 103

Inner object arrays, 103

Intrinsic sorts, 132

Inverted index, 92

J

Java Virtual Machine (JVM), 229

JAVA_OPTS, 7

JSON documents, 50

K

key_as_string, 122

Kibana, 1

    bar chart, 34

    configuration, 14

    dashboard, 16

    data table, 36

    discover page, 138

    key features, 137

    metric, 35

    settings page, 32

    share options, 37

    time filter, 32

    user interface, 138

    visualization, 2, 4, 15

L

Language analyzer, 95

Leaf clauses, 80

Line charts

    log option

      bubble chart, 169
    log options

      circles, 174

      connecting lines, 166
      smooth lines, 165
      Y-axis data bounds, 169
      Y-axis extents, 168
      output, 162

    square root option, 163

Load balancer node, 50

Log analysis, 1

Log management, 2

Logstash, 3

    agent, 10

    codecs, 3

    configuration file, 11

    Elasticsearch, 3

    event pipeline, 13

    forwarder, 11

    function, 12

    input plugins, 12

    installation, 9

    logstash-output-mongodb plugin, 40

    output plugins, 13

    plugin development

      advantages, 39
      configuration, 44
      download and installation, 40
      execution, 44
      register, 44
      teardown, 45
    running, 9

Lucene query syntax, 141

M

Mapping

customization, 99

revision, 100

test, 101

Master node, 50

Match

attribute, 26

match_all query, 84

query, 85

timestamp, 10

mean_price metric, 110

Metadata information, 24

Metrics

based sorting, 133

visualization, 174

Microsoft Azure, 49

Multi_match query, 85

Multicast discovery mechanism, 202

Multi-level objects, 102

Multiline event configuration, 30

Multiple document retrieval, 61

Multi-tier correlation, 122

Multivalue bucket sorting, 132

Multi-value fields, 102

N

Newline character, 67

NoSQL document database, 50

O

Optimistic concurrency control, 69

Over-sharding, 213

P

Partial document retrieval, 60

Participating shards, 75

Pessimistic concurrency control, 69

Pie charts, 171

donut, 173

percentage, 181

Play field fragments, 102

plays.json, 73

Plugin

Packaging, 47

structure, 41

Post filter, 131

Prepackaged analyzers, 94

Price range histograms, 116

Primary and replica shards, 201

Production environment, 228

  backups

    cancel, 263
    deletion, 262
    index, 262
    indices, 262
    monitoring, 263
    shared filesystem repository, 261
  cluster, 244

    backup, 260
    statistics, 255
  disks, 228

  index templates

    configuration management, 244
    creation, 244
    delete, 248
    file system, 246
  individual nodes

    F5 and network sections, 256
    fieldsdata circuit breaker, 256
    gc section, 255
    index statistics, 257
    indices section, 251
    JVM section, 254
    OS and process sections, 253
    output, 251
    pending tasks, 257
    threadpools, 255
  Java virtual machine, 229

  logging

    debugging problems, 258
  memory, 228

  monitoring, 248

  network, 229

  restoration

    cancel, 264
    monitor operations, 264
    rolling restarts, 259

  slowlog, 259

  troubleshooting, 248

Q

Query documents, 129

  clause construction, 79

  DSL, 79

  filter, 129

  mashup, 78

  string version, 77

  validation, 88

Quick time filter, 139

R

RabbitMQ topic, 24

Range searches, 142

Ranger filter operators, 83

relations and tuples, 49

Relative time filter, 140

Reloading configuration file, 30

run method, 43

S

scaling capabilities

  maximizing throughput, 213

over-sharding, 213

Scaling capabilities. *See* Elasticsearch
    cluster

    data slicing, 213

Scripted fields, 138

Searching data

    criteria combinations, 76

    document Id, 75

    Elasticsearch, 71

    filter and query, 81

    hits, 75

    lite, 77

    pagination, 77

    performance concerns, 82

    search without parameter, 74

    took field, 75

Shipping events, 27

Sorted Term List, 92

sprintf format, 22

Standard analyzer, 94

Standard error, 116

store and index documents, 51

Structured query, 72

T

Throughput/fast searches, 215

Tile maps

    geohash grid options, 176

    map, 175

    shaded circle markers, 175

Time filter, 139

Time series aggregations, 120

timed_out field, 75

Tokenizers, 94

    filters, 94

U

U.S. Department of Energy (DOE), 17

Unicast discovery, 203

Universally unique identifiers, 58

Updating documents partially, 63

V

Vertical bar chart

    bar chart, 179

    bar charts, 182

    percentage, 181

    X-axis, 179

Visualization

    advanced options

        JSON input, 147

bucket aggregations, 152

canvas

  aggregation designer, 152
  key elements, 149
  load option, 188
  new visualization button, 148
  preview, 149
  refresh button, 151
  save option, 151
  share, 151
data table, 161

desaturate map tiles

  checkbox, 178
  option disabled, 179
  tile map, 179
heat map, 177

line charts

  log option, 165
  output, 162
  square root, 163
markdown widget, 170

metric, 170

pie charts

  donut, 173
  percentage, 172
  split charts, 171
search data source, 149

search source options, 148

step-by-step approach, 152

toolbar page, 184

W, X, Y, Z

Whitespace analyzer, 95